AN INTRODUCTION TO
BRITISH ECONOMIC STATISTICS

AN INTRODUCTION TO
BRITISH ECONOMIC STATISTICS

BY

ELY DEVONS

*Professor of Commerce (with special reference to International Trade)
in the University of London*

CAMBRIDGE
AT THE UNIVERSITY PRESS
1961

PUBLISHED BY
THE SYNDICS OF THE CAMBRIDGE UNIVERSITY PRESS

Bentley House, 200 Euston Road, London, N.W. 1
American Branch: 32 East 57th Street, New York 22, N.Y.
West African Office: P.O. Box 33, Ibadan, Nigeria

First printed   1956
Reprinted   1958
                1961

First printed in Great Britain by
William Clowes and Sons, Limited, London and Beccles
Reprinted by offset-lithography by Billing and Sons Ltd., Guildford

PREFACE

MOST universities now quite rightly require students of economics and commerce to include a course on economic statistics as part of their studies. Such courses normally cover both elementary statistical theory and the sources and uses of British economic statistics. On elementary statistical theory the student has several books to choose from which cover the subject quite adequately; but on the sources and uses of British economic statistics he is faced with a bewildering long list of books, White Papers, Blue Books, statistical reports and publications, and articles in journals. Few students have the time, let alone the inclination, to consult such a wide variety of sources. In any case many of these publications are written for the specialist statistician and are hardly appropriate for the first or second year student. There is clearly a need for a book which provides the student with a gerral survey of the main British economic statistics—tells him where they can be found, what they mean, what problems arise in using and interpreting them, and guides him in further reading and in consulting the original sources themselves. In this book I attempt to fill this need. Although it is designed principally for students of economics and commerce, I hope that it will also be useful to others, in academic life, business, politics, the public services, and journalism, who use economic statistics and feel the need for some guide through the maze of statistical information with which they are regularly confronted in their work.

The best way of acquiring some capacity in handling economic statistics—knowing exactly what they mean, the margins of error in them, securing comparability between different sets of figures, and adjusting them to suit the particular purpose in hand—is to go as often as possible to original statistical sources to try to use the figures for oneself. No amount of reading other people's comments on economic statistics will give the student the insight into problems of using them that he will get from actually getting into contact with the primary material himself. If students use this book as a way of escaping from this need to become familiar with the original statistical sources, it will have failed in its purpose. For it is meant to guide the student in using these original sources, rather than merely to enable him to acquire a superficial acquaintance with them at second-hand.

I have not attempted to cover all British economic statistics. This would not be appropriate in an introduction to the subject, and in any case a comprehensive treatment would need a work in many volumes. I have selected the major topics of general economic interest, which I think all students of economics should know about, and which they are likely to meet in other parts of their economic courses. To some extent the list is arbitrary. A glaring exclusion is public finance, which I finally decided to leave out because of the peculiar difficulty and intricacy in interpreting the available statistics. On the other hand I have included a chapter on national income and expenditure, even though this means discussing problems which first and second year students may find difficult to follow. National income analysis now plays such a central role in economics and in public discussion of economic policy that I felt bound to include some treatment of this subject, albeit brief and inadequate, even in an elementary book on economic statistics.

There is a continuous flow of new statistical information, week by week, and a book of this kind is bound to be out of date in some respects even when it is first published. I have tried to make it as up to date as possible by including in an appendix notes of the important new statistics which have appeared since the main text of the book was prepared for the press. An asterisk (*) in the main text itself indicates that there is a further reference to the subject in this appendix.

At every stage in writing this book I have had most generous and valuable help from my colleague, Mr K. S. Lomax. Professor Cairncross read and commented on some of the chapters. Members of the staff of the Central Statistical Office read the manuscript and provided me with some very helpful comments. Professor Gluckman very generously helped with the arduous task of proof-reading. My secretary, Mrs Bertenshaw, has most efficiently and patiently typed successive versions of the manuscript, and helped me in preparing it for publication. To all these I am most grateful.

Manchester   E. D.
September 1955

PREFACE TO SECOND IMPRESSION

THE Appendix drawing attention to the most significant revised and new statistics which have appeared since 1955 has been extended to cover the period to mid-1958. Since there is now a reference in the Appendix to every chapter in the main text the asterisks which were included in the first impression have been omitted.

E. D.

Manchester
August 1958

CONTENTS

CHAPTER I

INTRODUCTION

In the last century, and at an accelerating rate in the last twenty years, more and more statistics have been collected and published describing and analysing our economic affairs. Any discussion of social and economic problems, any argument about economic policy, is incomplete unless conducted against a background of statistics. Statistics play an increasingly important role in academic study in the social sciences. Business uses them more and more in controlling its internal operations and in exploring the market for its products and services. No student of economic affairs can get very far nowadays without some knowledge of economic statistics.[1]

In the sense used here, 'statistics' implies little, if any, elaborate mathematical analysis. The term is, indeed, almost synonymous with 'figures'. When we talk about 'employment statistics' or 'trade statistics' we use the term 'statistics' to cover the whole mass of figures about trade or employment. But although no elaborate mathematical analysis is involved, proper use of economic statistics is not easy. The statistics about any particular subject are usually scattered over a wide variety of sources, and the information available may be frequently changed or extended. It is, therefore, often difficult to discover what statistics there are about a subject and to know where to find them. Then there is the whole range of questions that arise in using the figures: what exactly the figures cover; whether the definitions have been changed from time to time and, if so, how this affects their use and meaning; whether they can be compared with other figures; and what margin of error there is in them. Unless we know the answers to questions of this kind, we may easily be deceived rather than enlightened by the statistics we use.

In addition to the basic statistics about any subject, economic

[1] For a discussion of the uses of economic statistics, especially in Government policy, see C. F. Carter and A. D. Roy, *British Economic Statistics* (Cambridge, 1954).

statisticians have developed secondary statistical information in an attempt to measure important economic relations. For example, from the original statistics of prices of particular commodities and services, economic statisticians attempt to measure changes in the general level of prices by constructing price index numbers. In the field of population analysis, statisticians attempt to throw light on significant changes by constructing mortality rates, fertility rates and reproduction rates from the basic material of numbers in the population, and of births, deaths and marriages. The exact basis and significance of secondary statistics such as these, what they attempt to measure and how successful they are in achieving what they attempt, must be understood if they are to be used properly.

This book provides an introductory guide to the most important British economic statistics covering the main issues raised in the last two paragraphs. Seven main subjects—population, employment, production, foreign trade, prices, incomes and national income—have been selected; for each the main sources and nature of the statistics are described and some of the problems that arise in their use and interpretation are discussed. But there are some statistical publications that cover a wide range of topics, and some of the problems of interpretation are common to all economic statistics whatever they are about. Before turning to deal in turn with the particular topics chosen for analysis, it will be useful, therefore, to review in general terms the sources and nature of British economic statistics and to discuss some of the common problems in using them.

THE MAIN SOURCES OF ECONOMIC STATISTICS

Economic statistics can be divided into those collected by the Government, those arising from the working of business and other economic organizations, and those collected by private individuals. Statistics collected and published by central and local government are of two kinds: those which are obtained from specifically statistical enquiries and those which are collected as part of the working of some administrative control or system of taxation. Although this distinction can usually be made without difficulty when one enquires how the statistics started, the two may overlap in later development. For statistics which started merely as an accidental offshoot of some administrative control, may later be developed and extended for the knowledge and information they give about some aspect of economic affairs.

Historically, most of our economic statistics are a by-product of administration or law. Statistics of foreign trade originally arose from the control of imports and exports; statistics of income from the operations of the Board of Inland Revenue in assessing incomes for tax purposes; statistics of the consumption of a wide range of commodities, for example tea, beer and tobacco, from the operations of the Customs and Excise; statistics of employment and unemployment from the schemes of compulsory insurance against unemployment.

Administrative and legal control will not be maintained or continued merely because it yields useful statistics, and changes in administration and law will usually be made without regard to the convenience of those who use the statistics. This means that there are frequently sudden changes in the continuity and coverage of statistics derived from such sources. Thus the abolition of food rationing in 1954 makes it more difficult to estimate changes in food consumption; the abolition in 1946 of the death duty on estates up to £2000 has left us with practically no information about the smallest holdings of capital; and the abolition of exchange control, if it ever happens, would make it much more difficult than at present to calculate figures of the balance of payments.

Statistics collected directly as part of a statistical enquiry mainly for their informative value are in a different category. For here the questionnaire used, the coverage of the enquiry, and the tabulation of the results can all be designed mainly from the point of view of the usefulness of the information that will be obtained. The first major official statistical enquiry of this kind was the Census of Population taken in 1801. Since then a population census has been taken every ten years, except in 1941. The first Census of Production was taken in 1907 and has been taken annually since 1948, and a Census of Distribution was taken for the first time in 1950. These three censuses now form the major statistical enquiries undertaken by the Government. There are many other smaller enquiries, such as the employment and the budget enquiries made by the Ministry of Labour, and the monthly statistics of production collected from industry by the Board of Trade. Some of the statistics first obtained as an off-shoot of administration have now been extended in range and

3

detail in such a way that they ought perhaps to be considered as statistical enquiries in their own right. Examples are the foreign trade statistics collected by the Board of Trade and the employment and unemployment statistics collected by the Ministry of Labour.

Most economic organizations, public and private, need to keep statistical records if they are to run efficiently, and some of these records form a most important source of economic information. For example, most of our information about the movement of wholesale prices came, until recent years, from the records of transactions kept by internationally organized produce and raw material exchanges. The records of transactions on the stock exchange, the published accounts of the banks and other public companies, provide valuable information about the operation of a large section of business. Most figures of wage rates and hours of work are based on the collective agreements made between trade unions and employers' associations or on decisions given by statutory wage-fixing authorities. In many industries, private trade organizations collect statistical information of great economic interest. Much of this is published or passed on to interested government departments for inclusion in official publications. For example nearly all the detailed statistics that we have about iron and steel production and employment are collected by the Iron and Steel Federation from its members.

THE PUBLICATION OF ECONOMIC STATISTICS

The great mass of statistical information which now appears is published in a wide variety of sources. Apart from specifically statistical publications, practically every government report, trade journal or business publication, has some figures of interest, and important information is often given in answer to parliamentary questions. There is, unfortunately, no single index of all this information[1] to which one can go to discover what is available on any

[1] In the period between the wars a most useful *Guide to Official Statistics* was published each year, indexing in detail the whole of the statistical information contained in official publications issued during the year. The *Guide* was first issued for 1922; it was suspended during the Second World War and has not been resumed since. In Carter and Roy (*op. cit.*, pp. 171–81) there is a useful list of the principal British economic statistics, giving the source, where published, the frequency of the series, and the approximate time-lag.

particular subject. There are, however, some general statistical publications in which an attempt is made to gather together and summarize in a convenient form the main information about the most important aspects of economic affairs.

Undoubtedly the two most useful general statistical publications are the *Annual Abstract of Statistics* and the *Monthly Digest of Statistics*, both compiled by the Central Statistical Office and published by the Stationery Office.[1] These bring together in a convenient form the most important statistics relating to economic and social affairs. Many of the tables give in summary form statistics available in more detail in other publications, but they also include figures on many topics which are not published anywhere else.[2] The *Annual Abstract* has a much more extensive coverage than the *Monthly Digest*, for it includes many figures which are available only on an annual basis. The two give figures for the whole of the United Kingdom or for Great Britain. Since April 1953 a separate half-yearly statistical digest has been published for Scotland, and the first of an annual series for Wales was published in 1954.

Once a year a supplement is issued to the *Monthly Digest*,[3] explaining in some detail the definition, coverage and meaning of the series included, together with references to other sources which give the figures and explanations in more detail. There is no such supplement to the *Annual Abstract*, but an index of sources is included, showing the department and official publication or other source from which each series is obtained. Since many of the series in the *Annual Abstract* are the same as those in the *Monthly Digest*, but on an annual basis, the annual supplement to the *Monthly Digest* can also be used in association with the *Annual Abstract*.

One of the difficulties in using the *Annual Abstract* and *Monthly Digest* is that, for some of the series, later figures may come out and earlier figures be revised in other publications between issues of

[1] Since November 1953 an abbreviated popular version of the *Monthly Digest*, with charts, has been published under the title *Economic Trends*.

[2] Two of the most important topics not covered elsewhere are detailed figures of output of manufactured goods, and supplies, consumption, and stocks of raw materials and food.

[3] *Monthly Digest of Statistics, Supplement: Definitions and Explanatory Notes*. This supplement is issued with the January number of the *Monthly Digest*.

these general digests. This is particularly important in the case of the *Abstract*, and one certainly cannot rely on its figures being the most accurate or the most up to date available. For example, between any two issues of the *Abstract*, there are two publications on national income and expenditure giving figures for a later year and revising, sometimes substantially, figures for earlier years.

The *Monthly Digest* usually gives monthly figures for two years, with annual figures for five previous years, including a pre-war figure where available. The *Annual Abstract* gives a run of figures for ten years with a pre-war year for comparison. Thus, in the *Annual Abstract* for 1954, most of the tables include figures for 1938, and for each year from 1944 to 1953.

The *Annual Abstract* issued since 1946 is a continuation, although in a substantially altered form of presentation and coverage, of the pre-war series of *Abstracts* which extends back to 1854. The *Monthly Digest* is a post-war innovation, the first issue coming out in January 1946. In the pre-war period, apart from the *Annual Abstract*, the only review of economic statistics issued officially was in a brief quarterly supplement to the *Ministry of Labour Gazette*.[1]

The *Bulletin* of the London and Cambridge Economic Service has always included a summary of the most important series of economic statistics. When the Service first started in 1923 the *Bulletin* was issued each month, but this was soon changed to a quarterly basis. This quarterly *Bulletin*, however, continues to give monthly figures. Nearly all series given in the *Bulletin* also appear in the *Monthly Digest of Statistics* and the *Annual Abstract of Statistics*. But in each issue of the *Bulletin* there is a longer run of monthly figures than in the *Monthly Digest*, and figures for more previous years than in the official *Annual Abstract*. The authors of the *Bulletin* are also more ready to make adjustments to the original data in order to provide a run of figures on a comparable basis, and there is always a text which comments on significant changes in events which the figures portray. The *Bulletin* ceased separate publication in November 1951. Since then it has been published as a supplement in the March, June, September and December issues of *The Times Review of Industry*.

From the beginning of 1947 *The Economist* issued a weekly

[1] Statistics forming the basis of charts illustrating the course of trade, output, prices, wages, finance and investment.

supplement, called *Records and Statistics*, which included the most important series of regular economic statistics for the United Kingdom. In addition each week new statistics appearing in government publications, trade association reports, in answer to parliamentary questions or other sources, were noted and commented on. This publication was thus most useful for anyone wishing to keep abreast of the voluminous mass of economic statistics appearing week by week. Unfortunately, however, publication ceased in the middle of 1953. Instead there is now a statistical appendix to *The Economist* itself, but this gives only a few general series.

In addition to the publications which cover extensively or in summary the whole field of economic activity, there are a large number giving statistics on particular subjects. First of all there are the publications, weekly, monthly and annual, of government departments, and of special government committees or commissions. Two of the major economic departments, the Board of Trade and the Ministry of Labour, have their own journals, the *Board of Trade Journal*, a weekly, and the *Ministry of Labour Gazette*, a monthly, each of which includes extensive statistics on the subjects within the department's responsibility. The *Ministry of Labour Gazette*, for example, gives in detail figures of employment and unemployment, by industry and region, which are given only in summary in the *Monthly Digest of Statistics*. Some departments which have no regular monthly statistical publication issue duplicated statistical statements; this is done by the Ministry of Fuel and Power and the Ministry of Transport and Civil Aviation. Advance press statements of important statistics are often issued by departments before their normal publication. This is usually done for monthly figures of foreign trade, coal production and stocks, and employment and unemployment.

Many departments issue annual reports, which are mainly or partly statistical. Examples are the *Statistical Digest* of the Ministry of Fuel and Power, and the *Annual Reports* of the Board of Inland Revenue, H.M. Customs and Excise, the Chief Inspector of Factories, the Ministry of Education, the Ministry of Labour and the Ministry of National Insurance. Then there are the specifically statistical publications such as the reports of the Registrar General, the *Trade and Navigation Accounts*, the White Papers on *United Kingdom Balance of Payments*, and *National Income and Expenditure*. The results of the three main censuses, on

Population, Production and Distribution, are published in great detail.

In addition, official committees reporting on an economic subject usually find it necessary to collect and to bring together statistical material on the subject they examine, and at least a summary of these statistics is included in the published reports. An outstanding example of this is the statistical investigation and analysis undertaken by the Royal Commission on Population. The tables in the main report and in the *Reports and Selected Papers of the Statistics Committee* give the best and most convenient set of statistical tables on demographic trends in the United Kingdom.

Some of the boards of nationalized industries publish regular monthly statistical bulletins,[1] and all give a great deal of statistical information in their annual reports. There are other statutory bodies which have power to collect statistics from industry and some compile most valuable statistical summaries for the industries they cover; the outstanding example here is the Cotton Board. Many trade associations issue regular monthly and annual statistical publications covering the sphere of economic activity in which their members are interested. These often include not only summaries of relevant official figures but also statistics which the association collects from its members. Examples are the *British Iron and Steel Federation Monthly Statistical Bulletin* and the *Monthly Statistical Review of the Society of Motor Manufacturers and Traders*, or the statement on shipping and shipbuilding compiled and issued by Lloyds.

One of the best ways of discovering what current statistical information there is on any industry or trade is to look at recent issues of the appropriate trade journals, for such journals will usually notice and comment on statistical information about the industry.

GENERAL PROBLEMS IN USING ECONOMIC STATISTICS

The main problems that arise in using economic statistics are: First, to find out exactly what the statistics mean and cover. Second, if a series is being used over a period of time, to make sure that the figures are comparable, or if they are not comparable

[1] Examples are *Coal Facts*, published by the National Coal Board, and *Transport Statistics*, published by the British Transport Commission.

to attempt to ensure comparability by allowing for changes in definition and coverage. Third, to assess the degree of accuracy and reliability in the figures published. Fourth, to adapt the statistical information to the particular purpose for which one wants to use it, for statistics are rarely published in the form which is exactly appropriate to the use one has in mind. And last, where there is no published statistical information, to try to make estimates on the basis of the data which are available. The best way of explaining how to deal with these problems is to discuss them in relation to the statistics on some particular subject. The later chapters of this book do this for some of the most important sections of British economic statistics. But there are certain general issues which recur in many different fields of economic statistics and these are discussed in the remainder of this introductory chapter.

Statistics arising from the administration of some scheme of control or from the operation of the law, inevitably reflect the peculiar and changing features of such administration and law. They cannot, therefore, be used properly without knowledge of the administrative and legal system from which they arise. Thus the figures of income distribution in this country are not collected in a special statistical enquiry. They arise from the operations of the Board of Inland Revenue in assessing individuals' incomes for the payment of income-tax and surtax, and therefore reflect the legal and administrative rules according to which such assessments are made. One cannot use the published figures of income distribution sensibly without knowing something about these rules and the changes in them over the period for which one wishes to use the figures. Or, take the monthly figures of unemployment published by the Ministry of Labour. These do not result from a special statistical enquiry into unemployment, but record the number of persons who register as unemployed at the labour exchanges. This registration is much influenced by the coverage of state unemployment insurance and the conditions governing the payment of unemployment benefit; these have varied a great deal since the first state unemployment insurance scheme was introduced before the First World War. Without considerable knowledge of these changes the published figures of unemployment may easily be misinterpreted.

It is not easy to discover how the detailed peculiarities of administration and law affect the meaning of statistics of this kind.

Detailed, painful research is often necessary, for the authorities issuing the statistics are themselves not always fully aware of the administrative practices which may affect the figures.[1] It is rare for figures of this kind to correspond in definition and coverage to what is wanted in economic and statistical enquiry. And one of the problems in using these figures is to make adjustments to them so that they are more appropriate to the purpose in hand. Thus the figures of income distribution published in the Board of Inland Revenue reports cover only incomes assessable to tax, and, therefore, exclude incomes below the tax-exemption limit and that part of income, such as interest on saving certificates, which is by law exempt from taxation. But for most purposes of economic analysis one wants, if possible, to include these categories of tax-exempted incomes, and one would try therefore to adjust the official figures, difficult though this may be.

Where the statistics are the result of an enquiry specially undertaken to obtain the information, it is easier to find out what exactly the figures cover, and they are more likely to correspond to what is wanted for economic analysis. The official reports in which the results of such enquiries are published usually include a full explanation of the exact nature of the enquiry and questions asked, how it was conducted, and how the results were analysed and tabulated. It is always advisable to study the explanatory introduction and notes before using the statistics. Useful hints about the meaning and reliability of the figures can often be got from examining the questionnaire which was used in the enquiry. This also gives some clue to the further material which may be available but is not published. Unfortunately, a copy of the questionnaire used is not always given in the published reports, but it can usually be obtained without difficulty from the department responsible for the enquiry.

Some of the grossest errors in the use of economic statistics arise from ignoring the most elementary problems of comparability. A regular pitfall arises from ignorance whether the figures being used cover the British Isles, the United Kingdom, Great Britain or only England and Wales. The variation in territorial coverage is a most irritating feature of British official statistics.

[1] See, for example, H. A. Turner, 'Measuring Unemployment', *J. R. Statist. Soc.*, series A, vol. 118, pt. I (1955), for a discussion of the effects of the administration of unemployment insurance on the meaning of the published unemployment figures.

There has been a tendency to try to secure uniformity, with the United Kingdom as the normal basis, but many official figures are still published covering Great Britain only. Even greater confusion is possible in dealing with regional statistics, for although there is now a standard set of regions, these have only been introduced since the war and they are not used in all official statistics.

When statistics are improved in scope and definition one usually has to pay a price in lack of comparability with the past, for it is rarely possible to go back and revise earlier figures on the improved basis. Thus the introduction in 1948 of the standard industrial classification for most Government statistics was a great step forward. But the improvement itself to some extent destroyed comparability with statistics before 1948. For example, the Ministry of Labour adopted the new classification for its figures of employment, earnings and hours of work, and it is now difficult to compare the figures on these subjects for the periods before and after 1948.

It is never easy to assess the exact degree of accuracy and reliability in any set of published statistical data, and official publications give little help in such an assessment.[1] There are three main kinds of error. First, error occurs in the original statistical material, either because people who should do not provide returns, or because some provide figures which are inaccurate. The second kind of error arises in statistics which are not merely summaries or tabulations of original data, but attempt to make secondary estimates on the basis of incomplete statistical material. Typical statistics of this kind are the figures of the national income and expenditure or the balance of payments. Lastly, there is the extent of error in using statistics as if they measure something slightly different from what they actually measure. A typical example is the error involved in using figures of the average value of imports, based on customs declarations, as a measure of changes in the prices of goods imported into this country.

The error in the original statistical material can usually only be assessed, and then often with difficulty, from detailed knowledge of the source of the statistics and the way they were analysed and tabulated. One often gets a useful clue about the reliability of figures by looking at the original form or questionnaire and asking whether the questions are so framed that reliable

[1] For a discussion of the treatment of error in British economic statistics see Carter and Roy, *op. cit.*, pp. 113–23.

answers can and will be given. Thus the Census of Population volumes give figures of the non-employed population in this country in three categories: those out of work, the unoccupied who are retired, and other unoccupied people. These figures are based on the answers given about each person's occupation on the census form. The notes to this column on the census form state 'if occupied for payment or profit, state precise occupation or calling. If out of work or wholly retired, state usual former occupation, and add, "out of work" or "retired".' How would this question be treated by a man aged 65 who had lost his job and is not sure whether to try to live on his pension or to look for another job? Would he call himself 'retired' or 'out of work'? There is no clear dividing line in such cases between being 'out of work' or 'retired', and the way in which individuals in similar circumstances may describe themselves may be quite different. Or, again, suppose a married woman had had a job for some years ten or fifteen years before the Census enquiry. Would she describe herself as 'retired'? If one examines the original questionnaire in this way one may come to the conclusion that for certain categories and age groups the figures of those 'out of work', 'retired', or 'otherwise unoccupied' must be treated with great caution.

Where statistics arise from law or administration, their accuracy and reliability will in part be a reflection of the efficiency of the administration. If, for example, the statistics arise from the operation of taxation, one can assume that the taxation authorities have the power to investigate the accuracy of the information on the basis of which such taxation is assessed. The accuracy of the statistics will therefore reflect the honesty of those subject to the taxes and the efficiency and thoroughness with which the authority exercises its power of investigation. If there is an *ad valorem* duty on imports, the Customs and Excise can require information to satisfy themselves that the importer is not trying to evade payment of tax by undervaluing the goods, and can, if necessary, insist on its own assessment for tax purposes. It is this valuation for customs duty which is used in the trade statistics published by the Board of Trade. If the customs authority is lax in checking import valuations, then importers may be tempted to undervalue goods in their customs declarations, and in countries where this happens figures of import trade would be correspondingly unreliable. In the same way statistics of income derived from taxation authorities reflect, in part, the efficiency of the taxation authorities in assessing incomes for tax purposes and the honesty of the citizens in declaring their full incomes as required by law.

Where the published statistics depend on estimation, one ought to try to discover the element of estimation in the figures and the exact way in which the estimate was made. This is often extremely difficult because British official statistical publications give little information about how estimates are arrived at. The annual National Income Blue Book is full of estimates, but there is little indication of the methods used in arriving at them. At present one must proceed from general knowledge of the available material to work out for oneself how the official statisticians probably make their estimates and then attempt to assess how reliable they are.

Assessment of error and accuracy cannot be expressed in precise numerical terms, since it is usually a matter of personal judgment. The assessment of a margin of error in statistical terms would imply much more accurate knowledge of the error in the figures than is usually available to the statistician. Indeed, the kind of information which would usually enable one to quote precise figures of margins of error would often itself enable one to reduce the extent of error in the figures. Thus the kind of knowledge which would enable one to state with precision the margin of error due to evasion in the Board of Inland Revenue's estimates of income, would itself enable the Board to reduce the amount of evasion.

The significance of error in the basic statistics or in estimates derived from them varies according to the use to which they are put. Thus if you are using the Registrar-General for Scotland's figures of population, births and deaths, to work out changes in birth-rates and death-rates, they can be used with confidence as highly reliable and accurate. But if the same figures are used to work out estimates of migration to and from Scotland,[1] the results would be subject to a wide margin of error.

There is often a tendency to exaggerate the extent of reliability in published statistics. For when figures are well presented in

[1] Such estimates would be made by taking population at the beginning of the period, plus births minus deaths during the period, minus the population at the end of the period. For a more detailed discussion of migration estimates, see pp. 42 ff.

neatly printed tables, the reader is usually inclined to assume that they are accurate, especially if the publication is an official one. And official publications rarely give sufficient information to enable the user to distinguish easily between the more and less reliable figures, unless he is himself an expert in the subject. It is true that in some publications one can gather from the notes and explanations which accompany the tables that the figures are no more than 'reasoned guesswork' or are subject to 'a wide margin of error'. But statistics and the notes which explain and qualify them are easily parted, and the same figures may appear in another publication without any mention of the cautionary warnings about error. For example, there are voluminous notes in the Balance of Payments White Paper explaining and defining the terms used and in some cases indicating the uncertainty in the figures. But most of these qualifications and notes have disappeared, perhaps inevitably, when the figures are given in the summary tables on the balance of payments in the *Annual Abstract of Statistics*. The unwary reader of the *Abstract* might assume, quite wrongly, since there is no mention of error, that all the figures are equally reliable or unreliable.

It must be clear to the reader already that there is no easy way of learning how to use economic statistics correctly. There are no simple rules which will enable one to become an efficient expert in the use of the language. At every stage there are difficulties and pitfalls, and one can only acquire skill by practice and caution in actually handling the statistics oneself.

CHAPTER II

POPULATION

IN this chapter we shall consider statistical information about the size and structure of the population; the movement of births and deaths; and the problems that arise in analysing this information and in making forecasts of the population in the future. This branch of statistics is often referred to as 'vital' or 'demographic' statistics, and the whole subject of the analysis of such statistics as *demography*. Other aspects of the condition of the population, for example statistics of employment and unemployment, will be dealt with in later chapters.

THE CENSUS OF POPULATION

Most of the statistical information about the population comes from two sources—the Census of Population and the reports of the Registrars General for births, deaths and marriages. The Census of Population was first taken in 1801 and has been taken every ten years since, excepting 1941. The questions asked in the Census have gradually been extended [1] and the latest Census for 1951 will provide information about the size, fertility, distribution, nationality, education, employment, language, place of work and housing conditions of the population. [2]

The mass of information which is obtained in the Census takes several years to tabulate and publish. First there is the *Preliminary Report*, published very soon after the Census is taken—

[1] For a detailed explanation of the coverage of the Censuses for England and Wales and Scotland, 1801–1931, see *Guides to Official Sources No. 2. Census Reports of Great Britain, 1801–1931* (H.M.S.O., 1951). *The Census Explained* (H.M.S.O., 1951) gives a useful popular explanation of the origins, methods and purpose of taking a Population Census.

[2] A copy of the 1951 Census questionnaire is given in *Census 1951, Great Britain, One Per Cent Sample Tables* (H.M.S.O., 1952), Part I, p. xix.

in 1951 three months afterwards [1]—which gives the total population (males and females separately) for the main regions, counties, county boroughs, municipal boroughs and urban districts, and rural districts of the country,[2] with comparative figures of the population at the previous Census and estimates of migration. Some time later the County Volumes are published; these appear in parts dealing with single counties or group of counties and contain statistics of special interest and value for local government. Detailed figures are given of population in wards and local authority areas by age and sex, and of private families, dwellings and housing conditions.

Then come the National Volumes dealing with special subjects of major interest for the country as a whole. For the 1931 Census there were volumes on occupation, industry, housing and ecclesiastical areas, and a volume of general tables giving national summaries of certain important figures. For the 1951 Census there will also be volumes on fertility, work-places, and an index of place-names. Finally, there is a *General Report* which comments on the Census as a whole and may include certain significant tabulations not given in the earlier reports.

The complete results of the Census have not been available in the past for some years after the Census was taken,[3] and it will be some time before we get the full results of the 1951 Census. In the past this delay made the results of the Census more useful in research and historical analysis than in dealing with current administrative, social and economic problems. For on many aspects of Census enquiries substantial changes take place between the taking and publication of the Census.

An innovation in the tabulation of the 1951 Census goes some way towards remedying this defect. For the first time a sample one per cent of the schedules have been analysed before the main

[1] *Census* 1951, *England and Wales, Preliminary Report* (H.M.S.O., 1951). *Census* 1951, *Scotland, Preliminary Report* (H.M.S.O., 1951).

[2] In addition, in the 1951 Census figures are given for Greater London and five major provincial conurbations. A detailed description of the areas included in these conurbations is given in *Conurbations for Statistical Purposes* (August 1951). This has not been published but can be obtained from the Central Statistical Office.

[3] The last of the National Volumes for the 1931 Census was published in 1935, the last of the County Volumes in 1940, and the *General Report* in 1950. Some of this delay in publishing the *General Report* was due to the work being interrupted by the war.

POPULATION

tabulation. The results of this sample analysis are published in
two parts.[1] The first covers the distribution of the population by
age, sex, marital condition, occupation, industry and housing
conditions; the second deals with the social and economic
characteristics of households, social class, education, fertility,
birthplace, nationality and language. The published figures are
subject to the normal errors in a sample of this size[2] and should
be used with this qualification in mind; yet they provide a most
useful advance summary of some of the most important information obtained in the Census.

The Censuses for England and Wales, Scotland,[3] and Ireland
are compiled and published separately. This brief description of
the publication of the results applies to the Census for England
and Wales. For Scotland there is also a *Preliminary Report* and
a series of county and national volumes, but these do not cover
exactly the same topics, nor are they presented in the same
tabular form as those for England and Wales. It is not always
easy, therefore, to add together figures for England and Wales
and Scotland to arrive at figures for Great Britain as a whole.[4]
The one per cent sample results of the 1951 Census are, however,
a joint production of the two Registrars-General and give figures
for Great Britain as well as for England and Wales and Scotland
separately.

The Census for Ireland has always been taken quite separately
from those for England and Wales and Scotland, and it is often
extremely difficult to obtain figures for the United Kingdom or
the British Isles, especially when dealing with detailed subjects.
No Census was taken in Ireland in 1921 and 1931. A Census was
taken in both Northern and Southern Ireland in 1926, in the
Irish Republic in 1936 and in Northern Ireland in 1937. The

[1] *Census* 1951, *Great Britain, One Per Cent Sample Tables*, Part I and
Part II (H.M.S.O., 1952).

[2] Part I of the *One Per Cent Sample Tables* has a useful general introductory discussion of the basis of the sample and the interpretation of the
results (pp. iv–xii).

[3] A separate Census for Scotland was taken for the first time in 1861.
Since then the enumeration and publication of the results for Scotland
have been the responsibility of the Registrar-General for Scotland.

[4] For some of the more important topics, e.g. total population, the
reports for England and Wales also give figures for Scotland, Great
Britain, the United Kingdom and the British Isles.

17

1951 Census was taken in Northern Ireland and the Irish Republic on the same day as the Census for Great Britain, and for Northern Ireland the questionnaire was the same as that for Great Britain. It should thus be easier to obtain figures for the whole of the United Kingdom[1] or the British Isles, or to make accurate comparisons between its parts, from the 1951 reports than from earlier Census results.

THE REPORTS OF THE REGISTRARS-GENERAL

The reports of the Registrars-General are mainly concerned with statistics of births, deaths and marriages, but they also include estimates of the population for non-Census years.[2] The reports of the Registrar General for England and Wales are published in three series: a weekly report which gives merely the number of births and deaths in the country as a whole, and in each of the main towns; a quarterly report which gives estimates of population, births, deaths, and birth- and death-rates for counties and over 300 towns; and an annual report which covers the whole field of vital statistics in great detail. The annual reports are published in three sections: Medical Tables; Civil Tables; and the Text.[3] The Medical Tables are primarily taken up with a detailed analysis of deaths, by place, age, occupation, and cause; the Civil Tables with births, marriages and fertility. These volumes also give the latest detailed estimates of the population of England and Wales, together with figures for the main countries of the world.[4] The Text comments in detail on the movement shown by the figures and gives the results of special demographic analysis

[1] The most convenient source for population figures for the United Kingdom—although this only covers a few general topics—is the *Annual Abstract of Statistics*. See, for example, *Annual Abstract of Statistics*, No. 90, 1953 (H.M.S.O., 1953), Tables 6–11, pp. 7–14.

[2] For a discussion of these estimates, see pp. 19 ff.

[3] Recently the 'Text' volumes have also been subdivided into separate volumes covering the 'Medical' and 'Civil' fields; but they have not been issued annually.

[4] There are also statistics on subjects which are not part of 'vital' statistics, but which are the responsibility of the Registrar General's office, e.g. statistics of Parliamentary and Local Government electors and the results of the latest elections, and figures about the weather—rainfall, sunshine, etc.

undertaken by the Registrar General's department into the significant factors affecting mortality and fertility.

The weekly and quarterly reports are issued promptly, very soon after the period to which they relate, but there is a longer interval before the issue of the annual reports. The Registrar General is still faced with the problem of overtaking the arrears caused by the war and no regular interval before publication has been established in the post-war period.

The weekly and quarterly reports published by the Registrar-General for Scotland are similar to those for England, but the annual reports cover a narrower range of subjects than those for England, and the analysis of deaths, births and marriages as well as the commentary are included in one annual volume.

The separate publication of their statistics by the two Registrars-General makes it difficult to obtain figures, especially on detailed topics, for Great Britain as a whole. This makes the series of tables published by the Royal Commission on Population for Great Britain as a whole of great value.[1] These tables give details of population by age, sex and marital condition, and figures of births, marriages and deaths over the last 100 years. The series end in 1947 or 1948, but it is not too difficult to bring them up to date from the *Annual Statistical Abstract* and the reports of the Registrars-General.

ESTIMATES OF THE SIZE OF THE
POPULATION

The Census of Population gives us accurate and detailed figures of the population once every ten years.[2] For intervening years estimates can, however, be made, and for this country these have reached a high standard of reliability.[3] In principle these estimates start with the latest Census figures and then allow for births, deaths and migration since the date of the Census. Births and deaths are known with great accuracy, but information

[1] 'Summary of Demographic Statistics for Great Britain', *Papers of the Royal Commission on Population*, vol. II; *Reports & Selected Papers of the Statistics Committee* (H.M.S.O., 1950), pp. 188–212.

[2] Except for 1941.

[3] For a comparison of the Registrar General estimates and the results of the Census, see *Census 1951, England and Wales, Preliminary Report* (H.M.S.O., 1951), p. xi.

about migration, especially internal migration,[1] is much less reliable.[2]

There are three or four quite distinct definitions used in estimates of the population, and since each of them may be loosely referred to as an estimate of '*the* population' without qualification, use of figures on different bases as if in fact they were the same often leads to error. The Census attempts to include every person in Great Britain on the night when the count is taken. In the words of the Census report 'The *de facto* population thus recorded comprises all persons enumerated on land, in barges and boats on inland waters, in all vessels in ports and at anchorages at Census midnight other than ships of foreign navies, and also persons in boats on fishing or coastwise voyages which returned to port during April not having proceeded from a port outside Great Britain, Ireland or their adjacent islands'.[3] This basis is used not only in the Census but also in all the Registrar General's estimates for the pre-war period. Since the figures refer to all people in this country they include all armed forces at home, whether British or foreign, but exclude British forces overseas.

The difficulty of keeping an accurate check on movements of the population—especially the armed forces—after the outbreak of the war, made it impossible to continue with this basis after 1939 and two new definitions were adopted. The first covered the 'total population' and differed from the 'Census population' in that it included the armed forces and merchant navy both at home and overseas but excluded Commonwealth and Allied armed forces in this country. The second estimate referred to the

[1] Internal migration must be known for inter-Census estimates of the population of towns, counties, etc. After 1939 the National Register and Food Office records provided substantial information about internal migration. Before 1939 internal migration was estimated from a wide range of sources. For a detailed discussion of the basis of the estimates, see the *Registrar General's Statistical Review of England and Wales*, 1936, *Text* (H.M.S.O., 1938), pp. 166–70, and *Statistical Review*, 1946–1950, *Text, Civil* (H.M.S.O., 1954), pp. 5–23. Also M. P. Newton and J. R. Jeffery, *Internal Migration: Some Aspects of Population Movements within England and Wales* (General Register Office, Studies on Medical and Population Subjects, No. 5, H.M.S.O., 1951).

[2] For a discussion of migration statistics, see pp. 42-5.

[3] *Census 1951, England and Wales, Preliminary Report* (H.M.S.O., 1951), p. x.

'civilian population' and excluded the armed forces altogether. During the war and the immediate post-war years, the Registrar General for England and Wales published figures for both the 'total population' and 'civilian population' for the country as a whole, but all the estimates for individual areas—regions, counties, towns, etc.—related to the civilian population only.[1]

Recently the Registrar General has gone back in his main estimates to a basis which follows the Census definition quite closely. These estimates are called the 'home population', which is defined as the civilian population, the armed forces—British, Commonwealth and allied—stationed in this country, plus all merchant seamen in home waters. The 'home population' is now the basis of the Registrar General's detailed estimates of population by regions and towns; but for the country as a whole figures are also given for the 'total' and 'civilian' population.

The bases in current use, therefore, are:

(1) *The Census or home population*—briefly, the population actually in the country. This includes all the armed forces stationed in this country and the mercantile marine in home waters. This basis is sometimes referred to as the '*de facto*' population.[2]

(2) *The civilian population*—the home population less the armed forces stationed in this country.

(3) *The total population*—the civilian population plus United Kingdom armed forces both at home and overseas, but not including any Commonwealth and Allied armed forces in this country.[3]

The Registrar General's estimates of the population are published in summary in the quarterly reports and in more detail in the annual reports. Since there is considerable delay in issuing

[1] Between 1943 and 1947 the mercantile marine was excluded from the 'civilian' population. Between 1940 and 1942 and from 1948 onwards it has been included.

[2] Figures corresponding to those of the home population published by the Registrar General are described as the '*de facto*' population in the *Annual Abstract of Statistics* and the *Monthly Digest of Statistics*.

[3] The difference between the 'total' population and 'home' population does not therefore give figures of the United Kingdom armed forces overseas.

the annual reports, the Registrar General has started a new series of publications giving in advance his estimates of the population of the administrative areas of the country for June of each year. The series was started in 1949, relating to 1947, and now comes out about eight months after the date to which it relates.[1] There is no comparable advance publication of population estimates by the Registrar-General for Scotland.

Because of the changing basis of the estimates of population during the last few years, one has to exercise great care in using the figures. To take one example: the population of Aldershot given in the Registrar General's estimates for 1948 is 27,780, and in the estimates for 1949 is 39,050. This increase is not due to a sudden migration of population to Aldershot, but merely reflects the fact that the estimate for 1948 is for the 'civilian population' only, while that for 1949 is for the 'home population', i.e. the civilian population plus the armed forces stationed in the area.

In using the population figures for individual towns or small areas one has also to keep in mind the particular time of the year to which the figures relate. For example, the population of Blackpool in August will normally be substantially higher than in December; to compare the population in August in one year with December in a later year will not, therefore, tell us whether Blackpool's population has increased or decreased in the normal sense. For this reason one has to be careful in comparing figures for the 1921 Census which was taken on June 19th, when holiday travel already had some effect, with later Censuses taken in March or April.

Temporary movements of local populations can to some extent be met by basing the figures on the *normal* residents of each area, although this raises some knotty problems of how to define 'normal residence'. As far as possible the Registrar General's estimates of local population are on a 'normal residence' basis. The Census itself is based on the 'enumeration' principle, i.e. it relates to the places where people were on the night when the Census was taken. But in recent Censuses a question has also been asked about the place of 'normal residence' and this has made possible estimates on a 'residence' basis as well. At a time

[1] The first of the series, for 1947, gave information by age distribution as well as sex for each administrative area. Recent ones give total population only.

when there are substantial movements of the population—for example, during the popular holiday months, or the evacuation period immediately after the outbreak of war in 1939—the difference between the actual, or enumerated, population and the normal, or resident, population of a particular area may be quite substantial.

In many areas there is a big difference between the day and night population. The City of London has a day population many times greater than its night population. Each of these figures is useful for different purposes. The Census and the Registrar General's figures in principle refer to the night population. But in 1921, and again in 1951, the Census asked for information about each person's place of work, and it should thus be possible to make estimates for these years of the day population and of the extent of daily travel to work in the large cities of the country. Such estimates are of great value in dealing with problems of housing, transport and re-siting of industry.

ANALYSIS OF POPULATION STATISTICS: (I) DEATHS

OR MORTALITY

Changes in the total population of any area are the net result of deaths, births and migration. If, therefore, we wish to discover the causes of such changes we must proceed by analysing these three factors separately. Such separate analysis is also necessary if we wish to use the evidence of past trends to make estimates of the size of the population in the future. In addition an examination of changes in deaths and births often throws much light on many important social and economic problems.

Crude death-rates

The number of deaths by itself provides us with little information of significance. It is perhaps of use to undertakers and to those concerned with estimating the cemetery space needed in the country. But if we are interested in the figures as a measure of changes in conditions of health, either over time or in different areas, industries or occupations, we must relate the number of deaths to the population at risk. The simplest and crudest way of doing this is to express deaths per unit of the population, or since it is more convenient arithmetically, per 1000 of the population. This gives us the *crude death-rate*.

Specific mortality rates

The moment we come to consider the meaning and significance of movements in the crude death-rate we meet one of the most important problems in population analysis—how can we take account of the changing age composition of the population? For if two populations have a different age structure, a comparison of the crude death-rates may not be a good guide to the comparative health conditions of the two populations. A population with a lot of old people and a few young people may have a much higher crude death-rate than a population with a lot of young people and a few old people; and yet the first population may be healthier, age for age, than the second. The death-rate at each age—called the *specific mortality rate*—in the first population may be lower than in the second population and yet the overall death-rate much higher. For the crude death-rate is merely the average of the specific death-rates weighted by the population at each age. In the first population the weighting of the older age groups, in which the specific death-rates are higher, is much greater than in the second.

This point may be clearer if one takes an extreme hypothetical example. Suppose that everyone left Manchester on reaching retiring age and went to live in Southport, and suppose that the population of Southport consisted only of these retired people. In these circumstances the population of Manchester would be relatively young, few people would die there and Manchester's death-rate would be low; Southport's population would be old, the number of deaths and the death-rate relatively high. But this would not mean that Manchester was a healthier place to live in than Southport. It would merely reflect the fact that Mancunians went to Southport to die!

Differences in age composition are not trivial in their effects on the movements of the crude death-rate,[1] and the use of the crude

[1] For example, the crude death-rate for England and Wales in 1941 was practically the same as in 1911 (15·7 compared with 15·6), although there had been substantial falls in the death-rates for every age between the two dates. This was because the age structure of the population in 1941 was very different from that of 1911.

death-rate in making mortality comparisons over time, between countries or towns is most dangerous. What statistical devices are there for eliminating the effects of age and sex[1] composition from comparisons of death-rates? The simplest device is not to use a total death-rate but to make all comparisons on the basis of specific mortality rates—that is, the death-rates for particular age and sex groups. For many purposes this is the most instructive and convenient method to follow. These figures are in any case of importance because they reveal significant information about the mortality conditions of the population. For example, the figures for England and Wales[2] show quite clearly that the mortality rates for men and women from the ages 5 to 55 are now so low that there is little scope for further reduction. Measures to reduce mortality can now only affect the rates among babies and young children, and extend people's lives after the age of 55.[3] One specific mortality rate—*the infant mortality rate*—is of considerable importance because it is a sensitive indicator of changing social and health conditions. The infant mortality rate relates the number of deaths of babies under one year to the number of births during the year, and is expressed, as are other mortality rates, as deaths per 1000.

Standardized death-rates

There are, however, disadvantages in using specific mortality rates. If one wants to examine the trend of mortality over a series of years,[4] one would have to look at a very large number of figures and it might become difficult to see any of the broad general trends that are in operation. Further, on many occasions the specific mortality rates would not all move in the same direction or to the same extent, and one would still want some method of summing up or averaging the varying movements.

The commonest method of dealing with this problem is to

[1] Sex composition is important as well as age composition, because in most populations women live longer than men.

[2] See *Annual Abstract of Statistics, No. 90, 1953* (H.M.S.O., 1953), Table 21, or *Registrar General's Statistical Review of England and Wales, 1952, Tables, Part I, Medical* (H.M.S.O., 1953), Table 4, pp. 6–8.

[3] This fact is important when one considers the effect of further reductions in mortality on the size of the population or its age structure in the future.

[4] Or between occupations or areas for a single year.

B

25

relate the specific mortality rates year by year to a fixed population by age and sex. Before 1938 the Registrar General for England and Wales used the population of England and Wales in 1901 as the standard for calculations of this kind. For each year he calculated a death-rate based on the specific mortality rates of that year, but related to the population of 1901. This gave an annual series of death-rates all related to the same population—that of 1901—but based on the specific mortality rates of the year in question.[1] It was thought that average death-rates arrived at on this basis, known as the *standardized death-rate*, would not be influenced by age and sex structure, since they were all based on the same population. The Registrar-General for Scotland also calculates a standardized rate, but uses as his fixed population 'a standard division by age and sex fixed for the purpose by the International Statistical Institute'.[2]

It was soon discovered that standardizing death-rates by this method did not in fact eliminate the effects of age and sex structure from mortality comparisons. For the final result of the calculation still depends on the age and sex structure of the population in the particular year chosen for the fixed standard, and using different years as a standard gives substantially different results. This can be seen quite clearly if one compares mortality in 1901 and 1939. A standardized death-rate, based on the 1901 population, would show a reduction from 16·9 to 8·5 per thousand; but if the 1939 population is chosen as the basis for standardization, the fall would be from 19·6 to 12·1 per thousand—in the first case a fall of 50 per cent compared with only 38 per cent in the second.[3] Unless the population of 1901 was more normal in its age and sex structure than the population of 1939, there is no reason for preferring the first basis of standardization to the second. In fact, it soon became clear that the 1901 population was highly abnormal. It contained an unusually high proportion of young people, and death-rates based on this

[1] If the total death-rate is thought of as a weighted average of specific rates, then the crude rate is an average with varying weights—the weights varying with the year—, while the standardized rate has fixed weights—the weights being the population of 1901.

[2] See *Annual Report of the Registrar-General for Scotland*, 1952 (H.M.S.O., 1954), pp. 14–16.

[3] See *Registrar General's Statistical Review of England and Wales*, 1940–45, *Text, Vol. I, Medical* (H.M.S.O., 1949), p. 6.

population as a standard gave undue importance to the down-ward movement of mortality at the younger ages. The stan-dardized death-rate, therefore, tended to exaggerate the extent of the fall in mortality.

Comparative mortality indices

For this reason the Registrar General for England and Wales decided in 1941 to introduce a more up-to-date basis for stan-dardization. The year 1938 replaced 1901 as the standard, but since 1938 would also get out of date in time and since, in any case, there were no grounds for assuming that the age and sex structure of the 1938 population was normal, it was decided to use the average of 1938 and the year in question as the basis for stan-dardization. The final result was not expressed as a death-rate, but as a comparison with the death-rate for 1938 calculated on the same population basis. This comparison is called the *comparative mortality index*. The comparative mortality index for 1952, for example, takes the specific mortality rates for 1952 for each age and sex, weights them by the average of the population of each age and sex for 1938 and 1952,[1] and expresses the result as a ratio of the specific rates for 1938, also weighted by the average of the population at each age and sex for 1938 and 1952.

The formula for the calculation can be expressed in more general terms applying to any year.

If

m_x = the specific mortality rate for each single age and sex group in year x.

m_{38} = the specific mortality rate for each single age and sex group in 1938.

p_x = the proportion of the population in each particular age and sex group in year x.

p_{38} = the proportion of the population in each age and sex group in 1938

then the comparative mortality index for the year x is

$$\frac{\Sigma m_x(p_x + p_{38})}{\Sigma m_{38}(p_x + p_{38})} .$$

[1] Since the size of the total population changes, the average of the ratios of each age and sex group to the total population is taken as the weighting basis.

The comparative mortality index for 1938 is obviously 1, and the comparative mortality indices for later years are expressed as a ratio of unity. The comparative mortality index is now published annually in the *Registrar General's Statistical Review of England and Wales, Text, Medical*,[1] and has been calculated back to 1841.

The comparative mortality index compares each year with 1938, but the Registrar General publishes a further calculation which compares the mortality index for each year with the comparative mortality index for the previous year, thus making it easy to see by how much mortality, measured on this basis, goes up or down, year by year. This calculation is called the *mortality ratio*. Thus the mortality ratio for any year x is

$$\frac{\text{C.M.I. for year } x}{\text{C.M.I. for year } x-1}$$

This new basis for standardizing death-rates over time, which was introduced by the Registrar General for England and Wales in 1941, has not been adopted by the Registrar-General for Scotland, who continues the older system as the basis for calculating a standardized death-rate.[2]

The comparative mortality index does not completely or satisfactorily solve the problem of eliminating age and sex structure from mortality comparisons. First, because it is an average which is still substantially influenced by the age and sex structure of the current year and to this extent corresponds to the crude death-rate; and secondly, because there are no grounds for assuming that the population of England and Wales in 1938 was 'normal' in its age and sex structure.

Life table death-rates

Another way of attempting to eliminate the effect of age and sex structure is to calculate the 'death-rate for a stationary population'. Suppose we take the specific death-rates for any

[1] See *Registrar General's Statistical Review of England and Wales, 1952, Tables, Part I, Medical* (H.M.S.O., 1953), Table 3, pp. 4–5. For a more detailed explanation of the Comparative Mortality Index see *Registrar General's Statistical Review, 1941, Tables, Part I, Medical* (H.M.S.O., 1945), Appendix, and *Statistical Review 1940–1945, Text, Vol. I, Medical* (H.M.S.O., 1949).

[2] See p. 26.

year and assume that they continue year by year, and that in each year the number of births is just sufficient to offset the deaths. Then eventually the population would settle down to a stable level, not only in total numbers but also in numbers of each age and sex. The crude death-rate of such a stationary population would not reflect any abnormalities in age and sex structure, since the population would have settled down to a normal unchanging structure. If, therefore, we use the specific mortality rates of any year to work out what the average crude death-rate would be for a stationary population with such specific mortality rates, we have a measure of average mortality in that year which is not influenced by any abnormalities in the age and sex structure of the population. For example, suppose we take the specific mortality rates by age and sex for 1953, and work out what the crude death-rate would be for a stationary population which had those specific mortality rates. Then we have a figure summarizing mortality experience in 1953 which is not influenced by any abnormalities in the actual age and sex structure of the population in 1953. We can then compare such a 'stationary population death-rate' for 1953 with similar calculations for other years, and be sure that the comparison is not affected by abnormalities in the age and sex structure of the populations.

The best way of working out the stationary population death-rate for a given set of specific mortality rates is by constructing a life table, and such a death-rate is therefore also called the *life table death-rate*. A life table sets out to show how many people would die, and therefore how many would survive, year by year, if they experienced a given set of specific mortality rates. As well as giving the basis for calculating a life table death-rate, life tables have many other uses, especially in insurance.

A life table usually starts with a 100,000 children at birth,[1] and then shows on a given set of mortality rates, what is the chance of death before reaching age 1, also what is the chance of survival to age 1; therefore how many will die between 0 and 1 and how many of the original 100,000 will survive to age 1. The calculation is then repeated for mortality between 1 and 2 for those who remain out of the 100,000; and so on year by year until the whole of the original 100,000 have died out. Having done this calculation we can work out the number of years on average that each

---

[1] Since mortality rates are different for males and females, separate life tables are usually calculated for each.

person in such a population would live.[1] This figure is known as the *average expectation of life*, since it tells us the number of years of life that on average can be expected, given the mortality rates used in the calculation. A similar calculation of average expectation of life can be done for those who survive to later ages. Such figures for later years will then tell us the number of further years of life that on average can be expected by those who survive to a particular age. To say, for example, that the average expectation of life at age 5 is 60, means that given the set of mortality rates used, those who survive to age 5 will on average live a further 60 years each.

From the average expectation of life at birth, we can work out the death-rate for a stationary population or the life table death-rate. Suppose the average expectation of life, on a given set of mortality rates, is 65 years. Then in a stationary population, with births equal to deaths and a stable age structure, 1/65th of the population will die every year, thus giving a death-rate per 1000 of 15·4.

Life tables can be constructed for any given assumed set of mortality rates, and are a convenient and enlightening way of summarizing and expressing the implications of such mortality rates. They can be calculated for actual mortality rates experienced in the past or for any hypothetical set of rates. To calculate them accurately for actual mortality experience accurate information is necessary about the total population and deaths by age and sex, and they can therefore be compiled most reliably for years in which there is a Census of Population. The Registrar General publishes a detailed volume of life tables in connection with the *Census of Population*.[2] A special set of life tables for Great Britain in an abbreviated form was calculated for the Royal Commission on Population for the years

----

[1] Suppose that the life table shows that 5000 of the 100,000 die between 0 and 1 and 1500 between 1 and 2. If we assume that the deaths are spread evenly throughout the year, the 5000 will have lived 2500 years between them (5000 × ½ year each) and the 1500, 2250 years (1500 × 1½ years each). In total the 6500 will have lived 4750 years. If we continue such a calculation for all ages we shall have the total number of years lived by the whole 100,000; and if we divide this by 100,000, the average number of years lived by each.

[2] *Registrar General for England and Wales, Decennial Supplement*, 1931, Part I, *Life Tables* (H.M.S.O., 1936).

1942–4.[1] Abridged life tables, based on current mortality rates, are now published each year by the two Registrars-General[2] and in the *Annual Abstract of Statistics*.

The life table death-rate is not favoured as a measure of mortality by the Registrar General,[3] and although some figures are usually given in the *Registrar General's Statistical Review, Text, Medical*, they are not published regularly elsewhere in the Registrar General's reports. They can, however, be calculated quite easily from the figures given in the published life tables.

Comparison of local death-rates

So far we have discussed ways of eliminating the effects of age and sex structure in comparing death-rates over time. Similar problems arise in making comparisons between places or occupations.[4] Comparisons of occupational mortality can only be made for Census of Population years, since it is only for these years that there are figures of the population by occupation. Occupational mortality rates are published in the *Registrar General's Decennial Supplement*.[5] One of the methods of allowing for differences in age structure between occupations is to compare the death-rate in each occupation with what the death-rate would be for the people in that occupation if they were subject to the same specific mortality rates by age and sex as the average for the country as a whole. This gives a ratio, called the *standardized mortality ratio*, between the actual deaths for a given occupational group and what the deaths would have been if by age and sex they had

---

[1] *Papers of the Royal Commission on Population, Vol. II, Reports and Selected Papers of the Statistics Committee* (H.M.S.O., 1950), pp. 54–8.

[2] See *Registrar General's Quarterly Return for England and Wales, quarter ended 31st December*, 1953 (H.M.S.O., 1954), Appendix A, p. 30, and *Annual Report of the Registrar-General for Scotland*, 1952 (H.M.S.O., 1954), p. 21.

[3] For the arguments against the use of the life table death-rate see *Registrar General's Statistical Review of England and Wales*, 1940–45, *Text, Vol. I, Medical* (H.M.S.O., 1949), p. 12.

[4] There are in addition other problems, especially the attribution of deaths to particular areas and occupations. The former is especially difficult when there is considerable internal population movement, as for example during the war, and the latter is especially difficult for retired persons.

[5] The latest being for 1931.

suffered the average mortality rates for the country as a whole. Such ratios can then be compared for different occupations.[1]

In the *Decennial Supplements* the Registrar General for England and Wales makes comparisons between regions, by calculating for each region what deaths would have been if the region had experienced the life table death-rates for the country as a whole[2] and then relates this to the actual deaths in the region. For non-Census years the Registrar General calculates an *area comparability factor*[3] which is used to correct the local or regional death-rates for the effects of differences between the age and sex structure of each locality and that of the country as a whole. After 1934[4] the area comparability factor has been calculated for England and Wales on the following basis: calculate for each area the average death-rate that would occur in that area if it experienced by each age and sex group the specific national mortality rates for 1930, 1931 and 1932; compare this with the average national death-rate for the same period. The difference between the two will be due to the difference between the age and sex structure of the region and that of the country as a whole. If we use the ratio between these two rates to adjust the actual local death-rates, any remaining difference between localities should then reflect factors other than age and sex composition.

In theory we should have a different 'area comparability factor' for each year, for the relation between the national and local age and sex distribution may vary considerably even over short periods. In fact it is not possible to do this, because the age and sex composition of the population of each locality is not known accurately every year. For the years 1934–8 the Registrar General used the years 1930–2 as the basis for calculating this factor. It was revised in 1939 on the basis of mid-1939 population and mortality estimates. The publication of the A.C.F. was suspended from 1940 to 1947, but was resumed in the reports for

[1] For a more detailed discussion of this method and explanation of other methods of allowing for differences in age and sex structure, see *Registrar General for England and Wales, Decennial Supplement, 1931, Part IIa, Occupational Mortality* (H.M.S.O., 1938), p. 14.

[2] Called the 'expected' deaths.

[3] Frequently referred to as the 'A.C.F.'

[4] For methods of standardizing local rates before 1934, see *Registrar General's Statistical Review of England and Wales, 1934, Text* (H.M.S.O., 1936), pp. 4–6.

1948.[1] The reliability of the adjusted local death-rates will clearly depend on how up to date the basis of the area comparability factor is, and whether one can assume that there have been no significant changes in the relation between local and national age and sex structure since that date. Great care must, therefore, be taken in making use of these rates.[2]

A different method is used by the Registrar-General for Scotland in arriving at standardized death-rates. The local specific mortality rates by age and sex are applied to a standard population structure to arrive at comparable adjusted local death-rates. The standard population used for this purpose is that of Scotland in 1931.

ANALYSIS OF POPULATION STATISTICS: (II) BIRTHS OR FERTILITY

Crude birth-rates

The same problem of allowing for the changing age and sex structure of the population occurs when we use birth statistics. The crude method, which merely relates the total number of births to the total population—the crude birth-rate [3]—does not enable us to tell whether changes are due to a tendency for people to have more or less children or merely reflects a temporary change in the ratio of the child-bearing population to the total. If there is an unusually large proportion of the population at the child-bearing ages, we would expect the birth-rate to be high, even though each mother was having relatively few children. Such a high birth-rate

[1] The A.C.F.s now used in the Registrar General's reports—see Table 17 of the Medical Tables or Table E of the Civil Tables—are different from those used in the 1939 Reports and are presumably based on more recent population and mortality rates than those for 1939, but no indication is given in the Reports of the basis now used.

[2] The A.C.F. only deals with comparisons for any particular year. The Registrar General has also worked out a method for combining this adjustment with an adjustment for changing age and sex structure in each area over time—the *time comparability factor*—the adjustment for the two together being called the *combined comparability factor*. For details of this see the *Registrar General's Statistical Review of England and Wales, 1938 and 1939, Text* (H.M.S.O., 1947), pp. 6 and 7.

[3] There are many tricky points involved in calculating even the crude birth-rate—whether to include or exclude still births, whether to base the rate on actual occurrences or registrations during the period, and so on.

would be deceptive, because as the age structure of the population changed and the proportion at the child-bearing ages dropped the birth-rate would fall, even though the number of children born per mother remained the same.

General, specific, and total fertility rates

Just as with death-rates, therefore, if we wish to use the figures to examine the deeper underlying factors, we must eliminate the effect of changing age and sex structure. The simplest way of doing this is to relate the number of births to the population of child-bearing age only, taken as either the females aged 15–50 or 15–45. This measure, known as the *general fertility rate*, is published annually by the Registrars-General.[1] But this measure only allows for the changing ratio of women aged 15–45 to the total population, and takes no account of changes within the age group 15–45. These changes may be significant and may have a substantial influence on fluctuations in the general fertility rate because there is a preponderance of births at certain ages within that group.[2] This difficulty can be overcome by using the figures of birth-rates for each age or age group, known as the specific fertility rates. These rates can only be calculated if the age of the mother is known at the time of the registration of the birth, and such information has been obtained in this country only since 1938. Since that date specific fertility

---

[1] See *Registrar General's Statistical Review of England and Wales*, 1950, *Tables, Part II, Civil* (H.M.S.O., 1952), Table C, p. 8; and *Annual Report of the Registrar-General for Scotland*, 1952 (H.M.S.O., 1954), Table 8, p. 85.

[2] The rate of live births per 1000 females in the population at various ages within the group 15–45, for England and Wales in 1950, was as follows (*Registrar General's Statistical Review of England and Wales*, 1950, *Tables, Part II, Civil*) (H.M.S.O., 1952), Table EE, p. 145.

Live Births per 1000 females of the population	
15–19	22·18
20–24	126·25
25–29	136·21
30–34	89·40
35–39	48·25
40–44	14·20
45–49	1·08

rates as well as a mass of other new statistics on fertility have been published by the Registrars-General in their annual reports.

There are the same objections to the use of specific fertility rates as there are to the use of specific mortality rates. One has to look at a very large number of figures to make comparisons over a series of years, and in any case one would still wish to combine upward and downward movements in a single figure.

There are two ways of doing this. The first proceeds on the same basis as the life table. We calculate the number of children that would be born to 1000 females if they had children at the specific fertility rates of the year we are dealing with. If the specific fertility rates are given per thousand females for each age, this total can be obtained simply by adding up the specific fertility rates.[1] If we compare figures on this basis—known as the total fertility rate—for successive years, we are making comparisons of fertility which are not influenced in any way by the age distribution of the population. A different method, used by the Registrar General for England and Wales,[2] is to compare the actual recorded births each year with the births that would have occurred if the population of the year in question had been subject to the specific fertility rates of some standard year, 1938 being chosen by the Registrar General as the standard year. Calculations on this basis are published in the annual reports.[3]

Other measures of fertility

All these adjustments deal only with the effect of age and sex distribution on the number of births, and are designed to eliminate the effects of abnormalities in this distribution. In the case of death rates, when we eliminate the effects of abnormal age and sex structure we arrive at rates which reflect fundamental changes in mortality, but this is not true with birth-rates. For even specific fertility rates may reflect abnormal temporary phenomena and these may mask for a time the underlying forces affecting the

[1] If the rates are given in five-yearly age groups, then we must multiply each rate by five, since 1000 females would experience each group fertility rate for five years.

[2] See *Registrar General's Statistical Review of England and Wales, 1940–45, Text, Vol. II, Civil* (H.M.S.O., 1951), pp. 64–5.

[3] See *Statistical Review, 1938–39, Text* (H.M.S.O., 1947), Table CVI, p. 189 and *Statistical Review, 1940–45, Text, Vol. II, Civil* (H.M.S.O., 1951), Table XXIX, p. 65.

population's attitude to having children. If, therefore, we use specific fertility rates as a measure of these underlying forces, we may get a misleading picture. Some of the important temporary changes which may affect the specific fertility rates are changes in the proportion of the population who marry, the age at which they marry, and the rate at which they have children.

Let us take as an example the age at which people marry and see how this may affect specific fertility rates. Suppose that the age at which women marry falls for some reason. Then in the period in which this fall takes place the number of marriages will increase and for a time thereafter specific fertility rates will increase. Take an extremely simplified hypothetical case. Suppose that the age of marriage for all females in the population was 24 and had been 24 for some time, and that suddenly all females started getting married a year earlier, at age 23. In the year in which this change occurred the number of marriages would double, since in that year both the group reaching 24 and the group reaching 23 would marry. In the years immediately following, the number of births and the specific fertility rates would be abnormally high, even if there were no change in the number of children which each woman had throughout her married life. The higher specific fertility rates would merely reflect the fact that women were having their children earlier in their lives as the result of marrying earlier, not that they were having more children. Unless therefore we allow for this factor we may be misled in our interpretation of the higher fertility figures. We may mistake what is merely a temporary phenomenon, resulting from a change in the age of marriage, for a fundamental change in the forces affecting fertility. Similarly, if married couples have their children earlier in their married lives, this would show as an increase for a time in specific fertility rates, even if they had no more children in total.

It is thus clear that if there are substantial changes in the proportion of the population who get married, or in the age of marriage, or in the rate at which people build up their families, conclusions about fertility trends which are based on specific fertility rates may be quite misleading. The answer to this difficulty is to measure trends in fertility in what we regard as the basic factor—the size of the family or the number of children which married couples have in the course of their lives. If we could say, for example, that on average couples married in 1850 had eight children, those married in 1900 five children, those married in 1930 three children, and those married in 1950 two children, then we have a measure of fertility which 'eliminates' age distribution, rate and age of marriage, and the rate of family building.

There are two difficulties in making such calculations, one fundamental and one connected with the availability of statistical information. The first is that we cannot arrive at the size of the family of married couples until in fact they have passed the child-bearing age. This means that a complete assessment of fertility on this basis must be very much out of date. We can say with accuracy in 1950 what the average size of a family born to couples married in 1930 is, since by 1950 practically all the women married in 1930—twenty years earlier—will have had all the children they are going to have. But we can say very little about the average size of families of couples married in 1950, since a large part of their families are still unborn. A way to overcome this difficulty is to measure fertility only in terms of 'completed families', but then we are in fact not measuring *present trends*, but something in the past, since the present size of completed families reflects attitudes and social conditions over the past twenty years. In fact the position is not quite as difficult as this, because we know that most married couples have the major part of their families in the early years of their married lives; and we can assume with fair certainty that if the number of children born to married couples in, say, the first five years of their married lives is increasing, there will also be an increase in the size of the completed families.

The other difficulty in assessing changes in fertility in terms of family size is the availability of statistical information. For one needs to be able to relate births each year to the year of marriage of the mothers and to the number of previous children born. Some information on these lines has been available since 1938, but not sufficient to make complete calculations of family size. This was one of the reasons why the Royal Commission on Population thought it necessary to take a sample family census as part of its investigations into population trends. From the material collected in that census the Royal Commission was able to analyse changes in family size for the thirty years before 1947.[1] The

[1] See *Report of the Royal Commission on Population* (Cmd. 7695, H.M.S.O., 1949), pp. 51–9, and *Papers of the Royal Commission on*

annual reports of the two Registrars-General also contain substantial analysis of births in relation to date and duration of marriage.[1] The Census of Population for 1951 asked for information about date of marriage and date of birth of children and it will be possible to make a more detailed analysis of fertility when the results of that Census become available.

ANALYSIS OF POPULATION STATISTICS: (III) THE MEASUREMENT OF REPLACEMENT

So far we have considered the measurement of mortality and fertility separately. How can the two be combined so that we can assess whether one is more or less offsetting the other, whether fertility is sufficient to balance mortality? The crudest method is to compare the number of births and deaths year by year. But such a comparison may be highly misleading since such figures, as we have already explained, may be influenced by temporary factors. For example, if, owing to high birth-rates in the past, there is a relatively young population, for the time being there will be a low death-rate and relatively few deaths, and an abnormally large number of births because of the high proportion of young marriageable people in the population. We want to know whether births will balance deaths given the continuation of fertility and mortality trends, once this abnormality has passed. Measurements of replacement attempt to eliminate such 'abnormalities' and to tell us whether each generation will replace itself on the basis of the fundamental factors influencing mortality and fertility. Such measurements of replacement tell us only whether in the long run the population will increase or decrease, given existing mortality or fertility rates. It may be quite a long time before the abnormalities disappear, so that a population

Population, vol. II, *Reports and Selected Papers of the Statistics Committee* (H.M.S.O., 1950), 'The Family Census: a Preliminary Report', pp. 87–133.

[1] *Registrar General's Statistical Review of England and Wales*, 1950, *Tables, Part II, Civil* (H.M.S.O., 1952), 'Fertility Analyses' Tables AA–YY; and *Statistical Review 1946–1950, Text, Civil* (H.M.S.O., 1954), pp. 98–114; and *Annual Report of the Registrar-General for Scotland*, 1952 (H.M.S.O., 1954), Tables 10–14, pp. 88–92.

may not be replacing itself and yet go on increasing for some time.[1]

Gross reproduction rate

Different measures of replacement can be calculated depending on the abnormalities in the population that are eliminated before arriving at an assessment of fertility and mortality. The earliest and most commonly used measure is that which eliminates only age and sex structure. This can be done quite easily by combining figures of total fertility and the measurement of mortality as calculated in a life table. The total fertility rate shows how many children would be born to 1000 women if they experienced the specific fertility rates of the year or series of years which are being examined. There is one further calculation that has to be made before this figure can be used as a measure of replacement. The number of children born to 1000 women on the basis of this calculation will include both male and female children, but if we are considering whether the births are sufficient to replace the existing generation of women we must include only female births.[2] This will give us the total number of female children that would be born to 1000 females during the course of their child-bearing life if they have the number of children year

[1] For a detailed discussion of the measurements of replacement rates and their meaning, see *Report of the Royal Commission on Population* (Cmd. 7695, H.M.S.O., 1949), Chapter 7, 'The Question of Replacement', and Appendix 3, 'The Measurement of Reproductivity'; *Papers of the Royal Commission on Population*, vol. II, *Reports and Selected Papers of the Statistics Committee* (H.M.S.O., 1950); 'Introductory Memorandum of the Statistics Committee', 'Fertility Measurements and the Reproduction Rate' 'Births, Marriages and Reproductivity, England and Wales 1938–1947', and Report by J. Hajnal, especially Section C, 'The Measurement of Reproductivity'. See also *Registrar General's Statistical Review of England and Wales*, 1940–1945, *Text, Vol. II, Civil* (H.M.S.O., 1951), pp. 65 ff., and Appendix III, pp. 204 ff.; and *Statistical Review* 1946–1950, *Text, Civil* (H.M.S.O., 1954), pp. 79–86, and Appendix III, pp. 210–225.

[2] Since the number of boys born is slightly more than the number of girls, this means reducing the total figure by rather more than half. This adjustment can be made either by using specific fertility rates of female births only, or by reducing the total fertility rates by the ratio of female births to total births for the year in question.

by year shown in the age-specific fertility rates of the year we are measuring. If we express the result in terms of the number who would be born to each female instead of per 1000 females, we arrive at the measure known as the *gross reproduction rate*.

Net reproduction rate

The gross reproduction rate takes no account of mortality, but it is a simple matter to combine the life table measure of mortality with the specific fertility rates used for the gross reproduction rate. From the life table we can work out how many females, from, say, 1000, would survive year by year if they experienced the mortality rates of the year we are dealing with. If we then apply the female specific fertility rates to the number of females who would survive from the original 1000 year by year through the child-bearing period, we get a figure of female children born which takes account both of fertility and mortality. The result tells us how many female children would be born to 1000 females, if the 1000 females survived according to the mortality rates and had children according to the age specific fertility rates of the period we are measuring. If the result is divided by 1000, thus giving a figure per female instead of per 1000 females, we have what is known as the *net reproduction rate*.

The Registrar General for England and Wales publishes a reproduction rate which is arrived at by a slight variant of this method, called the *effective reproduction rate*.[1] The effective reproduction rate takes account of expected mortality rates in the future. Thus the *net reproduction* rate for 1950 would be based on the age-specific fertility rates and mortality rates for 1950, while the *effective reproduction rate* is based on the age-specific fertility rates for 1950, and on the mortality rates which females are expected to experience in the following 45 years in the light of recent trends.

Reproduction rates calculated on this basis only eliminate abnormal age structure, and they have the limitations and deficiencies which result from this fact. Such reproduction rates

[1] This is published in the quarterly reports of the Registrar General and in the *Statistical Review, Text, Civil*. The Registrar-General for Scotland calculates both gross and net reproduction rates, i.e., using mortality experienced in the year of the calculation. See *Annual Report of the Registrar-General for Scotland*, 1952 (H.M.S.O., 1954), Appendix I, p. 41.

will still reflect other temporary changes, and may therefore fluctuate even though there is no change in the fundamental forces influencing replacement. These other factors which will still influence the net reproduction rate are mainly on the side of fertility and have already been discussed.[1] Changes in the proportion of the population who marry, in the age and rate of marriage and in the rate of family building, will influence specific fertility rates and therefore the net reproduction rate, even though the size of family which each married woman has during the whole course of her married life remains unchanged.

Since these other factors, apart from age structure, seem to have had an important influence on births in the last ten years, the net reproduction rate has been severely criticized as a replacement measure and its usefulness questioned, especially by the Royal Commission on Population.[2] The Royal Commission attempted to calculate measures of replacement to take account of some of these other elements. The *marriage-standardized reproduction rate* attempts to take account of the rate of marriage and the rate of family building as well as age structure.[3] The Royal Commission also considered the alternative method of approaching the problem of measuring replacement in terms of the fundamental factor of family size. We have already seen how the measurement of family size bristles with difficulties,[4] and how difficult it is to measure what are the 'present habits' of family size. Yet the Royal Commission found it possible to make a tentative calculation on this basis.[5] But this is not a calculation which can be made every year, and the Registrar General's variant of the net reproduction rate is likely to remain the only

[1] See pp. 35–6.

[2] See reference on p. 39. Another objection to the net reproduction rate is that a calculation of replacement in terms of men (the *paternal reproduction rate*) often gives quite different results from that in terms of women (the *maternal reproduction rate*).

[3] The marriage-standardized reproduction rate involves the calculation of the number who would survive to each age, the number who would marry at each age and the number of children these married couples would have at each duration of marriage. The fertility rates used would thus be 'marriage-duration/specific' as well as age-specific, whereas the rates used in the N.R.R. are age-specific only.

[4] See p. 37.

[5] For the conclusions, see *Report of the Royal Commission on Population* (Cmd. 7695, H.M.S.O., 1949), paragraphs 155–8.

regularly published measurement of replacement. It is clear from the course of the statistics for the last ten years and the recent critical analysis of the reproduction rates, that the view that the net reproduction rate gives the complete answer to the measurement of replacement—a view which was quite common in the 1930's—is grossly erroneous. As long as its limitations are realized it is still of substantial value,[1] but it is quite clear now that any assessment of replacement tendencies in the population involves a detailed examination of all the demographic data available, and that this complicated question cannot be answered by a single figure.

ANALYSIS OF POPULATION STATISTICS:
(IV) MIGRATION

For any area migration statistics can be obtained in either of two ways: directly from statistics, if available, of persons moving into and out of the area; and indirectly from changes in the total population of the area and figures of births and deaths. If we take the natural increase in the population of any area, that is, the excess of births over deaths, and compare it with the actual increase, the difference must be due to migration. This method of arriving at derived figures of migration gives us only the net balance of movement to and from the area, and is compounded of the two separate movements of immigration and emigration.

External migration

Figures of external migration[2] from the United Kingdom are available on both the derived and direct basis. Derived figures of external migration are officially calculated for census periods and are published in the Census reports.[3] For other periods such

[1] For a defence of the effective reproduction rate from recent attacks, see especially *Registrar General's Statistical Review of England and Wales 1940–1945, Text, Vol. II, Civil* (H.M.S.O., 1951).

[2] For a comprehensive discussion and analysis of migration statistics since the beginning of the nineteenth century see N. H. Carrier and J. R. Jeffrey, *External Migration: A Study of the Available Statistics, 1815–1950* (General Register Office, Studies on Medical and Population Subjects, No. 6, H.M.S.O., 1953), also Brinley Thomas, *Migration and Economic Growth* (Cambridge, 1954).

[3] See *Census 1951, England and Wales, Preliminary Report* (H.M.S.O., 1951), p. xii.

derived figures can be obtained from the estimates of population and the figures of births and deaths. But unless the estimates of population have been arrived at on some independent basis, such derived figures will merely serve to reveal what has been assumed about migration in making the population estimates.

Even for Census periods the figure of net migration derived in this way may not correspond to what is normally understood as migration. The Census population measures the home population and if this is affected by, for example, the presence of larger foreign armed forces in the United Kingdom or by an increase in British forces overseas, these movements will be reflected in the net figure of migration. Similarly, if the period covered includes years of war and the figures of deaths used include only those deaths that occur in the United Kingdom, then the residual figure of migration will include as emigrants members of the armed forces who died overseas during the war. If one does not wish to count these members of the armed forces as emigrants, then one must add these figures of deaths to those of deaths at home during the period.[1]

The main source for direct migration figures is the record kept of passengers moving to and from the United Kingdom.[2] These include people who leave or come to the United Kingdom only for short periods on either business or pleasure; but for people leaving United Kingdom ports *by sea for non-European countries* a distinction is attempted between the temporary visitor and the emigrant or immigrant. Figures giving the volume of emigration and immigration separately according to country of destination, but only to and from countries outside Europe and bordering on the Mediterranean, are published quarterly in the *Board of Trade Journal* and are summarized in the *Annual Abstract of Statistics*.[3]

[1] This adjustment makes a substantial difference to the estimate of 'net migration' for the period 1911–21 and 1931–51. See *Census* 1951, *England and Wales, Preliminary Report* (H.M.S.O., 1951), p. xii.

[2] For a detailed discussion of the basis and interpretation of these figures see H. Leak and T. Priday, 'Migration from and to the United Kingdom', *Journal of the Royal Statistical Society*, vol. XCVI (1933), N. H. Carrier and J. R. Jeffrey *op. cit.*, and J. Isaac, *British Post-War Migration* (Cambridge, 1954), especially p. xv.

[3] See *Annual Abstract of Statistics*, No. 91, 1954 (H.M.S.O., 1954), Table 36, p. 38. The figures in the Annual Abstract cover migrants of Commonwealth nationalities only, but the Board of Trade Journal also gives figures for aliens.

A detailed analysis of these figures by age and occupation is also published in the *Board of Trade Journal*.

The most serious limitation of these figures is that they exclude migration to and from Europe. They also include non-United Kingdom residents, such as citizens of the Irish Republic, who emigrate via the United Kingdom. Migration is defined as covering anyone who changes his permanent residence for a period of twelve months or more. The figures will, therefore, treat as immigrants students or members of the United States forces and their families who come to the United Kingdom intending to stay for more than twelve months, even though they do not intend to reside permanently in this country.

Internal migration

Figures of internal migration can be obtained for Census of Population periods by relating 'actual increase' to 'natural increase', as is done in calculating external migration for the country as a whole. This will give a figure of the net migration only to or from each area, and will throw little light on the size of the total flow of people changing their residence from one part of the country to another. Net migration figures on this basis for the main regions of the country are published in the Census *Preliminary Report*,[1] and can, in principle, be calculated for smaller regions or individual towns or local authority areas without difficulty.[2]

During the war and post-war period national registration and food rationing records provided a new source of statistics of internal migration. These records have been used by the Registrar

[1] *Census*, 1951, *England and Wales*, *Preliminary Report* (H.M.S.O., 1951), Table C, p. xv.

[2] Changes in local authority boundaries, or in the other areas for which the statistical information is available, will in practice often make such a calculation difficult.

All these figures would be based, as are those published in the Census, on deaths occurring in the region. For the period 1931–51, therefore, the resultant figures would count armed forces deaths overseas as emigrants. To allow for this accurately one would need to have figures of such service deaths (240,000 for England and Wales) by area of normal residence in the United Kingdom. These are not available, but an approximate estimate could be made by apportioning the 240,000 according to the population or deaths of the areas concerned.

General to arrive at his annual estimates of the population of regions and towns,[1] and have also been specially analysed for the information they reveal on population movement inside the country. Some of this information has been published in the Registrar General's annual *Statistical Review*.[2] In addition, a special report[3] on internal migration based on these records has been published which throws an entirely new and most revealing light on the extent and character of internal population movement in England and Wales.

FORECASTS OF THE FUTURE POPULATION

In principle the method of population forecasting is quite simple. Suppose we are trying to forecast the population one year ahead. We start with figures of the population by age and sex now. In one year's time the population aged one year and over will consist of the population alive now, less those who die in the next twelve months. And all those who survive will be a year older. We can, therefore, obtain the population by age and sex over one year in one year's time, by moving the figures of each age and sex in the present population forward to the next age group and subtracting from each our estimate of likely deaths for each age and sex during the year. Babies between the ages 0 to 1 now who survive for the next year, will be between 1 and 2 in a year's time; and we can arrive at our estimate for this latter age group by moving the present figure for 0–1 to the age group 1–2 and subtracting our estimate of deaths for this age group during the next twelve months. Proceeding on this same basis age by age will give us a forecast of the population aged one year and over. For the age group 0–1 we have to estimate how many children will be born during the next twelve months and how many of these will still be living in twelve months' time. This still leaves the effect of migration. Since this is bound to be a hazardous estimate, it

---

[1] The use made of these records by the Registrar General in estimating total and local populations is explained in *Registrar General's Statistical Review of England and Wales*, 1940–45, *Text, Vol. II, Civil* (H.M.S.O., 1951), p. 9 and pp. 16–17.

[2] *Ibid.* p. 18.

[3] M. P. Newton and J. R. Jeffrey, *Internal Migration: Some Aspects of Population Movements within England and Wales* (General Register Office, Studies on Medical and Population Subjects, No. 5, H.M.S.O., 1951).

is best left to be added or subtracted from the estimate of the natural change in the population. In making the forecasts, therefore, we have to make assumptions or estimates of what we expect mortality, fertility and migration to be in the future.

All forecasts of the population are merely attempts to show the result in the future of given assumptions about the trends of fertility, mortality and migration. No amount of statistical analysis will enable us to forecast these trends with certainty. By analysing recent population history we may try to find certain fundamental movements which are so deep-seated and of such importance that we can assume with some confidence that they will continue to operate. But statistical analysis alone will not enable us to decide whether the trends are deep-seated or not. Population forecasts will be of interest in revealing the implications of the assumptions that we decide to make, and we can have as many forecasts as assumptions and varying combinations of assumptions that we care to use.

The further ahead the period for which the population forecasts are made, the greater the influence of the assumptions about fertility and mortality. For one of the most important factors about population forecasting is that for a considerable period ahead, a substantial part of the future population is alive now. A forecast of the population ten years ahead involves an estimate of the number who will die and the number of children who will be born in the next ten years. Even widely different assumptions about the course of mortality and fertility will make relatively little difference to the total result, since the number of deaths and births over the next ten years and the difference between them is relatively small in relation to the total size of the population. As one extends the period of the forecast the assumptions become more and more important, and over a sufficiently long period assumptions which differ only by a small margin will yield widely different estimates of the total population. In the extreme case a set of assumptions about mortality, fertility and migration which implied that each generation did not quite replace itself, if carried sufficiently far ahead, would show the population declining to negligible numbers; while a set of assumptions about mortality, fertility and migration which implied that each generation more than replaced itself even though by only a very small margin, if carried sufficiently far ahead, would show the population increasing to very large numbers.

For the United Kingdom and other Western countries greater confidence can be placed in estimates of future mortality than in estimates of fertility. This is partly because, as we have seen, it is easier to analyse and account for past trends in declining mortality, and because mortality rates have now fallen so low that variations in assumptions about the rate of further decline make little difference to population forecasts.[1] But there is much greater room for variation in assumptions about fertility and such variations have a much greater cumulative effect on the size of the future population. Even if we are able to overcome the difficult problem of deciding what is the best statistical measure of the fundamental aspects of fertility and can make our forecasts in terms of such statistics, we are still very ignorant about the influences which determine the movement of these factors. Suppose, for example, we decide that fertility is best measured in terms of family size and that we are able to analyse changes in family size over recent years, we have still very little basis to go on in making assumptions about what family size is likely to be in ten, twenty or thirty years' time.

This means that for Western countries we can place more confidence in that part of population forecasts which relies only on mortality assumptions than in the part which depends on assumptions of both mortality and fertility. Thus if we are using forecasts of the population twenty years ahead, we can use the figures of the population over 20 years of age with confidence, but we must be much more cautious in using the figures for the age group 0 to 20.

The most extensive recent forecasts of the population of Great Britain are those made by the Royal Commission on Population.[2]

[1] The biggest margin is now in estimates of the increase in expectation of life at the older ages. But the extension of life at these ages has only a once for all effect on the size of the population, since women at these ages are beyond the age of child-bearing. If the average expectation of life is increased from 70 to 80 it would cause a non-cumulative increase in the population, but if mortality is reduced between the ages of 0 and 45 it has a cumulative effect, since more girls then survive to be mothers and in consequence more children are born.

[2] The main sections of the *Report* which deal with population forecasts are Chapters 8 and 9. See also 'Population Projections for Great Britain, 1947–2047', *Papers of the Royal Commission on Population*, vol. II, *Reports and Selected Papers of the Statistics Committee* (H.M.S.O., 1950), pp. 213–54; and P. R. Cox, *Demography* (Cambridge, 1950) Chapter 13,

The Royal Commission worked on only two mortality assumptions: one that specific mortality rates will remain at the level of 1942–4, and the other that they would continue to decline over the following thirty years in accordance with the trends of the last fifty years. The range of assumptions about fertility is much greater. The Royal Commission worked in terms of the two factors of rate of marriage and fertility rates at various durations of marriage, in each case with five different alternative assumptions about future trends. Five different assumptions are made about the possible level of immigration or emigration.

If a projection were made for every possible combination of these alternative assumptions, the total number of projections would be 250. Of these 250 the Royal Commission chose sixteen as sufficient to illustrate the influence of the most important factors on the size and structure of the future population. The estimates of each of these selected combinations are published in substantial detail by the Royal Commission, for five-yearly intervals over the hundred years from 1947 to 2047. They form the most up-to-date collection of forecasts for Great Britain.

As has already been explained, the further ahead one takes population forecasts, the greater the effect of the particular assumptions made about mortality and fertility. As one would expect, therefore, the margin between the sixteen forecasts that the Royal Commission chose increases the further ahead we look. For 1957, ten years after the base date of the forecast, the margin between the highest estimate, 50,976,000, and the lowest, 48,762,000, is only 4 per cent,[1] while the margin for 2047, between 61,382,000 and 29,562,000, is 52 per cent.[1] There is nothing in statistical analysis of population trends which will tell us which is the most reliable forecast. In the estimate for 2047 the difference between the two sets of figures results entirely from differences in the fertility assumption; the lower figure results from assuming a continued fall in fertility until 1967 and a constant level thereafter at about 20 per cent less than that needed for replacement, while the higher figure results from assuming a rise until 1967 and a constant rate thereafter at about 20 per cent more than that needed for replacement. Thus our view of the likelihood of each of these two population figures must depend on what we think of

for a useful critical review of the main forecasts made during the last twenty years.

[1] Of the higher figure.

the likelihood of the fertility assumptions. It is clear that when we look more than one generation ahead small differences in fertility assumptions can make a big difference to population forecasts, and it is indeed doubtful whether much useful purpose is served in extending such forecasts more than fifty years ahead.

No more recent population forecasts have been published in the detail and on the extensive scale used by the Royal Commission. But the Government Actuary's Department in consultation with the General Register Office now makes each year a summary forecast of the population of England and Wales, by sex and main age groups, for 10, 15, 20, 30 and 40 years ahead. These forecasts are published in the December issue of the Registrar General's quarterly reports. A single set of assumptions is used in each year's forecast and these assumptions change a little from year to year. The assumptions used in the forecasts published in December 1953 were: that death-rates for ages under 45 would decline steadily for 25 years to about half their present level; that death-rates for ages over 45 would decline progressively less as the age advances; that births would average 640,000 during the next 25 years and fall to 600,000 in the following 15 years.[1] No similar forecasts are published for Scotland or Northern Ireland.

[1] The number of births in 1952 and 1953 was 673,000 and 682,000.

CHAPTER III

MANPOWER

MANPOWER statistics cover all aspects of the use of the labour force of the country in economic activity: such as employment, unemployment, hours of work, mobility, turnover, and industrial relations. The most important general sources of statistics on these subjects are the Census of Population, the Census of Production, the Census of Distribution, and the publications of the Ministry of Labour. The Ministry of Labour now provides the most up-to-date and regular manpower statistics and attention will therefore be concentrated here on describing and analysing the figures published by that department. But it is worth while first looking briefly at the manpower information available in the three censuses and particularly taking note of aspects of the use of manpower covered by them but not covered by the Ministry of Labour's publications.

THE CENSUS OF POPULATION

The distinctive feature of the manpower statistics derived from the Census of Population is that they give a most detailed and complete analysis. They cover everybody in the population, employers, self-employed and employees, in all branches of economic activity. Most other statistics of employment merely tell us the number of persons employed by industries, usually showing men and women separately. The Census gives us this analysis by industries, but in addition gives a vast amount of information about employment by occupation, age and marital condition, industrial status,[1] social class, region and town.

On many of these topics the Census is the only source of information. For example, there is practically no information analysing employment by occupations apart from that in the Census. An occupational classification of employment analyses workers according to the work which they do—for example,

[1] I.E. grouped according to employers, managers, operatives, articled clerks and apprentices, part-time workers, unpaid assistants, working on own account, out of work, or retired.

spinners, weavers, bricklayers, metal machinists, clerks or typists; while an industrial classification analyses them according to the products made by the firms for which they work—for example, agriculture, mechanical engineering, cotton textiles, railway transport or wholesale distribution. In considering problems of mobility and transferability of labour, an occupational analysis of the labour force is often more important than an industrial analysis, since it is a man's occupational skill rather than the industry in which he works which determines his suitability for alternative employment.

The Census of Population also gives us a complete analysis of the whole occupied population, whereas most other sources cover only a part. It is true that since 1948 some of the Ministry of Labour's statistics cover the whole occupied population, but they are divided only into very broad groups, and even these figures involve some rather hazardous estimates.[1]

Another distinctive feature of the Census of Population is that it is available for a longer period of time in the past than any of the other sources. Indeed, for most of the period before the early 1920's, when statistics from the unemployment insurance schemes started, the Census is the only source for general manpower statistics. Questions about occupations were asked in the first Census, for 1801, and the detail asked for and analysed has been gradually extended with each successive Census.[2] In the early Censuses the classification was a compromise between an occupational and industrial one, and it was not until 1911 that an attempt was made to distinguish clearly between occupations and industries. Since then separate analyses have been made and published in great detail in the Occupation and Industry Tables.

The great drawback to the Census data on manpower is that they are available only once every 10 years, and that the most recent figures are out of date even when they are first published. The *One Per Cent Sample Reports* for the 1951 Census go a long way towards remedying this deficiency. The occupational and industrial analysis contained in this advance publication serves

[1] See p. 62. They are also to some extent based on an extrapolation of the figures from the latest Census of Population.
[2] For a useful summary of the employment information obtained and published in each Census since 1801, see *Guides to Official Sources No. 2. Census Reports of Great Britain*, 1801–1931 (H.M.S.O., 1951), pp. 27–65.

both to supplement and to check information for that date that we have from other sources.

One of the important points to remember when using figures from the Census of Population is that they are based on forms filled up by householders and that their reliability depends on the accuracy with which these forms are completed. How far can one rely on householders describing accurately, according to a standard classification, not only their own occupations, but those of their wives and children? How can one secure a uniform distinction between being 'retired' or 'out of work', especially for people over 65? Such questions must always be kept in mind in using the Census statistics and comparing them with other manpower figures.[1]

THE CENSUSES OF PRODUCTION AND OF DISTRIBUTION

The Census of Production gives figures of employment for the field of economic activity it covers:[2] mining, manufacturing, building and construction, and gas, water and electricity.[3] The employment figures are given separately for operatives, and technical, administrative and clerical staff, a division which corresponds roughly to the division between wage and salary earners.

The Census of Production returns relate to individual factories, and it is therefore possible to analyse the figures of employment in different industries, according to the size of unit in which people work. The Census is the only source for information of

[1] No detailed comparison has yet been published of the Census sample results and Ministry of Labour estimates of the working population for the same date. A general comparison shows some substantial differences between the two sets of figures. Some of the differences can be accounted for by differences in coverage—e.g., the Ministry of Labour estimate of the 'total working population' includes all the armed forces, both at home and overseas, whereas the Census would include only those at home. But some of the differences, for example in the numbers of occupied women (7·4 million according to the Ministry of Labour and 6·9 million in the Census), seems to suggest substantial inaccuracy in one of the two sets of figures.

[2] For a more detailed discussion of the coverage of the Census of Production, see pp. 80–5.

[3] In 1949 roughly 10½ million people out of a total occupied labour force of 24 million in the United Kingdom were covered by the Census of Production.

this kind.[1] On the basis of the Census for 1935 Leak and Maizels conducted a further analysis of the size of units in British manufacturing industry, in terms of firms and the interconnections between firms, as well as factories.[2] This remains the most complete available analysis of the structure of British manufacturing industry.

One of the principal advantages of the Census of Production figures of employment compared with other sources is that one can be sure that the coverage of the employment and production data are identical. This makes the Census much more reliable than other sources for examining trends in productivity. Most other estimates of productivity trends in British industry depend on relating figures of employment and production obtained from separate sources,[3] and this often raises problems of comparability. With the Census figures, however, one can be confident that they have the same coverage, since the production and employment figures are entered on the same forms for the same unit.

Until the post-war period the Census of Production was taken at irregular intervals and, as with the Census of Population, there was a substantial time-lag between the taking of a Census and the publication of the results. The first Census of Production was taken in 1907 and full Censuses were taken for 1924, 1930 and 1935. Some of the information obtained in the Census, including employment figures, was collected for most manufacturing industries in the Import Duties Act Inquiries for 1933, 1934 and 1937. A partial Census was taken in 1946 and the first full post-war Census in 1948. Since then a Census has been taken every year, but there remains a substantial interval between the taking of the Census and the publication of the results.[4] A useful summary of the results, including figures of employment, has been

[1] Since the Ministry of Labour has been obtaining direct returns from employers, it has also been able to analyse employment by size of establishment. But the figures are confined to manufacturing only and are in much less detail than in the Census of Production. See 'Size of Manufacturing Firms', *Ministry of Labour Gazette*, December 1952, pp. 411–12.

[2] H. Leak and A. Maizels, 'The Structure of British Industry', *Journal of the Royal Statistical Society*, vol. CVIII, pts. I and II (1945).

[3] For example, the Central Statistical Office index of production and the Ministry of Labour figures of employment. For a more detailed discussion of productivity measurement, see pp. 110–14.

[4] For example, the first results of the 1951 Census were not published until the beginning of 1954.

published for 1948, 1949 and 1950,[1] but for figures for individual industries by size of unit or region one must refer to the detailed separate annual reports for each industry.

A Census of Distribution and Other Services[2] was taken in this country for the first time for the year 1950 and questions were asked about employment. Figures of employment have been included in all the reports so far published. The Census distinguishes between persons engaged full-time and those engaged part-time, and includes in the latter categories all part-time workers, whether paid or unpaid, who help in distribution. This makes it difficult to compare the Census of Distribution results with either those of the Census of Population or those published by the Ministry of Labour.[3]

MINISTRY OF LABOUR STATISTICS[4]

The Ministry of Labour now provides the most up-to-date and regular statistics of manpower. Most of this information is published in the *Ministry of Labour Gazette*, but there are useful summaries of the more important figures in the *Monthly Digest of Statistics* and the *Annual Abstract of Statistics*. Before the war the Ministry of Labour itself published an *Annual Abstract of Labour Statistics* which provided a most useful collection of manpower statistics and was especially valuable if figures over a period of years were wanted. But this publication was suspended during the war and has not been resumed since.

The Ministry of Labour now depends on two main sources for its manpower statistics: the National insurance schemes and

[1] *Censuses of Production for* 1950, 1949 *and* 1948, *Summary Tables*, *Part I* (H.M.S.O., 1953). For a more detailed discussion of the coverage of the Censuses of Production and Import Duties Act Inquiries, see pp. 80–5.

[2] For a more detailed discussion of the Census of Distribution, see Chapter V, pp. 122–6.

[3] See 'Summary of Results of Census of Distribution taken in 1951', *Board of Trade Journal*, 24 January 1951, p. 133, for some discussion of the difference between the Census of Distribution and Census of Population employment statistics.

[4] There are useful descriptions of the Ministry of Labour's manpower statistics in *Guides to Official Sources No. 1. Labour Statistics*, *revised, August* 1950 (H.M.S.O., 1950), and R. B. Ainsworth, 'Labour Statistics', in *The Sources and Nature of the Statistics of the United Kingdom*, ed. M. G. Kendall (Oliver and Boyd, 1952), vol. 1, pp. 75–86.

direct returns from employers. National insurance has covered the whole occupied population only since 1948 and the direct employment returns were first taken in 1940. The coverage of Ministry of Labour statistics was, therefore, very different before 1948 and 1939 from what it is now. The changing coverage of Ministry of Labour statistics since they first started in the period before the First World War is a most complicated story which cannot be told in anything like full detail here. Attention will be concentrated here on the current statistics and this will be followed by a brief discussion of the main difference between the figures published now and those available over the last thirty years.

Insured employees

The insurance system forms the main basis of the Ministry of Labour's statistics. Under this system every gainfully occupied person, whether an employer, an employee or person working on his own account,[1] is issued with an insurance card, on which stamps representing weekly contributions are fixed. Once a year when the card is full it is sent to the Ministry of National Insurance in exchange for a new card. These cards have on them a code letter indicating the industry to which the worker belongs. There is also the name of the local office from which the card is issued, and cards for employers, employed, and self-employed have different rates of contribution, as do those for persons up to and over 18.

When the cards are renewed, therefore, an analysis of the number of persons insured can be made along any of these divisions, that is, by industry, by locality, by status, and by broad age groups. The cards for the whole of the insured population are not now exchanged at the same time each year. The currency of the cards is arranged so that a quarter mature every three months. If the Ministry of Labour could rely on the accuracy of this exchange, and assume that each quarter was a random sample of the whole, a complete analysis of the insured population in these groupings should be possible. In practice considerable difficulties seem to have arisen in the use and analysis of the statistics derived from this quarterly exchange of cards. First, it

[1] The only important exceptions are employed married women who did not wish to contribute, but even in these cases the employer must pay his part of the contribution.

seems clear that even though all employers and self-employed are by law required to be insured by the Act of 1946, yet there are substantial numbers who have not yet taken out insurance cards. Certainly the information available about this group from the exchange of cards does not seem to be sufficiently accurate to provide a detailed analysis of employers and self-employed by industry and region. The detailed analysis of the insured population, published by the Ministry of Labour, refers therefore only to the number of *insured employees*. Secondly, the Ministry of Labour has not found it possible to use all four quarterly exchanges as a basis for the publication of details even of the number of all *employees*. Delay in the exchange of cards and uncertainties about the reliability of the industrial classification have prevented this. Before using the exchange of cards the Ministry of Labour finds it advisable to get a special return from employers of the number of insurance cards held by them, and since this is done only once a year, estimates of the number of insured employees are available only at annual intervals.[1] These estimates refer to the position at the end of May of each year. The main results, by industry, sex and broad age groups, are now published regularly in the issue of the *Ministry of Labour Gazette* in the following February. In the issue for March a regional analysis is given, but only in broad groups without any breakdown by industry; and in the issue for June a detailed analysis by age, both regionally and industrially, based on a sample of the cards exchanged.[2]

For two or three years after 1948 there was substantial revision each year in the figures for the previous years, and in the *Ministry of Labour Gazette* for February and March 1953 a final revised set of figures of the industrial and regional analysis was given for June 1948 and May 1949, 1950, 1951 and 1952.

It is important to remember that these annual May figures refer to employees only. They exclude employers and the self-employed, but they still cover the greater part of the working population. The occupied civilian labour force in Great Britain in May 1953 was estimated at 22·4 million and the number of insured employees at 20·9 million.

[1] For the fullest explanation so far published of how the Ministry of Labour makes these estimates, see *Ministry of Labour Gazette*, February 1954, p. 37.

[2] For the basis of the sample, see 'Age-Analysis of Employed Persons', *Ministry of Labour Gazette*, June 1951, p. 223.

These annual figures cover all insured employees, whether unemployed or not. But it is a relatively simple matter to subtract the number of unemployed [1] from the insured, in order to get a figure of the numbers 'employed' in each industry or region. It is important to be quite clear what is included in the figures arrived at by such a process of subtraction. Since only the 'unemployed' are subtracted the residual figure will include everyone not 'unemployed' within the official meaning of the term. If people are away from work but are not registered as unemployed and are therefore not in the unemployment figure, they will still be included in the residual figures of 'employed'. The figure of 'employed' arrived at on this basis will therefore include people away ill,[2] people on holiday, on strike, or away for any reason which does not lead them to register as unemployed;[3] this figure does not therefore represent the numbers of people actually at work. It would perhaps be better described as 'the number on the pay-roll of industry'.

Although the analysis for May of each year published in the *Ministry of Labour Gazette* refers to the insured, the numbers employed—arrived at by subtracting the number unemployed as explained above—were given for some years in another publication issued by the Ministry of Labour. This publication gave figures of the numbers employed in each industry, not only for Great Britain as a whole but also for each of the main regions of the country, and provided the main basis of our information about the changing regional distribution of industry. Unfortunately this set of tables has not been published since 1951, and the latest figures are for May 1950.[4]

[1] Unemployment statistics are discussed in more detail later in this chapter; see pp. 67–73.

[2] Some information about the number of insured workers absent from work because of sickness can be obtained from Ministry of National Insurance figures of the number drawing sickness benefit. See *Ministry of Labour Gazette*, July 1952, p. 253.

[3] For example, the large number of workers who were stood off during the fuel crisis of 1947 but were paid wages by their employers and therefore did not register as unemployed, would have been included in a figure of employment arrived at on this basis.

[4] *Tables Relating to Employment and Unemployment in Great Britain, 1948, 1949 and 1950: Regional and Industrial Analysis of Employees and Unemployed Persons* (H.M.S.O., 1951). The *Tables* do not therefore take account of the revisions made to the insurance figures since that date.

Monthly figures of employment

As has already been explained, the detailed analysis of all employees is only available once a year. But since 1940 the Ministry of Labour has been collecting figures of employment direct from employers for certain industries quite separately from the insurance schemes, and these have made possible monthly estimates of employment for a large group of industries. These direct employment returns, known as 'L' returns, are obtained from firms in manufacturing industries with more than ten employees and from a sample of firms in distribution and other services. This enables the Ministry of Labour to publish every month figures of employment in manufacturing industries, coal-mining, building, public utilities, distribution, and some services. The main categories of employment not covered by these monthly figures are: insurance, banking and finance, public administration and defence, professional services, domestic service, agriculture and certain sections of transport. The monthly figures in May 1953 covered 14,800,000 employees, out of a total for all employment at that date of 20½ million. The figures cover Great Britain only, whereas the annual estimates of insured employees in May are given for both Great Britain and the United Kingdom.

The Ministry of Labour does not publish the direct returns themselves but uses these to extrapolate from the latest annual estimates obtained from the insurance figures. Since the 'L' returns ask each employer for the numbers he employs both during the current month and in the previous month, the percentage change in employment for each month can be worked out, industry by industry, and these percentages can be applied to the basic figure for the previous May to provide more recent monthly estimates. This method makes it possible to use the information in the 'L' returns even if the sample of firms covered by them varies slightly from month to month.[1]

The reliability of these estimates depends of course on the

[1] Suppose, for example, that in one industry the 'L' returns for June 1953 showed employment of 110,000 for that month and 119,000 *by the same firms* for the previous month, May. Suppose further that the annual calculation of employment in that industry (i.e. total employees – unemployed) gave a figure of employment of 125,000 for May 1953, then the estimated figure of employment for June would be:

sample taken by the Ministry of Labour and the accuracy of the information given by the firms. The Ministry of Labour gives little detailed information about the size of the 'L' return enquiries and how promptly employers send in their returns. But it is clear from such information as is given that the statistics for manufacturing have a much wider coverage and greater reliability than those for distribution and services.

Since the annual end-of-May estimates are not available until the following February, at the maximum the original base used in these estimates of monthly employment is eighteen months earlier. But when a new set of May figures becomes available it is of course possible to go back and revise the last six months' figures on the new basis. Thus the estimates of employment for November 1953, published in January 1954, were based on an extrapolation from the annual figures for the end of May 1952. But in February 1954, when the annual estimates for the end of May 1953 first became available, it would have been possible to go back and revise all the monthly figures for June to November 1953, using the annual figures for May 1953 instead of those for May 1952 as the original base. In fact the Ministry of Labour published revised figures for October and November 1953 only. If these revisions alter the figures substantially, it is dangerous to use the new and old sets as if they were a continuous comparable series. But in recent years the actual revisions found necessary have been relatively small.[1]

Since the monthly figures of employment are an extrapolation from the latest figures of insured employees, in principle they should have the same coverage and meaning, for the industries

$$\frac{125,000}{119,000} \times 110,000 = 115,600.$$

If the 'L' returns for July showed employment in July of 105,000 and of 108,000 *by the same firms* for June, then the July employment figure would be:

$$115,600 \times \frac{105,000}{108,000} = 112,300$$

(i.e. the estimated June figures × the estimated ratio of change June/July).

[1] Some measure of the extent of the revision can be obtained by comparing the figures of employment for November or December on the original and revised basis. The following table (p. 60) gives such a comparison for November 1953.

Numbers Employed in Great Britain: Comparison of Original and
Revised Estimates for November 1953
(Thousands)

	Original estimate (*Ministry of Labour Gazette,* January 1954) Extrapolated from annual figure for May 1952	Revised estimate (*Ministry of Labour Gazette,* February 1954) Extrapolated from annual figure for May 1953
Coal Mining	783·3	783·1
Non-metalliferous mining products	336·2	340·2
Chemical and allied trades	499·1	499·2
Metal manufactures	547·1	554·9
Engineering, shipbuilding and electrical goods	1,912·2	1,932·4
Vehicles	1,114·2	1,117·6
Metal goods n.e.s.	490·1	493·8
Precision instruments, jewellery etc.	135·6	138·3
Textiles	999·4	992·6
Leather, leather goods and fur	75·7	73·7
Clothing	663·6	653·8
Food, drink and tobacco	862·6	860·2
Manufactures of wood and cork	299·5	301·7
Paper and printing	525·3	524·3
Other manufacturing industries	271·7	272·5
Building and contracting	1,311·8	1,299·3
Gas, water and electricity	375·5	375·8
Transport and communication	459·8	461·3
Distributive trades	2,241·3	2,264·6
Miscellaneous services	1,018·2	1,041·3

concerned, as the basic annual figures. As was explained earlier,[1] these annual figures of employment are derived by subtracting the number unemployed from the number insured. They relate only to employees,[2] and include in the residual figures of employed many people who are not actually at work, for example those away ill or on holiday. In principle the monthly 'L' returns are on the same basis and the monthly employment figures also have the same coverage. They relate to the number of people on the pay-roll and not to those actually at work. They do not reflect seasonal fluctuations in the amount of work done due to holidays, sickness or absence from work for other reasons.

The widespread working of short time in the textile industries in 1952 brought to light a further complication in the interpretation of the monthly employment figures. If, as seems to be the general practice, employers treat all short-time workers or others 'temporarily stopped' as still on their books, they will be included in the 'L' returns. The monthly employment figures derived from these will therefore include these categories as 'employed'. Some of these workers may, however, be registered as unemployed and drawing unemployment benefit. Many of the workers that the Ministry of Labour includes in the category of 'temporarily stopped'[3] are therefore likely to have been included by the firms in their figures of 'employment'. Accordingly, in 1952[4] the Ministry of Labour amended its description of the monthly employment figures and changed the basis of the extrapolation. The annual May figure now used is the insured less the 'wholly unemployed' only, and the figures are best described as representing the number of workers on the books of any firm whether they are being paid or not. Only those unemployed whom the firms do not expect to re-engage and whom, therefore, they have struck off their books, will be excluded. This point is of little significance when unemployment is at a very low level, but it becomes important in affecting the interpretation of the figures when unemployment, especially short-term unemployment, increases, as in textiles in 1952. It is indeed difficult to

[1] See p. 57.

[2] I.E. they exclude employers and self-employed.

[3] For a more detailed discussion of the unemployment figures see p. 67 ff.

[4] In the *Ministry of Labour Gazette*, September 1952, giving the figures for July 1952.

define at all exactly what the monthly employment figures for textiles in 1952 covered.[1]

Monthly estimates of the total working population

Both the annual and monthly detailed figures of employment cover employees only, and the monthly figures exclude certain important groups of industries. But in addition the Ministry of Labour estimates and publishes each month figures of the total working population, covering all industries and all classes of occupied persons—employers, self-employed, and employees. The industrial categories used in these figures are, however, very broad. The figures are useful mainly in giving a general picture of the manpower position. Figures are given for the total working population, covering those in the armed forces[2] and the unemployed as well as those in civil employment. The figures of civil employment are then analysed separately for 19 industries or groups of industries.[3]

It is difficult to judge the accuracy of these monthly figures of the working population, for the Ministry of Labour provides no detailed explanation of how the estimates are made. The two most difficult elements in the estimates are the allowance for employers and self-employed, and the estimates of employment for those occupations, such as some of the professional services or entertainment, where there are neither 'L' returns nor any other source of regular information about employment.

The importance of the estimates for employers and self-employed varies a great deal from one group to another. It is of little significance in manufacturing and mining, but of substantial importance in distribution, professional services, building and agriculture. In principle the accuracy of these estimates of the total working population could be checked by comparing the

[1] See H. A. Turner, 'Measuring Unemployment', *J. R. Statist. Soc.* series A, vol. cxviii, pt. I (1955).

[2] Including, apparently, the armed forces overseas.

[3] Mining and quarrying; gas, water and electricity; transport and communication; agriculture and fishing; chemical and allied trades; metal manufactures; vehicles; engineering, metal goods and precision instruments; cotton; wool; other textiles; clothing; food, drink and tobacco; other manufactures; building and contracting; distributive trades; professional, financial and miscellaneous services; national government service; and local government service.

Ministry of Labour figures with those given in the one per cent sample analysis of the Census of Population. Unfortunately such a comparison raises many difficulties of comparability and without a great deal of detailed analysis the Census figures could not be used as a check on the Ministry of Labour estimates. But in revising the estimates of the working population in February 1953, the Ministry of Labour stated that account had been taken of the figures of employers and self-employed published in the *One Per Cent Sample Tables* of the 1951 Census of Population.[1]

Since the estimates of the total working population are also basically tied to the annual estimates of the insured population at the end of May, these estimates, like the monthly employment figures, are revised each time a new set of insurance figures becomes available in February. As with the employment figures, revision is in principle required for every monthly figure since the previous insurance base; but in fact the Ministry of Labour publishes revised figures only for one or two months of the earlier year.

Summary of current manpower figures

It is not easy to avoid confusion between the various manpower figures and definitions currently published and it might be useful to summarize them. They are as follows:

(1) *Occupied population*—as defined in the Census of Population, covering all people in the United Kingdom actually with a job, employers, self-employed and employees, including those looking for a job and classifying themselves as 'employed' in the Census returns. These figures are fully analysed in the *Industries and Occupations* volumes of the Census.

(2) *Working population*—monthly estimates by the Ministry of Labour, including all employers, self-employed and employees, in the armed forces,[2] in civil employment or wholly unemployed (Great Britain only).

[1] Back figures on the revised basis were given only for 'End 1951' and October and November 1952. Presumably, however, the figure published in the latest *Annual Abstract of Statistics* for June of each year since 1948 also takes account of such revisions (see *Annual Abstract of Statistics, No. 90*, 1953 (H.M.S.O., 1953), Table 120, p. 99).

[2] Presumably both at home and overseas.

(3) *Civil employment*—monthly estimates, including all employers, self-employed and employees on the books of any firm (that is, excluding the wholly unemployed only) by 19 industrial groups (Great Britain only).

(4) *Employed population*—annual figures for the end of May of the estimated number of *employees*, whether with a job or unemployed, in detail by 164 industries (Great Britain and the United Kingdom).

(5) *Numbers employed*—monthly figures of the estimated number of *employees* on the books of any firm (that is, excluding the wholly unemployed only) for all manufacturing and a few other industries (Great Britain only).

Ministry of Labour statistics, 1939–48

The explanation given in the last few pages of manpower statistics published by the Ministry of Labour relates to statistics from June 1948 onwards. The introduction of the new comprehensive insurance scheme in that month caused a major change in the coverage of the Ministry of Labour's figures, and the pre-1948 figures are not at all comparable with those published since that date.

Figures of 'working population', 'civil employment', 'employed population', and 'numbers employed' were estimated from 1939 onwards and published in the *Ministry of Labour Gazette*, beginning in November 1945,[1] but all these figures had a very different coverage from those now published. Before June 1948 the monthly estimates of the working population and those in civil employment excluded men aged 65 and over, women aged 60 and over, and private indoor domestic servants, because of lack of information about these categories. In addition, each

---

[1] The most convenient sources for the figures from 1939 to 1945 are:

(a) 'Working population' and 'civilian employment': *Annual Abstract of Statistics*, No. 90, 1953 (H.M.S.O., 1953), Table 119, p. 98.

(b) 'Employed population'—all industries (annual figures), *Annual Abstract of Statistics*, No. 90, 1953 (H.M.S.O., 1953), Table 123, pp. 102–4.

(c) 'Numbers employed'—manufacturing and certain other industries, quarterly:
Statistical Digest of the War (H.M.S.O., 1951), Tables 19–30, pp. 17–28.

part-time worker was counted as one-half, but in current figures all workers are included on the same basis. It is also fairly certain that the estimates of the working population made before June 1948 were a good deal less reliable than those made since. For, as will be explained later, the insurance schemes had a narrower coverage and estimates had to be made for substantial parts of the total labour force on a very uncertain basis. The complete count in June 1948 revealed that there was a substantial margin of error in the estimates on the old basis.[1]

The annual estimates of insured employees before June 1948, which related to July each year,[2] are also not comparable with those since June 1948. For under the Unemployment Insurance Acts in operation until June 1948, many categories of workers were excluded from insurance.[3] Thus of the total number of insured under the system introduced in June 1948 amounting to 20·97 million in the United Kingdom, only 16·15 million would have been insured under the old scheme.[4] The comparability of the figures by industry before and after June 1948 is also affected by the introduction of the standard industrial classification.

[1] The figure on the new basis originally given for June 1948 was 23,146,000. Subtracting from this the categories not included in the pre-1948 basis (men and women over pensionable age, 950,000; 500,000 private indoor domestic servants; and half 800,000 part-time workers) would reduce this figure to 21,300,000. The figure actually published on the old basis was only 20,274,000. See 'New Series of Manpower Statistics', *Ministry of Labour Gazette*, February 1949, p. 40. In fact, the figure for June 1948 has been repeatedly revised since then and the latest estimate for that date (given in the *Annual Abstract*) is now 22,780,000.

[2] Under the pre-1948 system, the cards for all insured were exchanged once a year in July.

[3] The main categories of employees excluded in the period immediately before June 1948 were: men aged 65 and over and women aged 60 and over; private indoor domestic servants; non-manual employees with a rate of remuneration exceeding £420 a year; members of H.M. Forces; established civil servants; permanent employees of local authorities, railways, public utility concerns, etc.; teachers; police; female professional nurses; farmers' sons and daughters employed in agriculture.

[4] For a detailed analysis of the number of insured employees at July 1948 and the number insurable at that date under the old scheme see *Ministry of Labour Gazette*, February 1949, pp. 42–3.

Manpower statistics before 1939 ¶

Before 1939 there were no monthly 'L' returns, and little information about employment apart from that derived from the Unemployment Insurance Schemes. There were, therefore, no monthly estimates of the total working population and no monthly figures of employment. The only statistics were those which could be derived from the annual count of insurance cards in July. Two sets of figures were published regularly every year derived from this count. The first gave the numbers insured, industry by industry, and was published regularly in the *Ministry of Labour Gazette* for November; the second gave the numbers employed (insured, minus the unemployed) and was published regularly in December. This series of figures goes back to 1923. Although there were some insurance figures and direct employment returns before that date, they were not published in the same form and their interpretation raises many difficulties.[1]

The series from 1923 to 1939 reflect the changing coverage of the Unemployment Insurance Schemes, and are not always comparable from year to year.[2] As has already been explained, throughout this period the Unemployment Insurance Schemes excluded many important categories of workers. The insured and employed figures derived from the annual count of cards in July never covered more than about three-quarters of the total labour force in the pre-war period.

OTHER SOURCES OF EMPLOYMENT FIGURES FOR
INDIVIDUAL INDUSTRIES

The figures published by the Ministry of Labour are the only regular up-to-date figures of employment covering the whole economy. But there are other important sources for particular industries, and these often analyse employment in much greater

[1] See A. C. Pigou, *Aspects of British Economic History* 1918–1925 (Macmillan, 1947).

[2] The main changes in scope over the period 1921–47 were: 1928, persons 65 and over excluded; 1934, juveniles 14 and 15 included; 1936, agricultural workers included; 1938, domestic staffs in businesses not run for gain, chauffeurs and outdoor domestic servants included; 1940, women 60–64 excluded; 1940, non-manual workers earning between £250–£420 a year included.

detail than is done by the Ministry of Labour. Most of the nationalized industries publish a detailed analysis of the number of staff they employ in their annual reports,[1] and some give monthly figures in their regular periodical statistical bulletins.[2] The Ministry of Agriculture obtains figures of the numbers employed in agriculture from its quarterly agricultural returns,[3] the Ministry of Works collects employment figures for the building industry,[4] and the Treasury publishes quarterly figures of those employed in the civil service.[5]

Many trade associations or other trade organizations collect employment statistics from their members, and these are often given in monthly or quarterly bulletins available to the public.[6] Two of the most important of these are the *British Iron and Steel Federation Monthly Statistical Bulletin* and the Cotton Board's *Quarterly Statistical Review*. The British Iron and Steel Federation analyses employment in the steel industry in much greater detail than is done by the Ministry of Labour. One of the interesting features of the Cotton Board's statistics is an attempt to distinguish between 'the numbers on the books' and the 'numbers actually working'.

This is not meant to be anything like a complete list of sources, but merely an indication that for particular industries there is often important regular information other than that published by the Ministry of Labour.

UNEMPLOYMENT

All the unemployment figures that we have in this country are derived from the operation and administration of the Unemployment Insurance Acts, and since 1948 from the operation of the

---

[1] See, for example, *British Transport Commission Annual Report and Accounts*, 1952 (H.M.S.O., 1953), pp. 307–26; also *Statistical Digest of the Ministry of Fuel and Power*.

[2] See, for example, *Coal Facts*.

[3] See *Monthly Digest of Statistics*.

[4] Some of these are published in the *Monthly Digest of Statistics* and others in the *Housing Returns of the Ministry of Housing and Local Government*.

[5] *Staffs Employed in Government Departments* (H.M.S.O.).

[6] Very often more detailed figures can be obtained without difficulty by bona fide research workers.

National Insurance Acts.[1] The figures, therefore, reflect the changing coverage of these insurance schemes, the most important of which have already been discussed. In addition, however, they reflect the changing administrative procedures and regulations which govern a person's right to unemployment benefit. The introduction of the standard industrial classification in 1948 also affects the comparability of figures of unemployment by industry before and after June of that year.

The statistics of unemployment published by the Ministry of Labour are derived from the addition and analysis of insurance cards lodged with them by unemployed persons. The completeness and reliability of the Ministry of Labour's record will depend on how far workers actually register at employment exchanges when they become unemployed. The incentive to register arises from the fact that only by so doing can the worker obtain unemployment benefit, and also because if he registers the Ministry of Labour will try to find him another job. The main categories of workers not entitled to benefit are married women who opted out of the scheme in 1948. In any industry which employs large numbers of married women the record of unemployment in a slump may underestimate the number out of work.[2] But, apart from this, the record will obviously not include everybody away from work, for example, those on holiday, ill, or on strike. So, as has already been explained,[3] when we subtract, either in total or for any industry or region, the number 'unemployed' from the 'total labour force' we arrive at a figure which is better defined as those on the pay-roll of industry, rather than those actually at work.

As long as workers are being paid by their firms, even though they are idle, they are not likely to register with the employment exchange and, therefore, will not be included in the unemploy-

---

[1] Official unemployment statistics started with the introduction of unemployment insurance in 1911. Before that date the main information on unemployment is from Trade Union records. For a detailed discussion of these Trade Union statistics and their comparability with post-1920 insurance statistics, see W. H. Beveridge, *Unemployment, A Problem of Industry* (Longmans, Green, 1912), Chapter II, 'The Sources of Information', and by the same author, *Full Employment in a Free Society* (Allen and Unwin, 1944), Appendix B.3, pp. 328-37.

[2] This was certainly true in textiles in 1952.

[3] See p. 57.

ment figures. For example, in the fuel crisis of February 1947 many factories and other work-places had to close down completely for a short time, and as a result their workers were idle. Some of these registered as unemployed but others, especially those who were still being paid wages by their employers, did not register.[1] In using the figures of unemployment one must, therefore, always watch for any changes affecting the incentive to register.

The number of unemployed will obviously reflect in part the conditions under which unemployment benefit or other forms of assistance is paid. If the conditions change, the number registered as unemployed may change even though the number actually out of work may not have altered. For example, in 1932 there were substantial changes in the conditions under which unemployment benefit could be obtained. These changes affected married women particularly, and many of those who were unemployed ceased to register because they were no longer entitled to benefit and they saw little chance of the labour exchange obtaining work for them. So the unemployment figures over these months reflected to an appreciable degree a change in the system of recording rather than changes in the employment situation.[2]

The figures of unemployment now published every month by the Ministry of Labour include all the registered unemployed whether they are insured or not.[3] Before June 1948 they related to the insured unemployed only.[4] Before 1939 two sets of

[1] The number of registered unemployed increased from 401,279 on 13 January 1947 to 1,874,061 on 22 February 1947. The Ministry of Labour estimated that on the latter date there were a further 503,200 'stood-off' as a result of the fuel crisis who did not register (see *Ministry of Labour Gazette*, March 1947, p. 82).

[2] For a detailed explanation of the effect of these administrative changes see *Ministry of Labour Gazette*, December 1931, p. 457; February 1932, pp. 46 and 60; March 1932, p. 100; and April 1932, p. 128. A brief summary of the main administrative changes affecting the unemployment figures in the pre-war period is given in Beveridge, *Full Employment in a Free Society*, pp. 333-4.

[3] The number of uninsured unemployed registered with employment exchanges must, however, be very small indeed. Many of the uninsured unemployed—e.g. married women in the textile slump of 1951-2—do not register.

[4] In June 1948 there were 274,120 insured persons registered as unemployed, and this was the figure published as 'unemployed' by the

figures were published; the first gave the insured unemployed, and the second gave the total unemployed registered at the exchanges.

The insurance card has a code number showing the industry to which the worker is attached. This makes possible an analysis of unemployment by industry. Since the unemployment figures are built up by adding up the figures at individual local exchanges, an analysis of the total figure by local exchanges or groups of exchanges—towns, counties or regions—also presents no difficulty. And the length of time during which the card has been lodged at the employment exchange forms the basis of an analysis of the duration of unemployment. An analysis of the unemployed on these three bases—by industry, by region and main towns, and duration—is published each month in the *Ministry of Labour Gazette*.[1]

Further analyses of the unemployed are done by the Ministry of Labour at less frequent intervals, some of them based on an examination of a sample of those on the unemployment register. The most important of these analyses examines unemployment by duration and age in greater detail.

The number of unemployed in a particular industry or particular locality is by no means an unambiguous category. It is usual to classify the unemployed by industry according to the industry in which the unemployed person last worked. If it is fairly easy to get work in some industries for short periods of time, then these industries will tend to attract unemployment on this basis of definition. Suppose, for example, that in a period of fairly heavy general unemployment it is possible to get a job for a short time on road repair or other public authority work. Then large numbers of workers originally employed in other industries will

Ministry of Labour. In addition there were 11,946 uninsured on the registers and these were not included in the figure of 'unemployed'. The difference made to the unemployment figure in July 1948 by extending it to cover all the unemployed was thus quite small.

[1] More detailed figures, analysing the figures by smaller localities are available at the regional offices of the Ministry of Labour, but these are not published regularly. An annual industrial analysis of unemployment by region was published for a time in *Tables Relating to Employment and Unemployment in Great Britain: Regional and Industrial Analysis of Employees and Unemployed Persons*. But this has not been issued since 1950.

get short period jobs of this kind. When these jobs are finished and they become unemployed again they will be shown as unemployed in the industry in which they got temporary employment, and not in the industry to which they may consider themselves more permanently attached. It is partly for this reason that the number of unemployed in 'public works contracting' was very high during the 1930's. Local authorities provided short spells of work for many unemployed and when these spells were over those concerned would be shown as unemployed in 'public works contracting'.[1]

The figures of unemployment by small areas are difficult to interpret because the worker can register at any local employment exchange he chooses. If he thinks there is little chance of getting employment and is registering mainly to substantiate his claim to benefit, he will tend to register near where he lives. Or he may register with an exchange which is near to factories where there are likely to be vacancies in his occupation, for there is then a better chance of the employment exchange finding a job for him. The actual location of employment exchanges in relation to industrial or residential areas will also affect the local figures of unemployment. One has, therefore, to be particularly careful in using figures of unemployment for small areas.

Unemployment percentages

By relating the number unemployed to the employee labour force, the 'unemployment percentage' can be calculated. This percentage is now given every month in the *Ministry of Labour Gazette* for the main regions of the country.[2] The regional offices of the Ministry of Labour usually calculate these percentages for the main towns in their area, and these are often published in the

[1] In fact before July 1948 the unemployed were classified according to the industry in which they were shown as occupied when the last exchange of cards took place, i.e. in the previous July, and this general statement needs some qualification (see *Ministry of Labour Gazette*, August 1948, p. 260). It was still true, however, that certain industries and occupations tended to attract the unemployed.

[2] In the post-war period until the March 1949 issue, the *Ministry of Labour Gazette* gave the percentage of unemployed only for the country as a whole, but the regional percentages were published in the *Monthly Digest of Statistics* from July 1946 onwards.

local press.[1] Before the war the Ministry of Labour also published each month in the *Gazette* the unemployment percentage for each industry, showing males and females separately, but this was not resumed after the war. These percentages can, however, be worked out without any difficulty from the annual statistics of insured employees and unemployed.

The significance of the 'unemployment percentage' has varied a great deal with the coverage of the unemployment insurance and national insurance systems. The way in which the figures of unemployment reflect the changing legal and administrative basis of these schemes has already been explained. There is, in addition, the further point that in the past the section of the labour force covered by the schemes, and therefore the percentage of unemployment among them, was not necessarily representative of the labour force as a whole. In the period before 1948 it was generally true that the incidence of unemployment among the labour force not covered by the insurance scheme was very much less than among those included.[2] In such circumstances, the extension of the insurance system to these categories by itself resulted in a reduction in the unemployment percentage. This reduction can be seen quite clearly when the insurance system was extended to cover practically the whole labour force in June 1948. Take, for example, the unemployment percentage for Wales. In the *Monthly Digest of Statistics* for July 1948 the number unemployed on 14 June for that region was given as 39,200, and the unemployment percentage as $5\frac{1}{2}$.[3] In the issue for April 1949

[1] These local unemployment percentages for small areas may be misleading. The allocation of the insured and the unemployed to a particular area reflects the habits of the firms who exchange cards in bulk and of the unemployed and the location of particular exchanges. The number insured, to which the number unemployed will be related to get the unemployment percentage, is based on the last exchange of cards. Since the exchange of cards is usually done in bulk by employers, the number insured in the area will depend on the exchanges with which employers deal. The coverage of 'unemployed' and 'insured' for a small town or single exchange may therefore be quite different.

[2] Indeed, one of the reasons for excluding certain categories, e.g. permanent civil servants, local authorities officials and permanent employees of certain public utilities, from the scheme was that the risk of unemployment in these occupations was very slight.

[3] *Monthly Digest of Statistics*, July 1948, Table 22, p. 16. For some reason the regional percentages of unemployment were not published in the *Ministry of Labour Gazette* in the early post-war years.

the number unemployed in March 1949 was shown as 38,500[1]—
very little different from the earlier figure—but the unemployment percentage was now shown as 4·2. The difference between
the two percentages was due to the fact that the later figures took
the insured employees on the post-June 1948 scheme as its basis,
while the earlier figure took the insured employees under the pre-
June 1948 scheme. The 'percentage unemployed' fell because
the insured newly brought within the scope of insurance in June
1948 were not subject to the same degree of unemployment as
those previously insured. In other words, the extension of the
coverage of the insurance scheme in June 1948 added proportionately far more to the number insured than to the number
unemployed.

The unemployment percentage since the end of the war has
been relatively low for the country as a whole, and the extension
of the scheme in June 1948 therefore made little difference to
the absolute change in the figure. But it is of much greater importance if one is comparing present and pre-war unemployment
rates. A comparison on the basis of the unemployment percentages published at the time without adjustment for differences of
coverage exaggerates the differences. Thus a comparison of the
percentage of unemployment in December 1953, 1·5 per cent,
with the percentage of unemployment in September 1939, 8·7,
exaggerates the difference between these two dates. The December 1953 figure relates to all the registered unemployed and all
employees, while the percentage for September 1939 relates only
to the insured section of the population, which then excluded
large sections of the labour force where the incidence of unemployment was almost certainly very small. A truly comparable
figure for September 1939, covering the whole employee labour
force, would give a substantially lower unemployment percentage
for that date.[2]

OTHER MANPOWER STATISTICS

The Ministry of Labour collects and publishes other manpower

[1] *Monthly Digest of Statistics*, April 1949, Table 26, p. 16.
[2] For the same reason, even if the unemployment position became as
bad again as it was in the 1930's, the unemployment percentage, as now
calculated, would be substantially lower than at that time.

statistics as well as those on employment and unemployment. It is impossible to deal with all these in detail here, but a brief description is given below of a few of the more important which are frequently used in manpower analysis.

Labour turnover

The return which the Ministry of Labour obtains every month from industry includes the number of workers on the pay-roll who were taken on during the month. Since the return also gives information about the number employed at the date of the previous return as well as the date of the current return, it is possible to calculate by difference the number who left during the period.[1] The Ministry of Labour uses these figures of 'engagements' and 'discharges' to calculate month by month percentage figures of labour turnover for the industries that make 'L' returns. These have been published every month in the *Ministry of Labour Gazette* since October 1948.

The following points must be kept in mind in using these figures.[2] First, the figures exclude persons joining and leaving a firm within the four or five weeks covered by the return. Secondly, the figures include young people entering industry as 'engagements', and deaths, old people leaving on retirement and men called up into the armed forces as 'discharges', and the turnover percentage therefore includes these normal movements. Thirdly, they do not distinguish in any way between transfers from one firm to another in the same industry and movements between one industry and another. And lastly, there is no way of telling from the present figures whether a particular turnover percentage represents the movement of a small group of workers who change their jobs frequently, or a less frequent movement among a larger group of workers. Indeed, although the figures at present published are of some interest, they have largely served

[1] For example, the number who left during the four weeks ended 26 July 1952 would be those on the pay-roll on 28 June 1952 (the date of the previous return) plus those taken on in the four weeks 28 June to 26 July minus those on the pay-roll at 26 July.

[2] A brief description of the basis of the figures is given in the *Ministry of Labour Gazette*, October 1948, p. 341.

so far to demonstrate how ignorant we are about labour turnover in industry.[1]

Vacancies in industry

The work of the employment exchanges gives rise to a mass of information about the jobs which are vacant and the rate at which they are filled. The significance of this information will depend on the extent to which employers and workers use the labour exchanges and how far they use other channels. There has without doubt been a fairly strong tendency over the last generation for employers to make greater and greater use of the employment exchanges to get the workers they want, and as we have already seen, workers who are unemployed and are looking for a new job will have a strong incentive to register at the exchanges. A fairly high proportion of the unemployed will, therefore, find their next job through the exchanges.

It is fairly easy for the employment exchanges to keep a record of the demands for workers which they have from employers in their area, and the number of workers that they place in new jobs during any period of time. These figures of 'vacancies unfilled' and 'placings of labour' have been published in the *Ministry of Labour Gazette* every month since October 1947. The figures actually published give figures by industry for the whole country, and the total for each region.[2] But information in greater detail must be available at the regional and local offices of the Ministry of Labour.

Although these figures give some indication of the changing labour situation, particularly as to the relation between the demand for and supply of labour, they must be used with the greatest care. They certainly cannot be used as a precise measure of changes in the conditions of the labour market.

There is the general point that not all labour is engaged through the exchanges. It is true that at present the Notification of

[1] A very useful enquiry throwing light on some of the most important issues was undertaken by the Social Survey. The results of this enquiry have been made available to interested research workers in G. Thomas, *Labour Mobility in Great Britain*, 1945–1949 (Social Survey, undated).

[2] At first the figures were given only in summary form. The detail has been gradually extended. For example, 'unfilled vacancies' by industry have been given only since February 1952.

Vacancies Order, 1952 [1] requires that all engagements of workers, except certain exempt classes, [2] should take place through employment exchanges, and one might, therefore, expect that, apart from the exempt classes, the figures would be fairly complete. But it is doubtful whether this is so. The extent to which the Order is obeyed is questionable. In any case the Order designates other organizations than the local employment exchanges as scheduled employment exchanges, and the placing work of these—for example certain Trade Unions—is not included in the figures. [3] Further, between the lapsing of the Control of Engagement Orders in 1950 and the coming into operation of the Notification of Vacancies Order, 1952, employers were not under any legal obligation to engage their workers through the employment exchanges. Thus some of the changes in the figures over the last few years reflect changes in the law rather than changes in the labour market. For example, in the eight weeks ended 9 April 1952 average weekly placings were about 70,000 a week, compared with 40,000 a week in the previous three months. But this increase reflects the introduction of the Notification of Vacancies Order on 25 February 1952 rather than any quickening in the pace at which labour was being engaged by industry. Any further changes in the legal or administrative arrangements controlling labour engagements must clearly be kept in mind when these figures are used.

The number of unfilled vacancies which the Ministry of Labour has on its books will reflect in part the habits of employers rather than the actual labour situation. Thus, for example, if labour of a particular type is acutely scarce, an employer may tell the local exchange to let him know of any suitable worker in that category that comes to the exchange, but he may not give a specific figure of the number he would like to employ. Indeed, if he knows that the local manager of the employment exchange is familiar with the labour situation at his firm he may not submit

[1] This came into operation on 25 February 1952.

[2] Employment in agriculture, coal-mining, the merchant navy or sea-fishing, as a registered dock worker, in the police force or fire brigade, in managerial, professional, administrative or executive capacity is exempt from the Order. The Order only applies to full-time workers—male workers between 18 and 64 and female workers between 18 and 59.

[3] The figures, however, include placings by the Youth Employment offices of certain local authorities.

any specific figure of labour requirements at all. In such circumstances, even if there are a large number of unfilled vacancies at the firm they will not be included in the Ministry of Labour figures. In short, the Ministry of Labour figures result from adding up the specific statements of labour requirements that have been submitted to them by employers, not from enquiry at each firm about the number of workers they could and would take on if they were freely available.

Again, if an employer has submitted a demand for workers to the local employment exchange and the conditions of trade suddenly worsen, he is not likely to notify the employment exchange immediately that he no longer has vacancies. This will normally only become apparent when the Ministry of Labour offers workers to him and he refuses them because of the changed circumstances. It is only at that stage that his 'unfilled vacancies' will be written down to nil.

It will be seen that the response of the figures of unfilled vacancies to changes in the labour situation is not likely to be immediate or simple to interpret. This does not mean that the figure is useless. The movement in the figure of 'unfilled vacancies' month by month and the relation between such vacancies, unemployment, and placings is a suggestive indicator of what is happening to the demand for labour, but it must clearly be used with great caution.

Hours of work, overtime and short time

The only detailed regular figures of hours worked in industry are those collected on a voluntary basis by the Ministry of Labour in connection with its half-yearly inquiry into earnings.[1] The results of this inquiry, which are published in the *Ministry of Labour Gazette*,[2] include figures of the average hours worked in a week in April and October of each year for each industry, showing men and women separately.

The figures are based on a voluntary return, and the coverage for the industries included was about two-thirds of the

[1] For a detailed discussion of the earnings figures in this inquiry, see pp. 200–2.

[2] See, for example, *Ministry of Labour Gazette*, September 1954, pp. 300–6.

wage-earners in those industries.[1] The main industries excluded from the inquiry are agriculture, coal-mining, transport, distribution, entertainment, commerce and banking, and domestic service.

This inquiry has been taken on a half-yearly basis each April and October since October 1946.[2] It was taken also on a half-yearly basis during the war, but for January and July of each year. The inquiry only included information about hours worked from July 1943 onwards.

Before the war similar inquiries were undertaken, but on an irregular basis. Inquiries on earnings and hours of work, very much on the same basis as the current half-yearly inquiries, were undertaken in 1924, 1928, 1931, 1935 and 1938.

Once a quarter the 'L' returns ask for information about the extent of overtime and short-time working, and the results are published in the *Ministry of Labour Gazette*.[3] The figures refer to operatives in manufacturing industry only[4] and, as with other 'L' returns, do not cover establishments with less than ten employees. Even apart from these exclusions, however, the figures do not have complete coverage. The movement of overtime and short time is, however, a very sensitive indicator of changing business conditions, and the figures are of considerable value. They would be even more useful if the inquiries were made more frequently and the figures were, therefore, more up to date.

Strikes

Statistics about strikes have a long history. Indeed, for many years before 1914 a wealth of material was published in the Board of Trade *Reports on Strikes and Lock-outs*. Since 1914 the in-

[1] After April 1948 the classification was on the basis of the Standard Industrial Classification.

[2] The extent of coverage varies from industry to industry. Some indication of the coverage for each industry can be obtained by comparing the number employed as given in the earnings return with the number employed as shown in the Ministry of Labour's monthly employment figures. This is not, however, a fully satisfactory basis of comparison since the earnings inquiry covers operative staff only, while the Ministry of Labour monthly employment figures cover all insured employed.

[3] In the issues for January, April, July and October.

[4] Excluding shipbuilding and ship-repairing.

formation published has not been so complete. Practically the whole of it is given in a monthly summary and a more detailed annual analysis in the *Ministry of Labour Gazette*. Figures are given about the number of workers involved in stoppages and the number of working days lost, classified according to the duration of the stoppages, the principal cause, and the industry. The following are some of the points that should be kept in mind in using the figures:[1] First, the figures exclude altogether strikes involving less than ten workpeople or lasting less than one day unless the aggregate number of days lost exceeds 100. This means that the small 'lightning' strike tends to be excluded from the records. Second, the distinction between workers 'directly' and 'indirectly' involved must be an arbitrary one. Third, the number of days actually lost in an industrial stoppage may be extremely difficult to determine, especially if the strike peters out and there is a gradual return to work. Last, the classification by causes and results, because this inevitably involves subjective judgements, gives rise to particularly difficult problems of interpretation.

[1] For a detailed analysis of strike statistics, see K. G. J. C. Knowles, *Strikes—A Study in Industrial Conflict* (Institute of Statistics Monograph No. 3, Oxford, 1952), especially the Statistical Appendix, pp. 299 ff. This appendix has a useful detailed critique of strike statistics and a set of tables analysing British strikes from 1911 to 1947.

CHAPTER IV

INDUSTRIAL PRODUCTION

IT is frequently convenient in economic and statistical analysis to divide production into three sections. The first, *agriculture*, covers farming, fishing, forestry and hunting; the second, *industrial production*, covers mining, manufacturing, building and construction, and gas, water and electricity supply; and the third, *services*, is defined by difference as consisting of all other economic activities, including distribution, transport, commerce, finance, public administration, entertainment, and domestic service. These three categories are now often called *primary*, *secondary* and *tertiary production*.[1]

Industrial production plays a predominant role in the economy of the United Kingdom. There is also much more statistical information about industrial production than about services and distribution. This chapter will therefore be devoted to statistics of industrial production, and Chapter V will deal with agriculture, distribution and transport.

There are three main groups of statistics about industrial production: the Census of Production; statistics for particular industries collected and published by government departments or trade organizations; and index numbers of production which attempt to measure the general movements of industrial output.

THE CENSUS OF PRODUCTION[2]

Frequency of the Census

The first Census of Production was taken in 1907. Censuses were then taken for 1912, 1924, 1930 and 1935. The full results of the

[1] See C. Clark, *Conditions of Economic Progress* (2nd ed., Macmillan, 1951), p. 401.

[2] For a summary of the coverage of the Censuses between 1907 and 1935 see H. Leak, 'Censuses of Production and Distribution', in *The Sources and Nature of the Statistics of the United Kingdom*, ed. M. G. Kendall (Oliver and Boyd, 1952), vol. I, pp. 1–16. The coverage of the post-war Censuses is explained in detail in the 'Introductory Notes'

1912 Census were never published, but some figures for 1912 were included in the reports for 1924. The Import Duties Act of 1932 gave the Board of Trade power to obtain statistics from industries protected by tariffs, and these Import Duties Act Inquiries, which collected information similar to that obtained in pre-war Censuses, were taken for 1933, 1934, 1937 and 1938. Reports for 1933 and 1934 were published in full, but because of the outbreak of the Second World War, work on the inquiries for 1937 and 1938 was never completed. Some figures for 1937 have, however, been included in the Census reports published for 1948.

A partial Census was taken in 1946 and from 1948 onwards a Census has been taken every year. For the first time it was decided to take the Census on a sample basis for the years 1952 and 1953.[1] The Committee on the Censuses of Production and Distribution has recommended that a full Census should in future be taken every third year with sample inquiries for the two intervening years.[2] This recommendation has been adopted by the Board of Trade, and there was therefore a full Census for 1954, and there will be sample inquiries for 1955, 1956 and 1957, and a full Census for 1958, and so on.

Industries covered by the Census

A full Census of Production covers manufacturing, mining, building and contracting, and public utilities.[3] In 1948 the total number of persons employed in establishments included in the Census was 10·1 million compared with a total of 21·6 million in

published with each set of Census reports. There is a brief summary of the coverage of the Censuses in the *Report of the Committee on the Censuses of Production and Distribution*, Cmd. 9276, H.M.S.O., 1954, pp. 11–12.

[1] See *Board of Trade Journal*, 6 November 1954, p. 960, for an explanation of the basis of the sample for 1952, 1953 and 1955.

[2] *Report*, pp. 14–15.

[3] Some activities on the borderline of industrial production have been included in the post-war Censuses, but were not covered in the 1935 Census. These are textile converting, laundry work, dyeing and dry-cleaning, wig making, tea blending and coffee roasting, and the scrap metal trade. (In 1948 dealers in scrap metal were included, in 1949 the trade was left out altogether, and in 1950 and 1951 only scrap metal processing was covered.)

civil employment in all economic activity in June 1948, according to the Ministry of Labour's statistics.

The pre-war Import Duties Act Inquiries only covered some of the industries within the scope of the Census. Building and contracting, paper and printing, public utilities, and government departments, as well as some manufacturing industries, were excluded.[1] The coverage of the 1950 Census has been rather different from the other post-war Censuses. This was because a Census of Distribution was also taken for that year, and in some trades a large number of firms were within the field of both Censuses. It was decided to confine the Census of Production in these trades to establishments engaged wholly in production, and to ask for limited information even from these. Building and contracting and civil engineering were also excluded from the 1950 Census. For many industries and groups of industries, therefore, the results for 1950 are not comparable with those for other years.[2]

Size of units covered by the Census

In the first Census for 1907 an attempt was made to cover all establishments of whatever size and this was repeated in 1924.[3] But since 1930 the Census and I.D.A.I. reports have generally excluded units employing ten workers or less. Units employing ten workers or less have, however, to fill in a form giving a figure of employment to demonstrate that they are exempt from completing the full Census return. From these figures the importance, in terms of employment, of small units can be estimated for each industry. In the 1948 and 1951 Censuses rather more information was obtained from some trades in which firms with

[1] The coverage of the 1933 Inquiry was narrower than the later ones. In terms of employment the 1934 Inquiry covered rather less than one-half of the full Census of Production field. For a detailed analysis of the coverage of the 1934 Inquiry see *Report on the Import Duties Act Inquiry, 1934, Part II* (H.M.S.O., 1937), pp. 294-6.

[2] Apart from the complete exclusion of building and civil engineering the main trades affected are: wholesale bottling; fish curing; cattle, dog and poultry food; tea blending and coffee roasting; rice; bread and flour confectionery; milk bottling; pharmaceutical and toilet preparations and perfumery manufacture; constructional engineering; and metal scrap and waste products.

[3] The Census for 1912 excluded units employing less than five workers.

INDUSTRIAL PRODUCTION

ten workers or less were of special importance.[1] There was also a special form for firms in building and contracting employing between 11 and 24 persons. Throughout the post-war Census reports the term 'larger establishments' is used to describe figures which refer to firms employing more than ten persons, the term 'small firms' to figures referring to those employing ten or less, and the term 'all firms' to figures referring to the two groups together.

Territorial coverage of the Census

The Censuses for 1907 and 1912 covered Great Britain and the whole of Ireland. The Census for 1924 covered the United Kingdom of Great Britain and Northern Ireland only. The I.D.A. Inquiries for 1933, 1934 and 1937 also covered the United Kingdom. In 1930 and 1935 a separate Census was taken by the Northern Ireland Government, but the results were included in the Census reports for Great Britain.[2] Unfortunately no Census was taken in Northern Ireland in 1948, so that the 1948 reports relate to Great Britain only. From 1949 onwards a Northern Ireland Census has been taken on a similar basis to that for Great Britain,[3] and the final reports relate to the United Kingdom.[4]

Information collected in the Census

The original intention in taking a Census of Production was to obtain accurate information about the output of British industry.

[1] In 1951 these trades were: canvas goods and sacks; tailoring and dressmaking; boots and shoes; laundry, cleaning and job dyeing and carpet beating; motor vehicles and cycle (repairing); bread and flour confectionery; fish curing; ice; soft drinks, British wines and cider; printing and publishing; building and contracting; local authorities (building and civil engineering).

[2] The inclusion of Northern Ireland was treated differently in these two Censuses. In the 1930 reports the main tables relate to Great Britain and particulars for Northern Ireland are given separately; in the 1935 Census reports the Northern Ireland figures are amalgamated with those for Great Britain and all the main tables relate to the United Kingdom.

[3] The main difference between the Northern Ireland and Great Britain Censuses are (i) no information at all was obtained about firms employing less than 10 persons in Northern Ireland in 1950 or 1951, and (ii) mining was not covered in Northern Ireland in 1951.

[4] The results for Northern Ireland are published in a separate report as well as being included in the main Census reports.

83

Even in the first Census for 1907, however, supplementary information was obtained on employment, materials used, and engine power employed. Although the Censuses and I.D.A. Inquiries of the inter-war years asked for progressively more detail,[1] in general the questions were confined to the three main topics of output, materials and fuel used, and employment.

As a result of the recommendations of the Nelson Committee in 1945 [2] it was decided to extend the scope of the questions asked in post-war Censuses of Production and to take a Census every year. In the 1948 Census the usual questions about output and materials and fuel used were asked, but in much greater commodity detail. In addition, information was obtained on an entirely new range of subjects, including wages and salaries paid,[3] expenditure on plant and equipment, buildings occupied, stocks, sales by type of output and payments for certain services.[4]

Since 1948 both the subjects covered and the detail asked for has varied from year to year. In 1949 and 1950 totals only had to be given for output and materials and fuel used. Details for particular products had to be provided again in 1951, but not on the extensive scale used in 1948. The sample inquiries for 1952 and 1953 asked for totals only, and the detailed information about output was obtained next in the Census for 1954. This is now to become the regular practice—detailed information in the years of a full Census and summary information in the intervening years of sample enquiries.

The sections on services and sales by type of outlet were excluded in 1949 and 1951; and the sections on plant, buildings and services in the Census for 1950. A new range of questions on

[1] The detail about materials used was very much increased in the 1935 Census.

[2] See *Report of the Census of Production Committee* (Cmd. 6687, H.M.S.O., 1945).

[3] Information about wages had not previously been asked for in the Census of Production itself. But in 1924, 1930 and 1935 the Ministry of Labour undertook an inquiry on wage-bills and the results were published in the Census of Production reports. But this was a voluntary inquiry and the coverage of the figures varied widely between industries.

[4] Repair and maintenance on buildings and plant; hire of plant; advertising; research; postal services; insurance; and rates.

power equipment, fuel consumption, shift working and transport payments was included in the Census for 1951.[1]

Publication of Census reports

The Census results are now published in a series of reports giving tables for individual trades. For 1948 there were 156 of these separate reports. In 1949 and 1950, when much less detail was asked for, the results were covered in about twelve separate reports, but for 1951 there will be the same number as in 1948. For each Census there is a separate corpus of 'Introductory Notes' explaining in detail the coverage of the Census and the subjects on which information was obtained. But in the separate reports for each trade or group of trades the bare statistics are given without any textual comment or help in interpreting them. A report, however, has been published bringing together in summary form the main figures for 1948, 1949 and 1950.[2]

This is in striking contrast to the form of publication of the pre-war Censuses. These were published in four or five volumes, giving figures for groups of trades as well as for individual industries, with some comment and statistical analysis,[3] and in 1907, 1924 and 1930 a general review of topics of special interest [4] in a final volume.

There is inevitably a substantial interval between taking the Census and the first publication of the reports. The first reports of the Census for 1951 began to appear in the middle of 1954.

[1] For subjects to be covered in future Censuses see *Report of the Committee on the Censuses of Production and Distribution* (Cmd. 9276, H.M.S.O., 1954) especially pp. 17–19. The recommendations of this Committee have been adopted by the Board of Trade.

[2] *Censuses of Production for 1950, 1949 and 1948, Summary Tables Part I* (H.M.S.O., 1953). There is also a useful article in the *Board of Trade Journal*, 9 January 1954, commenting briefly on the figures.

[3] For example, estimates of changes in the volume of production.

[4] For example, in 1930 analyses of the degree of specialization and the regional distribution of industry.

SOME PROBLEMS IN INTERPRETING THE CENSUS
RESULTS[1]

Sales in the trade and sales of the principal products

The first point to get clear in using the results of the Census is that the basic unit to which the information relates is the establishment or factory. Establishments are allotted to trades according to the character of the goods that account for the major part of their activity. For example, all establishments which produce mainly textile machinery and accessories are grouped to form the 'textile machinery and accessories trade'. These factories make some other products apart from textile machinery; and other factories not in this group make textile machinery or parts, but this is not their main activity.

When production figures are asked for in some detail, as in 1948 and 1951, it is possible to distinguish between textile machinery and other products made by factories allocated to the 'textile machinery and accessories trade'; and it is also possible to trace in detail the output of textile machinery in factories not included in the textile machinery trade. We thus have two sets of figures for the production of textile machinery. The first will be the value of all goods produced by the group of establishments classified in the 'textile machinery and accessories trade'; and the second will be the total output of textile machinery products and accessories produced by the establishments in this group and by establishments in other groups. The first is called 'value of sales in the trade' and the second 'value of sales of the principal products of the trade'.

The precise way in which these two figures are related to each other is illustrated by the following figures taken from the report of the 1948 Census on *Textile Machinery and Accessories.*

	£
Value of sales of establishments in the textile machinery and accessories trade	56,919[2]

---

[1] This section is not meant to be comprehensive. It merely picks out a few problems as illustrations.

[2] See *Final Report on the Census of Production for* 1948, *Vol. 4, Table D, Textile Machinery and Accessories* (H.M.S.O., 1952) Table 23.

Less sales by these establishments of products other than textile machinery and accessories [1]
£
— 3,766 [2]

Plus sales of textile machinery and accessories by establishments classified to other trades
+ 4,486 [3]

Value of sales of principal products of the trade
57,639 [4]

Most of the tables in the Census reports, for example the summary tables, and those on regional distribution, employment, capital investment, or materials used, refer to the establishments allocated to the trade. But the main detailed tables of output and the comparison between output and imports and exports are based on figures of principal products.

The difference between the two figures of output or sales depends on the degree of specialization [5] in industry and the particular industrial grouping adopted in the Census. The proportion of 'principal products' in the gross output of each trade was used as a measure of specialization in the *Final Report* of the Census for 1930. [6]

Gross output and gross output free of duplication

The *gross output* of a trade is the selling value of the goods made and other work done during the year by the group of establishments in that trade. In pre-war Censuses this was obtained directly by adding up the value of the output of the separate units, for the returns gave figures of the goods actually

[1] This covers a very wide range of items, including agricultural machinery, machine tools, casting, other engineering manufactures, and manufactures of timber.

[2] *Ibid.* Table 10.

[3] *Ibid.* Table 9.

[4] *Ibid.* Table 8.

[5] If, for example, the group of establishments in the textile machinery trade produced nothing but textile machinery and accessories, and if no other establishments produced any textile machinery or accessories, then the 'value of sales in the trade' and the 'value of sales of principal products' would be the same.

[6] *Final Report on the Census of Production for* 1930: *Part V* (H.M.S.O., 1935), pp. 56–68.

produced during the year. Post-war Censuses asked for figures of *sales* during the year, since it was thought that it would be easier for firms to give these figures. But figures have also to be given for stocks of finished goods and work in progress both at the beginning and the end of the year. It is therefore possible to adjust the figure of sales for changes in the value of stocks and work in progress and so arrive at a figure of the value of goods produced, or the *gross output*, during the year.[1]

If sales and purchases of goods take place between any of the establishments within a single trade, then the gross output for the trade as a whole will include an element of 'duplication', that is, some of the output will be counted more than once. Similarly the addition of the gross output of two trades will include duplication if there are sales and purchases between the two trades. Take, for example, the figures for the cotton industry. This is grouped in two trades, 'cotton spinning and doubling' and 'cotton weaving'. If we add together the gross output of the two trades, there will be a large element of duplication in the result, for a large part of the cotton yarn produced is sold to cotton weavers, and this will be included twice: first, in the value of the output of the 'cotton spinning trade', and secondly as an element in the value of the output of the 'cotton weaving trade'.[2] There will also be some element of duplication in the gross output of the 'cotton spinning and doubling trade' itself, for when cotton yarn is spun to the stage of single yarn and then transferred or sold to another establishment to be doubled, it will be counted twice, once as single yarn on the return for the spinning establishment, and again as doubled yarn on the return for the doubling establishment.

If we can eliminate these transactions within or between trades, we arrive at a figure of *gross output free of duplication*, for any trade or group of trades. Such a figure is of great value for many purposes. If, for example, we wish to calculate the proportion of

[1] The resultant figure of 'gross output' reflects in part therefore the basis used for valuing stocks; in times of rising or falling prices it might include a substantial element of stock revaluation. The Census forms instruct firms to value stocks 'as for income-tax purposes'.

[2] The more the process of production is split up, and therefore the more frequently production is valued, the greater the gross output and the greater the element of duplication when all sections are added together.

the total output of the cotton industry which is exported, we would have to compare the value of exports with the value of the output of the cotton industry free of duplication.[1]

It is sometimes possible to trace this element of duplication from the figures of 'materials used' given for each trade. We know, for example, that the 'cotton yarn' shown in the table of materials purchased in the *Cotton Spinning and Doubling Trade* report must have been bought from other cotton spinners in the trade and will, therefore, be counted twice.[2] By using such information we can deduct the element of duplication.[3] In the Census of Production reports for 1935 figures of gross output free of duplication were given for trades and groups of trades where the element of duplication was thought important, but there are no such estimates in the Census reports for 1948[4] and later years.

Net output

Gross output, whether free of duplication or not, measures the selling value of the output of an industry and therefore includes the value of the materials, fuel and services bought from other industries. Thus the gross output free of duplication of the cotton industry excludes the value of transactions within the cotton industry, and estimates the value of total sales of cotton goods apart from these transactions. But the value of output thus calculated still includes the value of the raw cotton, fuel, and other

[1] Other adjustments would have to be made to the figures to get them on a comparable basis. For example, exports are valued f.o.b. whereas output in the Census is valued 'ex factory'.

[2] Except in so far as imported cotton yarn is bought by establishments in the cotton spinning and doubling trade for further processes, e.g. doubling or winding. This would normally be very small.

[3] Certain complications arise in making this adjustment. For example, the value of materials used will usually be greater than the corresponding value of gross output; the former relates to the cost paid by the purchaser and will include charges for transport, merchanting, etc., while the latter will be the value ex factory only. Something less than the value shown in the 'materials used' table must therefore be deducted from gross output in eliminating the element of duplication.

[4] The data on materials used in the 1948 Census are, however, so much greater than in 1935 that the calculation could be made with greater accuracy for 1948.

supplies bought from firms outside the cotton industry. We can get the value of the contribution which the firms in the cotton industry themselves make to production by deducting from their gross output what they pay for the materials and fuel[1] used in producing that output. The figure we then arrive at gives us the *net output* of the trade.[2]

Figures of net output are of prime importance in analysing production statistics. Since net output measures the value which the establishments in the trade add to the materials and fuel they buy, it is a criterion of the importance of the trade from the point of view of production.[3] The relative importance of different trades in the industrial economy of the country can therefore best be judged by the value of the net output which they contribute. Since net output is the value added by the productive activity of the firms in the trade, it is the source out of which they pay wages, salaries, interest, profits, rents, rates, taxes, and so on. As we shall see when we discuss the national income,[4] if we add the total net output of industrial production to the net output of other sectors of economic activity—agriculture, transport, distribution, and other services—we should in principle get the total national output or product. Figures of net output per person employed have also often been used as criteria of the relative efficiency of trades or groups of establishments of different size, but there are very serious dangers in using them for this purpose.[5]

This description of net output must be qualified in one important respect. Net output, as defined in the British Census of Production, does not relate exactly to the value added in the process of production by the group of establishments in the trade. Even after materials and fuel are deducted from gross output

[1] The figures of 'materials and fuel' in pre-war Censuses related to actual usage, whereas in post-war Censuses they relate to purchases. In post-war Censuses the figure has, therefore, to be adjusted for changes in stocks.

[2] The amount of indirect tax paid (for example in brewing or tobacco manufacture) is also deducted, and the amount of subsidy received (for example in grain milling or fertilizer manufacture) is added in arriving at the figure of net output. It is, therefore, net output at 'factor cost', (see p. 226).

[3] It is for this reason that net output figures are used as weights in calculating index numbers of production. See pp. 101–3.

[4] See Chapter IX, especially pp. 222–3.

[5] See pp. 113–4.

there are still elements in the residual net output which are contributions to production made by firms outside the trade. The most important of these are advertising and market research, work done for the firms by research associations, postal and other services bought by the firms, and repair and maintenance of plant and buildings. All these services have to be paid for out of net output. Unless we exclude these, the contribution of each trade to production is exaggerated; and if we add up net outputs for all economic activity on the Census definition we would be counting some production more than once. The 1948 Census of Production and some of the later ones give information about these other payments and they could also be deducted from gross output to arrive at a truer figure of net output. But the Census authorities do not do this; they leave the net output figure as the difference between gross output and materials and fuel used.[1]

Gross and net output, and gross and net product

It is important not to confuse the terms 'gross output' and 'net output' used in the Census of Production with the terms 'gross output' or 'gross product' and 'net output' or 'net product' used in national income statistics. The 'gross output' of the Census of Production is 'gross' in the sense that it relates to the selling values of the goods and therefore includes the element of value which is contributed by firms from whom materials and fuel are bought; and the 'net output' of the Census is 'net' in the sense that it excludes the value of such materials and fuel purchased. The 'gross product' or 'gross output' of national income statistics is only 'gross' in the sense that it includes in the value of output the total of all capital equipment produced whether it is needed for replacement or is a net addition to capital; and the 'net product' or 'net output' is 'net' in the sense that it excludes the value of capital equipment needed for replacement, that is, it is 'net of depreciation'.[2]

The 'net output' of the Census would correspond to the 'gross

[1] Presumably the main argument for doing this is to retain comparability with 'net output' in pre-war Censuses when no information was obtained about these 'other services'.

[2] The distinction between gross and net product in national income statistics is discussed further—Chapter IX, especially pp. 216–7, 223 and 228–30.

product' used in national income statistics, if we deduct from the Census net output payments to other firms for services as well as the payments for materials and fuel already deducted. If we go further and deduct depreciation from the Census net output as well, then we get figures equivalent to the 'net product' used in national income statistics. It is unfortunate that terms so similar should be used to describe such different measures, and it is hardly surprising that there is frequently great confusion in using the figures.

Materials and fuel used

The statistics of materials and fuel purchased by each industry are useful in giving some indication of the supplies necessary for any expansion of the final output of the industry. But the figures also have other important uses. They enable us to trace the relation between industries [1] and particularly to see who are the main customers for a particular product. Take cotton yarn, for example. By extracting the figures of cotton yarn purchased wherever it is shown among materials used in any trade in the Census, we can get a picture of which industries consume cotton yarn and of their relative importance as customers of the cotton spinning industry.

There are important points to keep in mind when constructing and using tables of this kind. First, some of the yarn used by industry may be imported and there is no way of distinguishing in the figures of materials used between purchases from home production and purchases of imports. [2] Secondly, some of the yarn may be sold outside the field of industrial production, in the case of cotton yarn as sewing thread to the final consumer or cotton yarn exported, [3] and will not therefore appear as 'materials purchased' by some other industry. But even with these qualifications the Census will throw considerable light on the markets for many industrial products and this is valuable in market research and demand analysis. Much more information of this kind can be got from the 1948 Census, when materials purchased were

[1] Particularly in the construction of input-output tables. For a discussion of such tables, see pp. 224-6.

[2] The importance of imports can, of course, be found from the import figures in the *Trade and Navigation Accounts*.

[3] The cotton yarn exported can of course be traced in the *Trade and Navigation Accounts*.

itemized in great detail, than from any of the pre-war Censuses. Unfortunately, however, the figures are not brought together in the Census reports and it is a very laborious task to hunt through every report to collect together all the figures for a product which is used in many trades.

Size of producing units

Since the Census is based on returns from individual establishments, it is possible to analyse distribution of output by size of unit. This is done in the Census tables, the average number of persons employed being taken as the criterion of size.[1]

An analysis of production based on the establishment throws light on the size of the technical unit of operation, but tells us nothing about the size of business unit, since more than one establishment is often controlled by a single firm. Only in the 1935 Census was an attempt made to analyse output by size of firm[2] as well as by size of establishment.

Comparability of statistics between censuses

Some of the difficulties of comparing statistics in one Census with those of another have already been discussed. But it may be useful to draw special attention to two further problems of comparability between the Censuses. The most serious is the adoption of the Standard Industrial Classification as the basis

[1] Analyses of size were published in the Censuses for 1924, 1930 and 1935, but since the basic unit for making returns was different in those Censuses, the results are not strictly comparable with those for 1948 and later years. For example, in 1930 one return covering all establishments in the same trade was accepted provided the establishments were located in the same geographical area, so that the analysis by size for that year is by 'size of return' rather than by 'size of establishment'.

[2] For this purpose a 'firm' included all businesses operated under the same trading name; companies that made returns under their own name were included as separate firms although they formed part of, or were associated with, large combinations for purposes of trading. A more elaborate analysis of the structure of industry dealing with groupings of firms under the same control was undertaken by Leak and Maizels on the basis of the Census information, supplemented by further enquiries. The results of this analysis were published in 'The Structure of British Industry', *Journal of the Royal Statistical Society*, vol. CVIII, pts. I–II (1945), pp. 142–99.

of grouping establishments into trades in the post-war Census. This makes it very difficult to compare pre-war and post-war figures for many trades, except for 1935 and 1937. For these two pre-war years figures are given in the 1948 Census reports on the same basis of classification as is used for that year. But comparison with earlier years—1924 and 1930—is in many cases impossible.

The territorial coverage of the Census has varied between Great Britain and the United Kingdom since 1924. In each Census report the figures for earlier years are adjusted where possible so as to give a comparison on the same territorial basis. Thus the Census report for 1935—on a United Kingdom basis—gives figures in most tables for 1924 and 1930 also on a United Kingdom basis; similarly the Census for 1948, which is on a Great Britain basis, gives comparable figures for Great Britain for 1935 and sometimes for 1937 and 1946. But it is not always possible to do this, either because it would reveal the figures for individual establishments in Northern Ireland or because the information needed is not available. For example, the 1949 Census reports are on a United Kingdom basis, but the figures given there for 1948 have to remain on a Great Britain basis because no Census was taken in Northern Ireland in 1948.[1] In any case the problem of securing territorial comparability still remains where one wants to use figures for more than two or three Census years.

OTHER SOURCES OF STATISTICS FOR PARTICULAR
INDUSTRIES

Even in the post-war period, Census statistics are only available annually, the results are published only after a substantial interval, and in some years there is little detailed information about output. But for some industries there are other sources of regular information, much of it on a monthly basis, and often extending back into pre-war years when the Censuses were less frequent. It is not intended to describe this information in detail or to deal with any of the problems of interpretation. But a summary of some of the main sources may be useful.

[1] Where particulars would not be disclosed for individual firms, figures are, however, given in the 1949 reports for Great Britain as well as for the United Kingdom.

There has been regular statistical information about the coal industry for many years.[1] Before the war this used to be published by the Mines Department of the Board of Trade in the *Quarterly Statistical Statement of Production, Proceeds and Profits of Collieries*, and in the *Annual Reports* of that department. Since the war the Ministry of Fuel and Power has issued a press statement each week which gives weekly output and employment figures for the industry in some detail. The quarterly *Statistical Statement* has been continued and there is now an annual *Statistical Digest*[2] with a full section on coal, including very useful and convenient historical figures. The National Coal Board issues a monthly bulletin, *Coal Facts*; and the *Annual Reports* of the National Coal Board also contain a wealth of statistical information about the industry. The annual *Statistical Digest of the Ministry of Fuel and Power* also covers electricity, gas,[3] coke, and petroleum refining. For electricity and gas there are also the *Annual Reports* of the Electricity Authority and the Gas Council.[4]

A great deal of statistical information about the iron and steel industry[5] is collected by the British Iron and Steel Federation from its members and some of it is published in the *Monthly Statistical Bulletin*.[6] There is a *Statistical Year Book*[7] which gives more detail than the *Monthly Bulletin*, and covers some

[1] See R. F. George, 'Coal Mining Industry', in *The Sources and Nature of the Statistics of the United Kingdom*, ed. M. G. Kendall (Oliver and Boyd, 1952), vol. I, pp. 87–94.

[2] The first *Statistical Digest* of the Ministry of Fuel and Power was issued in July 1944—*Statistical Digest from* 1938 (Cmd. 6538). Digests have since been published for 1945 (Cmd. 6930), 1946 and 1947 (Cmd. 7548), 1948 and 1949, 1950, and annually thereafter.

[3] For a detailed discussion of gas and electricity statistics see G. W. Daniel, 'Electricity and Gas', in *The Sources and Nature of the Statistics of the United Kingdom*, ed. M. G. Kendall (Oliver and Boyd, 1952), vol. I, pp. 199–220.

[4] Separate reports are published for each of the fourteen Area Electricity Boards and of the twelve Area Gas Boards.

[5] See R. M. Shone, 'Iron and Steel Industry', in *The Sources and Nature of the Statistics of the United Kingdom*, ed. M. G. Kendall (Oliver and Boyd, 1952), vol. I, pp. 151–74.

[6] The publication of the *Monthly Bulletin* was interrupted by the war; publication was resumed in January 1946.

[7] The *Year Book* is published in two parts; Part I gives the figures for the United Kingdom.

additional subjects. The *Year Book* also gives a useful run of historical statistics about the industry.[1]

The British Bureau of Non-Ferrous Metals collects information regularly about the industry, some of which is included in its *Monthly Bulletin*. A useful summary of these figures is also published regularly every month in *Metal Age*.

Lloyd's Register of Shipping has for many years published a quarterly and annual return giving information about shipbuilding both in this country and overseas. The annual return gives historical series over a long period of years—the *Annual Report* for 1950, for example, gave figures of the tonnage of ships launched in Great Britain annually from 1897 onwards. The publication of these returns was interrupted by the war, but was resumed in September 1945. At first they gave only summary information, but this was gradually extended and the quarterly returns now include some material not given in pre-war years.

The Society of Motor Manufacturers and Traders issues a *Monthly Statistical Review* which gives figures of production of all types of motor vehicles, agricultural tractors, electrical delivery vans and work trucks. Home registrations of these are analysed in great detail every month from Ministry of Transport statistics,[2] and the total number of vehicles in use is given once a quarter.

The Cotton Board now collects detailed information about the cotton industry, and the Wool Industry Bureau of Statistics about the woollen industry. Summaries of these statistics are published regularly every month in the *Board of Trade Journal*. More detailed statistics about the cotton industry are given in the *Cotton Board Letter: Quarterly Statistical Review*,[3] and about the woollen industry in the *Monthly Bulletin of Statistics of the Wool Industry Bureau of Statistics*. Monthly figures of rayon yarn production and use are published by the British Rayon

---

[1] For example, the *Year Book* for 1948 gives figures for pig iron and steel production, consumption, imports and exports annually back to 1900.

[2] Even greater detail is given in the Ministry of Transport's quarterly publication *Mechanically-propelled Road Vehicles—Great Britain*.

[3] For a more detailed discussion of statistics about the cotton industry and a bibliography of sources see A. C. Wild, 'Cotton Industry', in *The Sources and Nature of the Statistics of the United Kingdom*, ed. M. G. Kendall (Oliver and Boyd, 1952) vol. I, pp. 113–22.

and Synthetic Fibres Federation in their monthly *Statistical Tables*.[1]

Government departments also collect a great deal of regular statistical information about the production of individual industries. The most important figures are published regularly in the *Monthly Digest of Statistics* and *Annual Abstract of Statistics*. These publications also include a summary of the information for those industries already referred to. But for some industries the *Monthly Digest* is the only source of published production statistics. The most important of these are chemicals, engineering,[2] building[3] and building materials. Quarterly figures of supplies to the home market[4] of a large range of consumer goods are also published in the *Monthly Digest*,[5] and they give some indication of the level of activity in an important group of consumer goods industries. Some of the items included in this statement are hosiery, footwear, household textiles, floor coverings, pottery and brushes, metal furniture, and utility furniture.

This brief survey of the statistics about production in particular industries has dealt mainly with information which is regularly available now. It would take far too long to describe the historical material even briefly. The *Working Party Reports* are one of the most useful sources for the inter-war years, since most of the Working Parties had to review the history of the industry with which they were dealing and used the available statistical material. *Working Party Reports* were published for boots and shoes

[1] Figures of total production of rayon yarn are published monthly in the *Board of Trade Journal*.

[2] Including railway equipment, civil engineering, machinery for manufacturing industry, machine tools, steam engines, electrical equipment, etc.

[3] Figures of house building are available every month in the *Housing Summary* and more detailed figures in the monthly *Housing Return* of the Ministry of Housing and Local Government. The *Monthly Digest of Statistics* also gives figures of the output of building and civil engineering works, new factory building, building materials and components (cookers, wash boilers, etc.).

[4] For some goods there are figures for both production and home supplies.

[5] These figures used to be given in greater detail in the *Board of Trade Journal* (see *Board of Trade Journal*, 24 May 1952, for the last publication there), but now appear only in summary in the *Monthly Digest*.

carpets, china clay, clothing, cotton, cutlery, domestic glass-ware, furniture, hosiery, jewellery and silverware, lace, linoleum, pottery, and wool. The Monopolies and Restrictive Practices Commission usually finds it necessary to describe the recent history of the industry being examined and its reports nearly always include statistics about production. The articles on individual industries sponsored by the Royal Statistical Society [1] usually include a bibliography and references to historical data.

INDEX NUMBERS OF INDUSTRIAL PRODUCTION

General problems in constructing index numbers of production [2]

Index numbers of production are designed to measure at regular intervals changes in the volume of industrial production, in particular industries, groups of industries, and industry as a whole. There are special theoretical and practical difficulties in measuring the volume of monthly output in agriculture, distribution and services, and in most countries, including the United Kingdom, index numbers of production cover industrial production only.

In principle there is a choice between measuring two different concepts: either the volume of goods delivered for final use, or the amount of work done. If we use the first, we measure the flow of goods as they leave the sphere of industrial production—

[1] Some of these have already been referred to. The industries covered in the articles published in *The Sources and Nature of the Statistics of the United Kingdom*, ed. M. G. Kendall (Oliver and Boyd, 1952), vol. I, are coal-mining, rubber, cotton, brewing, oils and fats, iron and steel, tobacco, electricity and gas, sugar, motors, chemicals, merchant shipping and publishing. Further articles covering the following industries have since been published in the *Journal of the Royal Statistical Society*, series A: timber, vol. CXVI, pt. III (1953), pp. 298–322; food, vol. CXVI, pt. I (1953), pp. 57–84; petroleum, vol. CXV, pt. IV (1952), pp. 534–65; and clothing, vol. CXV, pt. III (1952), pp. 424–9.

[2] For a detailed discussion of these problems see C. F. Carter, W. B. Reddaway and Richard Stone, *The Measurement of Production Movements* (Cambridge, 1948). This includes an excellent bibliography up to 1948 (pp. 129–31). See also *Index Numbers of Industrial Production* (Studies in Methods by the Statistical Office of the United Nations, No. I, 1950, U.N. Publications Sales No. 1950. xvii. 4).

whether for export, investment or home consumption; if we use the second, we measure the volume of work done during successive periods, whether the goods are made ready for final use during the period or not.

Let us take building as an example of the distinction between these two measurements. On the first basis we would take as the criterion of output in successive periods, the houses, factories and other buildings *completed* during each period; half-finished building and intermediate products such as bricks, cement, etc., would be ignored. On the second basis we would take as the criterion, the amount of building work done during each period on both completed and uncompleted buildings.

In practice it is impossible to measure either of these precisely and nearly all index numbers of production are a compromise between the two. Output ready for final use cannot be measured regularly, because, although figures of production for many products are available month by month, one does not usually know how much of this production is to be used in further stages of production and how much has reached completion.[1] Nor can we measure the amount of work actually done accurately and precisely. We know the output of various products, but very little about changes in work in progress over short periods. We know, for example, the output of steel ingots month by month, but not whether the amount of steel at various stages of production in the steel mills at the end of any month is greater or less than at the beginning.[2] The compromise is to take the output of products at as many stages as possible, but inevitably to ignore changes in work in progress within each stage. The more stages included in

[1] For example, there are precise figures of coal output every month, but an accurate division of this output month by month between (i) production for use in other industrial output, and (ii) export, domestic consumption and general commercial use is impossible. If we are measuring completed industrial output we would have to have this information since only output under (ii) should be included; output under (i) is merely an intermediate stage in industrial production and would not therefore be included in an index of final output.

[2] Unless we know this we cannot measure the amount of work done. For the amount of work done in steel production in a month (as distinct from the amount of steel ingots produced) will be equal to steel production in the month ±the change in work in progress in steel mills during the month. We have information about changes in work in progress only for calendar years in the Census of Production.

the index the nearer we approximate to a measure of the amount of work done.

It is important to realize that on this basis production will sometimes be shown as increasing even if it does not, for the time being, result in useful output. For example, if during a particular month brick output increases, but the bricks cannot be used because other building supplies are not available, the increase will still be counted in the measurement of production.[1] In an economy in which production is out of balance on a large scale, production might yet on this basis be shown as increasing for a short time. On the other hand, since we are not accurately measuring work done, if there is a great switch-over in industrial production and many industries are occupied in the preliminary stages of re-tooling for the new output, this measure would shew a marked fall in production even though the amount of work done were unchanged. For in these circumstances there would be a temporary drop in the finished output of many factories.[2]

Wherever possible index numbers of production are based on physical units of output—tons of steel, pounds of cotton yarn, yards of carpet—both because this eliminates the influence of price changes and because the physical unit is usually the best criterion of the amount of work done in the process of production. Thus if the weight of cotton yarn produced by the cotton industry increases in a month by 5 per cent then we conclude that the output of the cotton spinning industry has increased by 5 per cent. We conclude this because the weight of cotton yarn is the best criterion of output and because we assume that the amount of work involved in the cotton industry in producing a pound of yarn is on average the same over the two months.[3]

For some industries, however, the physical quantities of goods

[1] In a measurement based on final output it would not be counted at this stage.

[2] For example, if the engineering industry switches to munitions production.

[3] Over longer periods these assumptions may be incorrect; the first because quality, for example, may change and an average pound of cotton yarn produced in 1954 may be quite different from an average pound in, say, 1948; the second because the amount of work done by the industry in producing a pound of yarn, even of unchanged quality, may change, because higher quality raw materials are used.

produced are not used as the measure of production, either because there are no such figures or because they would be a misleading measure of output.[1] In such cases output has to be measured in some other way. The three most common alternative measures are the value of output, the quantity of materials used, or the number of persons employed. If value of output is used, the figures have to be adjusted to eliminate the effect of price changes. This can be done by dividing the change in the value of output by an index number of prices. Here the main problem is to compile an index number of prices which reflects accurately the prices of the goods produced by the industry concerned. Where figures of materials are used, we are implicitly assuming that output moves proportionately with the consumption of raw materials.[2] And where employment is used changes in output per person employed are ignored.[3]

When figures representing the output of the whole range of industries and products have been collected there remains the problem of combining these for groups of products and industries, and industry as a whole. This problem can be dealt with in either of two ways. First, we can find the value of the various products by multiplying each set of quantities by the value added by each unit of quantity; we multiply the pounds of cotton yarn by the value of net output per pound of yarn, the tons of steel by the value of net output per ton of steel. When all the figures are then expressed in money values they can easily be added up month by month. And since we want to measure changes in the *volume* of output we choose a single figure of 'unit value added' for each product and use it for valuing the physical quantities for successive periods. We thus value the quantities of production of successive periods in terms of the 'net output per unit' of each product in some base period. We can then express the output for a product or group of products of any period as a

[1] This is true of machinery where numbers or weight of machines are not good indications of the real volume of machinery output.

[2] In fact figures are normally available only for the main raw material, not for all raw materials, used, and for the quantity of raw materials *delivered* to the industry, not the quantity actually *consumed*. Changes in stocks held by manufacturers are thus ignored.

[3] In addition, figures of employment usually relate to persons 'on the pay-roll', rather than to persons actually at work (see p. 61). So these figures have to be adjusted for holidays.

percentage of the earlier period which we use as our basis of comparison.

Alternatively we can work out, product by product, the percentage change in production compared with some base period. Then the problem is how to combine or average these percentages to give the percentage change for industries or groups of industries. The average must be weighted because of the varying significance of products and industries. The obvious method of weighting is to give each industry an importance or weight represented by the industry's contribution to production, that is, the net output of the industry.[1]

In practice, index numbers of production are always calculated in the second form. This is because there is not complete information about production in each industry, and the movements of output of particular products have to be used as indicators for the industry as a whole. Also, as has already been explained, in some industries the volume of output has to be measured indirectly from the movements of raw materials consumption, employment or deflated values. A calculation of the percentage change in each indicator and averages for groups of indicators follows naturally when the material is of this character. It is best, therefore, to think of the index as a weighted average of the percentage movements in the indicators and groups of indicators. The practical problems in constructing such index numbers are therefore the choice of indicators to represent the movement of output in different industries, and of the weights to give to each

[1] These two alternative methods will give the same results if the same figures are used and if they cover the whole of industry in both cases. Let

$q_1{}^1, q_1{}^2, q_1{}^3, \ldots$, be the quantity of output in year 1
   for product 1, 2, 3, $\ldots$
$q_2{}^1, q_2{}^2, q_2{}^3 \ldots$ be the quantity of output in year 2
   for product 1, 2, 3, $\ldots$
$p_1{}^1, p_1{}^2, p_1{}^3, \ldots$, be the 'net output per unit of output' in year 1
   for each product 1, 2, 3, $\ldots$

then $q_1{}^1 p_1{}^1 =$ total net output for the industry producing q_1 in year 1.

On the first basis the production index for year 2, with year 1 as 100 will be:

$$\Sigma q_2 p_1 \times 100 \Big/ \Sigma q_1 p_1. \qquad (1)$$

On the second basis

$$\Sigma \left(\frac{q_2}{q_1}\right) q_1 p_1 \times 100 \Big/ \Sigma q_1 p_1, \qquad (2)$$

and (2) reduces to the same as (1).

in combining them in industrial groups and for industry as a whole.

The weights used in the index will affect the final results. Since net outputs are used as weights, the basis of weighting is usually a recent Census of Production in which accurate net output figures for each industry are available. But the index will need to be revised as time passes and later Censuses of Production are taken. Such revisions may give substantially different results for the movement of production between two years, if there has been a big change in the relative movement of net output and the volume of output in different industries. A change in the relation between the total net output, that is, in the total importance, of different industries will not matter, as long as this goes with an identical relative change in the total volume of output. But if there has been a big change in the relative movement of volume and net output between industries, that is, if there has been a big change in *relative net output prices*, there may be a substantial difference between the indices calculated on the older and the more recent Census of Production.[1]

In theory, in comparing any two periods one has the choice of weighting on the net output of the base period or of the current period. In practice, base-period weighting is nearly always chosen because net output figures are not usually available for current periods and because a base-period index is easier to calculate. This means that when the index is revised and a new base year chosen for weighting, continuity is broken and there are a series of index numbers with different years as base. Usually there is an

[1] There is often confusion on this point. It is often suggested that changes in the relative size of different industries will affect the index. In fact such changes do not matter so long as relative prices (in terms of net output) do not change. Comparing two years (using the nomenclature of n. 1, p. 102), on the basis of the net output of the first year the index would be:

$$\Sigma\left(\frac{q_2}{q_1}\right)q_1 p_1 \times 100 \Big/ \Sigma q_1 p_1 \;=\; \Sigma q_2 p_1 \times 100 \Big/ q_1 p_1. \qquad (1)$$

On the basis of the net output of the second year the index would be:

$$\Sigma q_2 p_2 \times 100 \Big/ \Sigma\left(\frac{q_1}{q_2}\right)q_2 p_2 \;=\; \Sigma q_2 p_2 \times 100 \Big/ \Sigma q_1 p_2. \qquad (2)$$

(1) and (2) will give identical results if $p_2 = k p_1$; that is, if relative net output prices in the two years are the same.

overlapping period when the calculation is done both on the old and on the new basis. This makes it possible to link together the various indices over time. Although this is often convenient it does not really overcome the essential discontinuity in the underlying calculations, which is specially important when the structure of industry is changing rapidly. It is indeed very doubtful whether any precise meaning can be given to comparisons of the volume of production for widely separated years.[1]

Current British index numbers of production

An official monthly index number of production is compiled by the Central Statistical Office and is published regularly in the *Monthly Digest of Statistics*, the *Board of Trade Journal* and the *Annual Abstract of Statistics*. The index uses 1300 individual production series, measures the percentage change in output compared with 1948, and uses 1948 net output as weights.[2] This was first published in the middle of 1952, but monthly figures have been calculated back to the beginning of 1950 and annual figures back to 1946.

Figures of physical quantities produced or delivered are used for indicators covering about 55 per cent of the total weights in the index; value of deliveries or sales for about 26 per cent (mainly for china, engineering, instruments, clothing, and building and contracting); input of materials for 12 per cent (mainly for non-ferrous metals, food, printing and publishing, and rubber); and employment for 6 per cent (a miscellaneous group of industries such as motor repairs garages, boot and shoe repairing, etc.).

The proportion of industry directly accounted for by the series used is 85 per cent for industry as a whole. The two most important industries least adequately covered are chemicals (65 per cent) and engineering, shipbuilding and electrical goods (75 per

[1] There is the further difficulty that the information used in the index number—the indicators—is also changed, extended and improved when the weighting system is revised. This makes accurate comparisons even more difficult.

[2] The Census of Production figure of net output has been adjusted to exclude payment for repairs, hire of plant, advertising, research work, postage, insurance and local rates. For a detailed explanation of the basis of the Index and the indicators used see *The Index of Industrial Production* (H.M.S.O., 1952).

cent). This coverage should give the index a high degree of accuracy, but it will not be possible to check this accuracy precisely until the index is compared with a calculation on the basis of the more complete detail given in the Census of Production.[1]

The index is of the compromise form mentioned earlier;[2] it measures neither completed output nor the amount of work done precisely. The general tendency is to approximate to the latter basis, and for shipbuilding and building, where changes in work in progress are of great importance, an attempt is made to allow for these in calculating the index.

In the final results seasonal variations are not eliminated, and production is relatively low every year in the months which include Easter and Whitsun, in December and January, and in July and August which are the main summer holiday months. But the Central Statistical Office does attempt to allow for the varying length of months, and in principle the effect of this is to give figures of the average weekly rate of production in different months. It is because this allowance is made that production is usually high in February even though it has only 28 days. Since seasonal variations, especially holidays, have a substantial influence on the movement of production, it is often difficult to assess the significance of changes in the figures from month to month. The London and Cambridge Economic Service has worked out an estimate of the seasonal variation in the official index, and a seasonally adjusted index[3] is given in the *London and Cambridge Economic Service Bulletin*.[4] A seasonally adjusted index is also published each month in the City Editor's column of the *Manchester Guardian*.

The index is calculated and published for 18 industrial groups, as well as for industry as a whole. The groups correspond to the

[1] This should be possible when the results of the 1951 Census of Production are published. An index number of production for 1951 relative to 1948 could then be calculated on the basis of the Census of Production for both years and compared with the results of the official index number. (This cannot be done for 1949 and 1950 because details of output were not collected in the Census for those years.)

[2] See p. 99.

[3] For the total index only.

[4] See p. 6. For an explanation of the method used to arrive at this seasonally adjusted index see A. A. Adams, 'Industrial Production', *The Times Review of Industry*, December 1952, *London and Cambridge Economic Service Bulletin*, pp. iv–v.

orders of the Standard Industrial Classification. The detail given is not related to the importance of the industry. For example, a single figure is given for 'engineering, shipbuilding and electrical goods', which covers 16 per cent of the weights in the index. By contrast there are separate indices for 'precision instruments and jewellery', which accounts for only 1 per cent of the total index, and for 'leather and leather goods', which accounts for only 0·8 per cent.

The interim index of production

The present index replaced the earlier 'interim index number of production' which compared production with 1946 and gave figures monthly from the beginning of that year. The present index is a considerable improvement on the interim one.[1] The interim index was based on a much narrower range of indicators—400 compared with 1300 [2]—and was weighted by rough estimates of net output in 1946.[3]

The London and Cambridge index of production

The London and Cambridge Economic Service compiled and published an index number of production in the post-war period comparing production on a monthly basis with the average for the year 1946. This index was published by the London and Cambridge Economic Service [4] in detail every quarter with monthly figures given in *The Times*. The basis of the index [5] was similar to

[1] For a detailed explanation of the interim index see *Studies in Official Statistics, No. 1. The Interim Index of Industrial Production* (H.M.S.O., 1949).

[2] The interim index had a relatively low coverage in chemicals (50 per cent), engineering, shipbuilding and electrical goods (45 per cent), vehicles (60 per cent), miscellaneous goods (35 per cent), precision instruments (20 per cent), paper and printing (60 per cent), and building and contracting (65 per cent).

[3] Since there was not a full Census of Production for 1946, net output for that year was estimated from wage-bills, on the assumption that wage-bills were the same proportion of net output in 1946 as in 1935. The figures of wage-bills on which this calculation was made were themselves only rough estimates.

[4] Until November 1951; see p. 6.

[5] For a detailed explanation of the index see C. F. Carter, W. B.

that of the interim index of production; it used indicators of the same type and estimated net output in 1946 as weights. There were, however, important differences between the two indices and it is these rather than their similarities which are of interest. Because of lack of information the London and Cambridge index excluded munitions output. Two indices were given for the total, the 'A' index based on deliveries or production of final products in each industry, the 'B' index taking account of changes in work in progress in shipbuilding and building and contracting. Like the official index, the London and Cambridge figures for the individual industrial groups were meant in principle to reflect output per working week, but made no allowance for holidays. For the index as a whole, however, an additional set of figures was also calculated allowing for the incidence of holidays and aiming in principle at measuring output per working day. Even this index shows considerable seasonal variations, since there are important seasonal influences apart from holidays and length of the month. The London and Cambridge Economic Service also used a different industrial grouping from that in the official index.

There were a large number of other differences between the London and Cambridge index and the interim official index, some on important matters of principle, some on matters of detail.[1] When the official interim index was replaced by the present index, the London and Cambridge Economic Service decided that it was no longer worth while calculating a separate index of their own and they now publish the official index in the *London and Cambridge Economic Service Bulletin.*[2]

Comparisons of pre-war and post-war production[3]

Both the Central Statistical Office and the London and Cambridge Economic Service have published indices comparing

Reddaway and R. Stone, *The Measurement of Production Movements* (Cambridge, 1948). A shorter explanation is given in *London and Cambridge Economic Service Bulletin*, vol. XXVI (II) (May 19, 1948).

[1] For a detailed comparison of the two indices see *London and Cambridge Economic Service Bulletin*, vol. XXVII (III) (August 1949).

[2] Adding, as has already been explained, a seasonally adjusted index which is their own, and not the Central Statistical Office's calculation.

[3] For a more detailed discussion of this subject see E. Devons, 'British Industrial Production', *Lloyds Bank Review*, April 1950, pp. 43–6.

industrial production in 1935 with 1946.[1] The most accurate comparison can be made with 1935 because of the Census of Production information for that year. Even this comparison is, however, open to a wide margin of error because of the relative paucity of information for 1946 and the difficulty of securing comparability between this and the information for 1935.[2] There is the further problem that the structure of production had changed so much over the period that quite different results are obtained according to whether 1935 or 1946 net outputs are used. The difference between the London and Cambridge index and the official index is also much greater in this calculation than for the period since 1946.[3] If one wants to use these comparisons to link post-war indices of production with pre-war indices to form a continuous series, the usual device for escaping from the dilemma of the difference between the results of 1935 and 1946 weighting, is to take the geometric average of the two.[4]

The comparison with 1935 is made in both cases for the individual industrial groups as well as for the total. The Central Statistical Office has done a similar calculation for 1936, 1937 and 1938, but for these years figures are given only for the broad industrial groups.[5]

[1] The London and Cambridge Economic Service figures for 1935 were published regularly with the monthly figures for the current index. A detailed explanation of the comparison with 1935 is given in Carter, Reddaway and Stone, *op. cit.*, Chapter 9, p. 64. The official figures of the comparison with pre-war are given in *Studies in Official Statistics, No. 1. The Interim Index of Industrial Production* (H.M.S.O., 1949), Part II, pp. 42–52.

[2] It should be possible to make a more reliable calculation comparing 1935 and 1948 on the basis of the Census of Production for those years. But nothing has yet been published along these lines.

[3] The two sets of Indices are as follows:

Production in 1935 : 1946 = 100

	L. & C. index ('B' series)	Official index
Using 1935 weights	95·3	88
Using 1946 weights	101·5	95

[4] This is called a 'device' because it is a way of comparing statistically what is in theory not comparable in terms of a single set of figures.

[5] Mining and quarrying; manufacturing industries; building and contracting; and gas, water and electricity.

Indices of production before 1939

Before the war there were two regular index numbers of
production, one published by the Board of Trade and the other
by the London and Cambridge Economic Service. Both these
index numbers gave quarterly and annual figures for industry as
a whole and for the main industrial groups. The Board of Trade
index was first published in 1928 and compared production from
1927 onwards with 1924. It was revised in 1935 and changed to
a 1930 base.[1] The London and Cambridge index, first published
in 1924, gave annual figures for 1907 to 1913 and from 1920 onwards, and quarterly figures from 1923.[2] This index was also
revised from time to time and changed to later base years.[3]

Both these indices were based on very scanty material and
there were serious gaps in the field of production covered by
them. More reliable estimates could be made for 1907, 1924,
1930, 1933, 1934, 1935 from the Census of Production and Import Duties Act Inquiry reports for those years. Estimates for
these years[4] gave results very different from those in the two
annual index numbers.[5] Indeed, the differences are so great,
especially in figures for some of the individual industrial groups,[6]
that it is doubtful whether the two pre-war indices of the London
and Cambridge Economic Service and the Board of Trade should

[1] For a detailed explanation of the revised index see *Board of Trade
Journal*, 28 March 1935, pp. 515–17; the original index is explained in
detail in *Board of Trade Journal*, 26 July 1928, pp. 104–7.

[2] For a detailed explanation of the index see J. W. F. Rowe, *The
Physical Volume of Production* (London and Cambridge Economic
Service, Special Memorandum No. 8, October 1924).

[3] A description of the index in the immediate pre-war period is given in
London and Cambridge Economic Service Bulletin, vol. XVII (V) (1939),
pp. 227–31.

[4] The various estimates for these years made by N. A. Tolles and P. H.
Douglas, E. C. Rhodes, G. L. Schwartz and E. Devons have been con-
veniently gathered together and recalculated as a continuous series in
Carter, Reddaway and Stone, *op. cit.*, p. 125.

[5] See R. and W. N. Stone, 'Indices of Industrial Output', *Economic
Journal*, vol. XLIX (1939), pp. 476–85.

[6] It is true that the London and Cambridge index total agrees quite
well with the indices based on Census material for 1924, 1934 and 1935
(but not for 1907); but the group index numbers show such serious
discrepancies that this must be regarded largely as an accident, and not as
evidence of the reliability of the London and Cambridge index.

be used at all. For the time being one must do without complete annual figures for the inter-war years.[1]

Even greater difficulties are met in any attempt to estimate changes in the volume of production before 1907 when the first Census of Production was taken. But these difficulties have been daringly, one might almost say ruthlessly, met by Hoffman, who has calculated an annual index back to 1700.[2] A detailed analysis of the basis of this index and of its reliability would take more space than can be afforded in this general introductory study of British economic statistics. But one can safely say that it should be used only with the greatest caution and reserve.

MEASUREMENTS OF PRODUCTIVE EFFICIENCY[3]

The figures of production in the Census and the index numbers of production are often used together with figures of employment to measure the productivity and efficiency of labour. The

[1] One can, however, link the recent estimates for 1935, 1936, 1937 and 1938 made by the Central Statistical Office with the estimates made for pre-war Census and Import Duties Act Inquiry years. This would give a set of figures for mining; manufacturing; building; and gas, water and electricity, for 1907, 1924, 1930, 1933, 1934, 1935, 1936, 1937, and 1938.

[2] See W. Hoffman, 'Ein Index der industriellen Produktion für Grossbritannien seit dem 18. Jahrhundert', *Weltwirtschaftliches Archiv*, vol. XL (1934), pp. 383–98, and *Wachstum und Wachstumformen der Englischen Industriewirtschaft von 1700 bis zur Gegenwart* (1940); the latter has been translated into English and is being published by Blackwell.

[3] In this country Dr L. Rostas devoted more attention than anyone else in recent years to these problems of measuring productivity. The main results of his work are to be found in the following publications:

Productivity, Prices and Distribution in Selected British Industries (Cambridge, 1948).

Comparative Productivity in British and American Industry (Cambridge, 1948). (This includes a useful selected bibliography on the general subject of measurements of productivity as well as on international comparisons, on pp. 253–9.)

'Changes in the Productivity of British Industry, 1945–51', *Economic Journal*, vol. LXII (1952), pp. 15–24.

'Industrial Production, Productivity and Distribution in Britain, Germany and the United States', *Economic Journal*, vol. LIII (1943), pp. 39–54.

'Output a Head', *The Times*, 10 and 11 November 1948.

There is a useful and interesting discussion of some of Rostas's inter-measurement of efficiency raises innumerable theoretical and statistical problems of the greatest difficulty. The dangers of mis-interpretation are even greater than in most other fields of economic statistics. But this is such a vast and complex subject that it is impossible to do more here than give a general warning of the pitfalls in using the cruder calculations.

These calculations fall into two groups. Those which aim at measuring changes in productivity in an industry or groups of industries over a period of years; and those which attempt to compare the productivity of different industries or units within an industry in a particular year.

The common way of making comparisons over a period of time is to relate the movement of production year by year to the move-ment of employment. Since figures of employment usually relate to whole industries, and few industries produce a single homo-geneous product,[1] this is frequently done by dividing an index of the volume of production by an index of employment. Even if the statistics used are completely accurate and comparable, it is not easy to assess the significance of the results of such calcula-tions. For changes in total output, to which all factors of produc-tion contribute, are being compared with changes in the input of a single factor only—labour. Certainly the result does not measure, except in a purely arithmetical sense, the productivity or efficiency of labour. For changes in the relation between out-put and employment may be significantly affected by variations in capital equipment, the quantity and quality of raw materials used, and managerial ability, as well as many other factors. But

national comparisons by E. C. Snow in 'The International Comparison of Industrial Output', *Journal of the Royal Statistical Society*, vol. CVII, pt. I (1944), pp. 1–54.

A good example of the problems that arise in making comparisons between different units in the same industry is provided by L. H. C. Tippett, 'The Study of Industrial Efficiency, with Special Reference to the Cotton Industry', *Journal of the Royal Statistical Society*, vol. CX, pt. II (1947), pp. 108–22.

Most of the reports of the Anglo-American Productivity Council attempt some comparative measure of productivity in this country and the United States.

[1] In a few cases where output approximates to a single homogeneous product—for example, cement, cotton yarn or coal—calculations of productivity in terms of physical units of output per person employed have been attempted.

apart from this fundamental point, the quotient of changes in production and employment may be influenced by many variations in the deployment of the labour force. The sex and age distribution of the working population, hours of work, the extent of absenteeism and sickness [1] and the distribution of the employed population between various industries, are merely a few of the large number of factors which influence this quotient.

Such comparisons, therefore, merely tell us whether there is a *prima facie* case for further investigation. If we want to know the cause and significance of the movement, we must attempt detailed studies for particular industries, perhaps for particular processes. Only then shall we be able to assess the importance of the various factors which contribute to changes in the relation between employment and production. To use the figures glibly as measures of changes in efficiency is not very enlightening.

There is in addition the equally serious problem of the error in the statistics themselves. A margin of error of, say, 2 per cent in the production and employment statistics may not be of great importance when the figures are used separately, but when they are combined in an index of output per head such an error may be of great significance—it may indeed affect not only the magnitude but also the direction of the change in output per head.[2] We have already seen that there were substantial margins of error in the pre-war indices of production and even the post-war interim index seems to have been badly wrong for some industries. If one takes into account the margins of error in the employment figures, it is indeed doubtful whether any significance ought to be attached to small variations in the index of output per head over short periods of time, especially for individual industrial groups.

When comparisons are made over longer intervals—say comparing post-war and pre-war figures—we meet the problem that we may get quite different results according to the base years

[1] This is because nearly all figures of employment relate to 'numbers on the pay-roll' and not 'numbers actually at work'.

[2] Suppose, for example, that for two years production is estimated to increase by 10 per cent and employment by 8 per cent, and that there is a margin of error in these two estimates of 2 per cent, that is that the two indices of production and employment are between 108–112, and 106–110. The extremes of the indices for the movement of output per head would show an *increase* of 5·6 per cent or a *decrease* of 0·9 per cent.

used for weighting in measuring production. For some periods one basis may show an increase in output per head while another may show a fall. In making annual comparisons in the period before the war there was the further complication of having to fit together the classification used by the Board of Trade in the index of production and that used by the Ministry of Labour in the employment figures, and of adjusting the Ministry of Labour figures to allow for changes in the coverage of the insurance schemes. These two difficulties are less important in the post-war period, since the Ministry of Labour employment figures have complete coverage from the middle of 1948, and the standard industrial classification is used in both the employment figures and the production index.[1]

Equally difficult problems arise in comparing productivity between industries or between units within an industry. This can normally only be attempted for a Census of Production year. Comparisons between industries must be based on some measure of the value of output, since it is only on such a basis that the output of different products can be compared. Notwithstanding repeated warnings in notes given in the Census of Production, the net output per head of different industries is often used for this purpose. As already explained,[2] 'net output' as used in the British Census of Production is the difference between the selling value of output and the cost of fuel and materials used. The relation between this difference and the number of persons employed does not reflect differences in efficiency alone. The capital employed,[3] other services purchased, the quality of the labour used and the prices which the industry can charge are some of the other factors which influence the net output per person employed. In the 1948 Census of Production additional information is given about expenses incurred by industry on such matters as advertising, repairs, and so on, and these could also be deducted,

[1] It would be a mistake to assume, however, that the adoption of the Standard Industrial Classification guarantees identical coverage in the two sets of figures. There are apparently still substantial discrepancies in some industries.

[2] See p. 89.

[3] For example, the net output per person employed in electricity undertakings and water undertakings is always relatively high because of the high ratio of capital employed, but this does not necessarily mean that these two industries are particularly efficient.

and a comparison made on a more narrowly defined 'value added' per operative. But there are still objections to using these figures as measuring efficiency.

Exactly the same difficulties arise in using the figures of net output per head for different units in the same industry as a measure of comparative efficiency within each industry. Where a group of firms produce an apparently homogeneous product, the alternative method has often been adopted of calculating the output per operative in terms of the physical units of the product.[1] But there are difficulties here, too. This method ignores differences in the other factors employed, particularly capital. It also takes no account of differences in the quality and amount of raw materials used.[2] Further, even with apparently homogeneous products there is a wide range of grades and qualities which ought to be allowed for.

This discussion of the statistical measures of efficiency has been highly critical and appears to lead to the conclusion that none of the available figures can be used with confidence. This is undoubtedly true. It would of course be very useful if simple and reliable measures of comparative efficiency could be devised, but the mere fact that they would be useful should not tempt us to assume that they are possible. At present the interpretation of economic statistics on this subject bristles with apparently insuperable difficulties; we must pay attention to these, not ignore them because everything would be so much easier if they did not exist.

[1] For example, tons of cement or coal, or pounds of yarn produced per operative.

[2] For example, it is possible to increase the output of cotton yarn within fairly wide limits, by using higher quality and more expensive raw cotton. This would give a higher output of cotton yarn per head but would not necessarily be economically more efficient.

CHAPTER V

AGRICULTURE, DISTRIBUTION AND TRANSPORT

BRITAIN is primarily an industrial country. Of the total value of the output of production and trade in 1953, industrial production —mining, manufacturing, building and public utilities— accounted for about 60 per cent.[1] For this reason considerable space has been given in the previous chapter to statistics of industrial production. In an introductory review of British economic statistics the other main sectors cannot be dealt with in the same detail. Statistics of the other main branches of production—agriculture, distribution and transport—will be covered only in broad outline. Agriculture accounted for about 6 per cent of the value of production and trade in 1953, distribution for about 14 per cent, and transport for about 9 per cent.[1]

AGRICULTURE[2]

Main sources of agricultural statistics

The two main regular sources of agricultural statistics are the annual returns taken by the three Agricultural Departments and the enquiries into farm management, expenditure and incomes conducted by the Agricultural Economic Advisory Departments attached to the universities. In addition there is a mass of miscellaneous statistics about output, use and prices which is collected by the Agricultural Departments and the Ministry of Food through the various controls, subsidy and general assistance schemes which now permeate British agriculture.

The annual returns taken by the three Agricultural Departments

[1] *National Income and Expenditure* 1946–1953 (H.M.S.O., 1954), Table 10 (i), p. 16.

[2] For the best comprehensive discussion of British Agricultural Statistics see Denis H. Britton and K. E. Hunt, 'Agriculture', in *The Sources and Nature of the Statistics of the United Kingdom*, ed. M. G. Kendall (Oliver and Boyd, 1952), vol. I, pp. 35–74. This includes an excellent bibliography.

cover all agricultural holdings of one acre and over.[1] The enquiries cover land use, equipment, stocks, methods of operation, employment and rent. The main return is taken once a year in June, but there are supplementary quarterly returns about livestock numbers and employment in September, December and March. A summary of the main results of the annual returns of acreage and output is first given in press reports and in the *Monthly Digest of Statistics*. Much more elaborate detail is given in the volumes of *Agricultural Statistics*. There are separate series for England and Wales, Scotland, and the United Kingdom. Each series is published in two parts. For England and Wales Part I covers acreage, livestock numbers, production, employment and machinery; Part II deals with prices only. Parts I and II in the volumes for Scotland have the same coverage as for England and Wales except that Part II covers output[2] as well as prices. Part I in the series for the United Kingdom covers the same subjects, although in less detail, as Part I in the separate country series. Part II in the United Kingdom series gives statistics of output not only for individual items but for agriculture as a whole, and analyses the use of farm products in a way which is not done elsewhere.

The returns for England and Wales, and Scotland, are a continuation of the series of *Agricultural Statistics* published before the war, but volumes bringing together the figures for the whole of the United Kingdom are a post-war innovation.[3] Before the war the volumes of *Agricultural Statistics* were published annually, but publication in the post-war period has been irregular and it is unlikely that annual publication will be resumed until arrears have been overtaken.

The Provincial Agricultural Economics Advisory Departments, which are responsible for the Farm Management Survey, collect accounts from a sample of farms in their area. The sample depends on the voluntary response of farmers and now covers about 2500 farms. An attempt is made to keep the sample representative of farms of different kinds and sizes, but the small farm is probably still unrepresented. On the basis of these accounts farm expenditure, sales, receipts, income and profits are

[1] For Ireland the limit is $\frac{1}{4}$ acre.

[2] For the significance of the distinction between 'production' and 'output', see p. 118.

[3] Some figures for the United Kingdom were, however, given in the series for England and Wales before the war.

analysed in some detail. The main results for England and Wales are now summarized each year by the Ministry of Agriculture and published by the Stationery Office.[1]

At present there is such a long interval before these major publications are issued that they are useful only for historical analysis and research. For light on what is happening currently one must rely on the summary information given in the *Monthly Digest of Statistics*, the *Annual Abstract of Statistics*, the journals of the Agricultural Departments,[2] and the trade press. Summary figures of production and farm income are also published at each annual review of farm prices.[3]

It is extremely difficult to secure accuracy in agricultural statistics. The large number of small units, the difficulty of defining terms precisely, the overlapping of the expenditure of the farmer and his household as consumers and their expenditure in operating the farm as a business, the arbitrary distinction between business farming and pleasure farming or gardening, all present the statistician collecting returns from farmers with peculiarly difficult problems. One has therefore to be particularly wary in using agricultural statistics, and it is especially advisable to enquire in detail how they were collected before using any set of figures.

Coverage of agricultural statistics

There are two main questions about coverage to ask in using agricultural statistics for this country: First, whether they cover all 'agricultural holdings' of whatever size, or whether they exclude the smallest below one acre. The official agricultural returns exclude these very small holdings and unless some estimate is specifically made for them, the published figures do

[1] *Farm Incomes in England and Wales: A Report based on the Farm Management Survey* (H.M.S.O.). The first number in the series, published in 1950, covered the years 1944-5 to 1947-8. The later annual issues give figures for the most recent year with some comparative figures for earlier years. A similar series for 1936 to 1943 was published in earlier years by the Agricultural Economics Research Institute, University of Oxford.

[2] *Agriculture* (journal of Ministry of Agriculture), and *Scottish Agriculture* (journal of Department of Agriculture for Scotland).

[3] See, for example, *Annual Review and Fixing of Farm Prices*, 1953, (Cmd. 8798, H.M.S.O., 1953), pp. 7-10.

not usually include them. Secondly, whether the figures refer only to farms, or whether the production of gardens, allotments, and so forth, is also included. Both these points are of substantial importance in affecting figures of vegetable, fruit or egg production. For example, in 1949–50 the production of eggs available for food on 'agricultural holdings' in the United Kingdom, as usually defined by the Agricultural Departments,[1] was 5991 million; in addition, it was estimated that 513 million were produced on holdings of one acre or less, and 1613 million by domestic flocks on non-agricultural holdings, giving a total production of 8117 million.[2]

Production and output

In most statistics the terms 'output' and 'production' have the same meaning and are used interchangeably as if they were synonymous. In agricultural statistics, however, there is an important difference between the two terms. 'Production' is used for figures of the total of goods produced whatever their use, while the term 'output' is used for that part of production which is not used in agriculture[3] and is therefore available for use in the rest of the economy or for export. The two main items included in 'production' but not included in 'output' are, therefore, seed and stockfeed, both of which account for a substantial part of agricultural production. The 'production' of wheat in the United Kingdom in 1949–50 was 2204 thousand tons, but the 'output' of wheat was only 1462 thousand tons.[4] All the figures given in the separate national *Agricultural Statistics*, in the *Monthly Digest of Statistics* and in the *Annual Review of Farm Prices*, relate to production; some figures of 'output' are given in the *Annual Abstract of Statistics*, but it is only in *Agricultural*

[1] That is, those which made returns, and were therefore more than one acre.

[2] See *Agricultural Statistics, United Kingdom, Part II*, 1943–1944 *to* 1949–1950 (H.M.S.O., 1953), Table 26, pp. 44–5.

[3] 'Output' includes that part of production which is consumed in farm households.

[4] The difference between 'production' and 'output' was accounted for as follows: seed, 200,000 tons; stock-feed, 514,000 tons; and waste, 28,000 tons. See *Agricultural Statistics, United Kingdom, Part II*, Table 17, pp. 34–5.

Statistics, United Kingdom, Part II, that figures of 'production' and 'output' are given side by side, and the margin between the two analysed in detail.

There is also an important difference in the statistical basis of the figures of 'production' and 'output'. 'Production' is always an estimate derived from a known figure of acreage sown or the number of livestock, multiplied by an estimated yield per acre or per unit of livestock. The figures of production are, therefore, subject to a considerable margin of error. 'Output' figures, on the other hand, are usually based on actual returns from millers, slaughterhouses, sugar refiners and the like.

Value of agricultural output

If the various items of output, defined in the special sense explained above, are valued at current prices, we get what the agricultural statisticians call 'the value of gross agricultural output'. Such figures do not correspond to 'gross output' as used in industrial statistics and in the Census of Production.[1] 'Gross output' in statistics of industrial production measures the selling value of all goods produced, whereas the figures of output, both of quantity and value, used in agriculture exclude goods used on the farm or sold for use by other farmers.

The gross value of agricultural output includes the varying contribution made by imported feeding stuffs, imported seed and stock animals. If we exclude these imports, we get what is called 'net agricultural output' in the official statistics. Again 'net output' used in agricultural statistics does not correspond to the meaning of that term when used in industrial statistics. 'Net output' in the Census of Production is obtained by deducting from gross output the value of all materials and fuel used. In the definition used in agricultural statistics the only items deducted from gross output are agricultural products—feeding stuffs, store animals and seeds. To get a figure corresponding to the Census of Production definition we would have to deduct the other materials, such as fertilizers and fuel, used by agriculture.

[1] If we think of all farms together as the national farm, then 'the value of gross agricultural output' corresponds to the value of goods sold by the national farm, that is, inter-farm transactions are eliminated. This corresponds to what is measured by 'gross output free of duplication' in industrial statistics. (See p. 87.)

Volume of agricultural output

Figures of gross output and net output are, of course, affected by changes in prices. Such price changes can be eliminated by using the prices of a single year to value both output and the inputs deducted in getting 'net output'. The prices of 1945–6 have been chosen for this purpose. The resultant figure of net output, at unchanged 1945–6 prices, is given as an index of the volume of agricultural output with the pre-war average as 100.[1] It is to this measure of output that the Government's target for the volume of agricultural output relates. As in any index number of this kind, this measure of the volume of agricultural output may be affected by the particular year's prices chosen for revaluing output and input. A volume index calculated in this way will also reflect changes in the quantities of fertilizers, fuel and machinery used, for these are not included in the inputs which are deducted in arriving at the revalued net output figures.[2]

Figures of the value of gross agricultural output and net agricultural output, both at current prices and revalued at the constant prices of 1945–6, are now published regularly in *Agricultural Statistics, United Kingdom, Part II*; they are not normally available elsewhere. The series is given for each farm year back to 1939–40, with a pre-war average for comparison.

Farm incomes

In the annual review and fixing of farm prices the Government makes estimates of farming net income, and these estimates are now published in an annual White Paper.[3] Estimates are made

[1] This is quite a different method of calculating the volume of output from that used in the index number of industrial production. In that index quantities are valued year by year at the net output per unit in the base year; in the index number for agriculture, output and input are revalued separately but only part of the inputs used are covered in the calculation.

[2] For a calculation of the volume of agricultural output on a narrower definition of net output, deducting fertilizers, fuel and machinery expenses in addition to feeding stuffs, as well as an alternative calculation with another year's set of prices (1950–51), see H. T. Williams, 'Changes in the Productivity of Labour in British Agriculture', *Journal of Proceedings of the Agricultural Economics Society*, vol. x, No. 4, March 1954, pp. 332–47.

[3] See *Annual Review and Determination of Guarantees*, 1954 (Cmd. 9104, H.M.S.O., 1954), Appendix II, pp. 10–12.

on two bases. First by taking figures of the value of gross output and deducting farm expenses; [1] and second by using the detailed analyses of farm accounts collected by the Provincial Agricultural economists. These cover only a sample of farms and they have to be 'raised' to give an estimate of income for agriculture as a whole.

Both sets of figures involve hazardous estimates and they give substantially different results. [2] For recent years the 'departmental' calculation gives much higher figures than the 'raised sample', but the proportionate difference varies from year to year. It is unfortunate that these estimates have such a margin of difference, for figures of farming income play a crucial role in Government decisions about subsidies and guaranteed prices for farming.

DISTRIBUTION

Distribution covers that section of the economy which is concerned with buying and selling goods and thus covers merchanting of all kinds, including the activities of wholesale trades and retail shops. Frequently such services as hairdressing, repairing, and some sections of catering are also included under this heading.

The two most important sets of statistics about distribution are the Census of Distribution and the indices of retail sales published each month by the Board of Trade. The Census of Distribution gives detailed information about the structure and character of distribution; the indices of retail trade about changes in the volume and type of sales.

[1] Gross output includes sales, subsidies and the increase in the value of farm stocks and work in hand; expenses cover feeding stuffs, fertilizers, other materials and services, labour cost, rent, interest and depreciation. Farming net income arrived at on this basis does not correspond to the figure of farmers' income given in the Blue Book on *National Income and Expenditure*. The basis used in the Blue Book is before allowing for interest and depreciation.

[2] No satisfactory official explanation of the difference has yet been published. The fullest published explanation of the methods used in the two estimates is given in *Annual Review and Fixing of Farm Prices* 1951 (Cmd. 8239, H.M.S.O., 1951), pp. 5–6. For a general criticism of these estimates and a discussion of their use in Agricultural Policy, see C. F. Carter and A. D. Roy, *British Economic Statistics* (Cambridge, 1954), Chapter VII, pp. 63–78.

E

The Census of Distribution

The first official Census of Distribution was taken in this country [1] for the year 1950. [2] As a result of the publication of the results of the Census we now know far more than ever before about the distributive trades of this country.

Taking a Census for the first time raised many extremely difficult problems and the results obtained necessarily reflect these difficulties. The Census covered all establishments engaged in selling goods and in certain specified service trades. [3]

Sixteen different types of questionnaire were used, according to the nature and structure of the business. [4] The general questions asked in each of these were much the same, but the amount of detail varied a good deal. Information was obtained on the kind of business, the type of goods handled, sales, purchases, stocks, employment, and wages and salaries paid. The detail about sales varied according to the size and type of business. Small retailers were asked for total sales figures only, distinguishing goods from meals and refreshments and charges for services.

[1] The Census covers Great Britain only, thus excluding Northern Ireland, the Channel Isles and the Isle of Man.

[2] An official Pilot Census of Distribution was taken for 1947, but none of the results have been published. A private trial Census of Distribution was taken for six towns for 1936 and the results were published in 1937 by the British National Committee of the International Chamber of Commerce under the title *Trial Census of Distribution in Six Towns*.

The Verdon Smith Committee on the Censuses of Production and Distribution recommended that the next Census of Distribution should be taken for 1960, and this recommendation has been adopted by the Government. (See the Committee's *Report* (Cmd. 9276, H.M.S.O., 1954), pp. 27–8.)

[3] Non-residential catering such as cafés, snack bars and canteens were included, but not public houses, clubs, hotels, and catering in hospitals or schools. The service trades covered were hairdressers, portrait photographers, funeral directors, pawnbrokers, shoe-repairers and other repair business for the general public.

[4] There are different questionnaires for wholesalers; large retailers; co-operatives; stallholders, street traders and pedlars; large motor traders; small motor traders; large caterers; small caterers; multiple caterers; canteens; pawnbrokers; service traders; boot and shoe repairers; other repair business. A specimen of the Census form for retailers is given in *Census of Distribution and Other Services*, volume II, pp. 325–30.

Large retailers were asked for figures for broad commodity groups; and multiples, co-operatives and wholesalers for sales by class of customer as well as by commodity group.

There are five publications summarizing the results of the Census. The first, *Britain's Shops*,[1] is not strictly part of the Census of Distribution, but results from the register of traders that had to be compiled by the Board of Trade so that they would have a list of firms to whom to send the Census forms. The publication gives the results of the analysis of this register of establishments by main type of goods sold, and by county, metropolitan borough and main town.

The first report of the Census of Distribution[2] proper gives a summary of the results for retail trade, analysing the number of establishments, sales, persons engaged, wages and salaries, in main commodity groups, by standard regions, size, and form of organization. The second report[3] analyses retail trade in more detail, with total figures of establishments, sales, employment and wages and salaries for each town with a population of 2500 and over, and by main commodity groupings for each town with a population of over 25,000.[4]

The third report,[5] which gives the greatest detail about retail trade, analyses trade by main economic characteristics such as type of trade, by size, by form of organization and method of trading. For most of the important tables figures are given for standard regions as well as for Great Britain as a whole and in one or two cases for main town-size groups as well. In this volume the results are analysed by retail organizations as well as by establishments. The last in the series of reports analyses the figures for wholesale trade.[6]

[1] *Britain's Shops, A Statistical Summary of Shops and Service Establishments* (H.M.S.O., 1952).

[2] *Census of Distribution and Other Services, 1950, Retail Trade, Short Report* (H.M.S.O., 1952).

[3] *Census of Distribution and Other Services, 1950,* vol. I, *Retail and Service Trades, Area Tables* (H.M.S.O., 1953).

[4] Towns are grouped into four categories—250,000 and over; 100,000 and under 250,000; 50,000 and under 100,000; 25,000 and under 50,000; with varying commodity detail according to the size group.

[5] *Census of Distribution and Other Services, 1950,* vol. II, *Retail and Services Trades, General Tables* (H.M.S.O., 1954).

[6] *Census of Distribution and Other Services, 1950,* vol. III, *Wholesale Trades* (H.M.S.O., 1955).

At the time of the publication of each of the Census reports an explanatory article has been included in the *Board of Trade Journal*.[1] This discusses the coverage of each report, gives summary figures, comments on some of the results and on some of the problems of use and interpretation. These are most useful supplementary articles on the Census results, and it would have been most convenient to have them included in the Census reports themselves.

The interpretation and use of the Census of Distribution statistics cannot be discussed here in any detail, but one or two of the major pitfalls will be mentioned briefly, if merely to emphasize how important it is to refer to the very full notes given with each report before using the figures.[2]

The first and most important point is the incompleteness of the published results for retailing and the services trades. There was less than one hundred per cent response to the Census, and the Board of Trade apparently decided that it would not be worth while prosecuting the appreciable number of small retailers who did not make returns. The Board of Trade has attempted, by sample enquiry, to discover the extent of the deficiency, and has estimated the coverage of the returns actually received. But the

[1] 'Summary of Results of Census of Distribution taken in 1951', *Board of Trade Journal*, 24 January 1953, pp. 129–34. (On *Retail Trade Short Report*.)

'Distribution of Britain's Shops and Service Trades', *Board of Trade Journal*, 29 August 1953, pp. 425–8. (On *Retail and Service Trades*, vol. I.)

'The Census of Distribution and Wholesale Trading', *Board of Trade Journal*, 13 February 1954, pp. 294–5.

'The Census of Distribution was much more than a count of Shops and Services', *Board of Trade Journal*, 24 July 1954, pp. 159–61. (On *Retail and Service Trades*, vol. II.)

'Census shows Wholesalers Handled Goods Value £13,049 million in 1950', *Board of Trade Journal*, 29 January 1955, pp. 217–20. (On *Wholesale Trades*.)

[2] For an interesting discussion of some of the uses of the Census, see: D. A. Clark, 'The Census of Distribution', *Applied Statistics*, vol. II, No. 1 (March, 1953), pp. 1–12.

Report of the Census of Distribution Committee (Cmd. 6764, H.M.S.O., 1946).

'The Value of the Census of Distribution to Business', *Board of Trade Journal*, 12 August 1950, pp. 341–2.

deficiency is not taken into account in the published reports; these give throughout figures based on the returns actually received. This is because the estimates of response are available only for trades as a whole, not for individual towns or commodity groups.[1]

The commodity classification of sales, purchases and margins, etc., is by the main kind of business undertaken by each establishment.[2] Thus the figure of sales of 'dairymen' relates to all sales by the establishments classified as dairymen, covering not only dairy products but also any other goods that such establishments sold. One cannot use the Census results, therefore, to discover the total number of retail outlets for particular products, nor for estimating the retail margin on different categories of sales.

Throughout Volume I of the report, which gives the detailed analysis of trade by area and town, figures are given of the 'persons engaged'. These figures include working proprietors, members of the owner's own family and friends, as well as paid employees. Part-time workers are included, no matter how short the time for which they worked. The inclusion of all part-time workers and unpaid family help may explain why the figures of people engaged in distribution given in the Census of Distribution are so much higher than those given in the Census of Population or published by the Ministry of Labour.

[1] The estimates of response are as follows:

	Percentage of total establishments	Percentage of trade
Retail trade	91	95
Catering (except canteens)	87	86
Canteens	76	..
Hairdressers	91	89
Funeral furnishers	76	..
Portrait photographers	84	..
Boot and shoe repairers	90	90
Watch and clock repairers ⎫ Other repairers ⎭	88	..
Motor vehicles, cycles and accessories; motor vehicle repairers and garages ⎫⎬⎭	84	88

[2] The basis of classification is explained in detail in *Census of Distribution and Other Services*, 1950, vol. I, Appendix C, pp. 145–51, and repeated in vol. II, Appendix C, pp. 305–11.

In Volume II, separate figures are given for employees, distinguishing part-time from full-time.[1] But the figures of the wage and salary bill cover both together, and it is not possible, therefore, to work out any significant figures of the average level of wages and salaries paid in different branches of distribution.

Indices of retail trade

The Census of Distribution sets out to analyse the structure and pattern of distribution in one year; the statistics of retail trade published each month in the *Board of Trade Journal* trace movements in trade month by month. These retail trade statistics are based on two sets of voluntary, and therefore partial, returns from retail distributors.[2] The first set, for 'large retailers', covers a sample of department stores, multiple shops and co-operative societies, and gives figures of weekly sales by main commodity groups, stocks,[3] and employment. The second set, for 'independent retailers', covers a sample of specialist shops, either individually owned or members of a small chain of less than ten units, and gives total sales only.[4] No food shops are included in this second group.

The sample of large retailers covered about £850 million of sales in 1950—about one-sixth of the total of the retail trade.[5] Comparison with the results of the Census of Distribution shows that the firms in the sample accounted for over half the sales of co-operative societies and department stores and more than a third of the sales of multiple shops.[6]

[1] The figures of numbers engaged and of the numbers of employees are only for the week ending 24 June. But an indication of the relation between these and the average employment for the year can be obtained from the 'employment factor', which is the wage- and salary-bill in that week expressed as a percentage of one fifty-second of the wage and salary-bill for the whole year.

[2] For the latest brief description of the source of these statistics, see 'Review of Retail Trade', *Board of Trade Journal*, 20 March 1954, p. 585.

[3] Stock figures are not given by co-operative societies.

[4] No figures were obtained by commodity groups, but shops were only included in the sample if at least two-thirds of their sales were of goods representative of the trade concerned.

[5] For more detail of the coverage of the sample of large retailers, see *Board of Trade Journal*, 5 July 1953, pp. 1–12.

[6] But they are not a random sample.

The shops included in the returns for independent retailers were selected by stratified sampling, but the sample is adversely affected by withdrawals from time to time. No figures have been published of the value of sales covered by this group of retailers.[1]

A summary of figures obtained from the two sets of returns is published each month in the *Board of Trade Journal*. Figures are given of the percentage change of sales for the main categories[2] and areas[3] of trade compared with the corresponding period a year earlier; also indices of sales monthly from the beginning of 1950 (based on 1950 = 100), and of the value of stocks and employment. The indices published each month are for Great Britain as a whole, but in the annual 'Review of Retail Trade'[4] indices are also given for the main trading regions, analysed according to principal categories of sales.

Figures are given in all the tables separately for department stores, co-operative societies and multiples as well as for 'large retailers' as a whole. The totals for the group merely represent the arithmetical addition of the actual returns sent in, even though these represent a varying sample for different commodities and for each of the three types of shop.[5] Where available, figures for 'independent retailers' are now given in the same set of tables. Here, when figures for particular trades are combined to give a total for a wider group,[6] the relative importance of each trade has

[1] For the number of shops, by trade, see *Board of Trade Journal*, 5 July 1952, pp. 1–12.

[2] A detailed explanation of the commodity classification used is given in *Board of Trade Journal*, 19 April 1947, p. 609.

[3] For a detailed definition of the main trading areas now used in the retail trade statistics, see *Board of Trade Journal*, 14 April 1951, p. 780.

[4] This is published in the *Board of Trade Journal*, usually at the end of March or beginning of April. The retail trade statistics year is February to January.

[5] The only exception to this is the treatment of the figures for footwear. It is known that sales of footwear are heavily overweighted in the sample, and in arriving at the national figures for 'clothing and footwear', 'non-food merchandise' and 'all merchandise', the footwear figures are divided by two. But this adjustment is not made in the area figures.

[6] For example, in combining sales by furniture shops, retailers of hardware, and radio and electrical goods, to give an index for sales of household goods.

been weighted by its total value estimated from the 1950 Census of Distribution.

No attempt is made anywhere in the published figures to combine the returns for the large and the independent retailers to give a series for retail trade as a whole.[1]

The retail trade figures are based on the actual value of sales and therefore reflect changes in prices as well as changes in volume. They are not easy to interpret when price movements are important, for there is no price index which is obviously appropriate for correcting the sales figures for price changes. The coverage, classification and weighting of the Ministry of Labour's retail price index does not in general correspond to that used in the retail trade figures. Perhaps the closest correspondence is between the price and sales indices for clothing, but even here the two sets of figures should only be used together with great caution.

Retail sales fluctuate greatly from month to month. The variation due to the length of the month is eliminated in the published figures, since they relate to four- or five-week sales periods and are based on sales per week during the period. But the major seasonal variation remains. The highest peak of sales is during the Christmas period, and the lowest in January and February; and there are substantial lesser fluctuations in the remainder of the year, especially in sales of clothing and footwear. The date of Easter and Whitsun and changes in the weather have an important influence on sales. Such seasonal factors are clearly not uniform in terms of the calendar from year to year, and it is, therefore, difficult to devise any convenient method of calculating the seasonal variation in trade and so arriving at figures of sales free from seasonal variation. Attempts have been made by the Board of Trade to calculate the pattern of seasonal movements,[2] but no regular calculations are published.

The origins of the present retail trade statistics go back to the

---

[1] In the 'Review of Retail Trade', however, charts are given of the :ombined sales of 'large retailers' and 'independent retailers' for clothing and footwear, household goods, and non-food merchandise, monthly back to 1950 (see *Board of Trade Journal*, 20 March 1954, p. 581), but the figures on which these charts are based are not given.

[2] See *Board of Trade Journal*, 1 April 1950, pp. 658–67, for an analysis of seasonal movements in sales of apparel and household goods in 1947–9 compared with 1936–8.

early 1930's when the Bank of England first started to publish figures collected from members of the retail distributors' associations.[1] The Board of Trade has always published monthly figures based on these returns in the *Board of Trade Journal*, but did not take over full responsibility for collecting and tabulating the figures until 1948.[2]

The coverage and detail of the figures have been much extended since 1930 and there have been substantial changes in the way they are analysed and tabulated. Originally the statistics referred to department stores only,[3] but were soon extended to the two other groups of 'large retailers'—the multiple shops[4] and the co-operative societies.[5] The figures were confined to 'large retailers' until the end of 1946 when the new series for 'independent retailers' was introduced.[6] From the beginning of 1946 to July 1952 the figures for 'large retailers' and 'independent retailers' were published in separate articles each month in the *Board of Trade Journal*, but since then they have been amalgamated into a single set of monthly tables.

At first the tables only included sales compared with the previous year. Index numbers of sales were introduced in 1934,[7] using 1933 as a base. The base of the index numbers has been changed three times since. The original base of 1933 was used until early 1939, when 1937 was introduced instead;[8] this was replaced by 1942 early in July 1944,[9] by 1947 in July 1949,[10] and by 1950 in July 1952.[11] The indices for independent retailers were originally based on 1947 = 100, but the base was changed to

[1] See I. Douglas, 'Retail Trade Statistics in Different Countries', *Journal of the Royal Statistical Society*, vol. XCVIII, pt. III (1935), pp. 455–96.

[2] In the early years the figures were first published officially in the *Bank of England Statistical Summary*, and the Board of Trade's figures were merely a reproduction of what was published there.

[3] *Board of Trade Journal*, 25 September 1930, pp. 360–1.

[4] In March 1931.

[5] In April 1931.

[6] See *Board of Trade Journal*, 19 April 1947, p. 608; and *ibid.* 24 May 1947, pp. 847–9.

[7] See *ibid.*, 15 March 1934.

[8] See *ibid.*, 9 February 1939, pp. 210–14.

[9] See *ibid.*, 1 April 1944, pp. 121–4.

[10] See *ibid.*, 16 July 1949, pp. 107–14.

[11] See *ibid.* 5 July 1952, pp. 1–12.

1950 = 100 in July 1952 in line with those for the large retailers. At each change of base monthly figures are given on the new base for a few previous years, and annual averages for some of the most important figures for a longer period.[1] The method of working out the indices was changed in 1952, and is now more reliable than the previous method.[2]

The figures for large retailers were changed to a weekly basis in 1947; previously they had been given on the basis of daily sales.[3] The figures for independent retailers have been on a weekly sales basis from the beginning. The areas used in the regional analysis of sales were changed in February 1951.[4]

Consumers' expenditure

The calculation of the national income and expenditure provides estimates each year of total consumer expenditure on goods and services analysed by broad categories.[5] The latest set of estimates gives figures back to 1946. The latest revised figures for 1938 are given in the *Annual Abstract of Statistics, No.* 90, 1953,[6] and for 1938 to 1945 in the *Statistical Digest of the War*.[7] The figures are given both in current prices and revalued at the prices of a base year. This makes it possible to estimate changes in the real volume of consumers' expenditure. At present 1948 prices are used as the base for revaluation. For revaluation up to, and including, the 1948 White Paper, the revaluation was based on 1938 prices. Figures on both bases are available for a few years so that it is possible to link the two sets of figures together to provide a continuous series of volume index numbers from 1938 onwards.

[1] For example, when the base was changed to 1947, annual figures were given on the new base for each main group by regions for each year from 1937 to 1948.

[2] For a comparison between the present and earlier method, see *Board of Trade Journal*, 5 July 1952, pp. 1–12.

[3] See *Board of Trade Journal*, 19 April 1947, p. 608. Sales on the two bases—per day and per week—are compared for 1946.

[4] For a detailed definition of the areas now used, see *Board of Trade Journal*, 14 April 1951, p. 784, and for a discussion of the effect of changes in areas see *Board of Trade Journal*, 12 May 1951, pp. 997–1001.

[5] See *National Income and Expenditure*, 1946–1953 (H.M.S.O., 1954), Tables 19 (i) and 19 (ii), pp. 30–3.

[6] Table 289, p. 271.

[7] Table 186, p. 203.

These figures are on an annual basis, and now appear in the Blue Book about nine months after the end of the period to which they refer. Figures on a quarterly basis, in rather less detail than those given in the annual Blue Book, are published in the *Monthly Digest of Statistics*, both on a current and revalued price basis.

Wholesale trade

The indices of retail trade and the figures of consumers' expenditure both relate to sales to final consumers, the final stage in distribution. The only published information about changes in trade at the wholesale level relates to textiles. Information collected by the Wholesale Textile Association and the Bank of England has been published each month in the *Board of Trade Journal* since May 1939.[1] The figures now published are based on returns of 145 firms with sales of £150 million in 1950. Sales and stocks in the current month are compared with a year earlier for seventeen categories of trade, and indices of sales and stocks are given for three major categories of home trade and for export trade as a whole.[2] The present base for the indices is 1950; in earlier periods 1947, 1943 and originally 1937 were used as the base. The returns were first collected in June 1934, and figures back to that date were given when the Board of Trade first started publication in 1939. As with the retail trade figures, the coverage and detail have been gradually extended since 1939, but the figures are still confined to textiles.[3]

TRANSPORT

The operation of transport has long been subject to some form of public control. Although this control yields a mass of statistical information, it is scattered in a wide range of sources and is nowhere brought together in a comprehensive publication on

[1] See *Board of Trade Journal*, 25 May 1939, p. 761, for the first publication of these figures.

[2] For a detailed explanation of the coverage of the statistics and the methods used in calculating the index numbers, see *Board of Trade Journal*, 10 January 1952, pp. 51–2.

[3] One or two categories of non-textile goods, for example sports and travel goods and boots and shoes, are shown but these refer only to sales of such goods by textile wholesalers.

transport. Little more can be done in this introduction than to mention some of the main sources of information about rail, road, shipping, and air transport.[1]

Railways

The railways have long been required by statute to publish regular statistics. Since the nationalization of the railways in 1948 these statistics have been published by the Transport Commission; monthly in a series called *Transport Statistics*, and annually in the reports of the Commission.[2]

One of the remarkable, and exceptional, features of railway statistics is the detailed information given about capital equipment, detail which exists for no other British industry. Figures of traffic rolling stock, locomotives, coaching and freight vehicles, containers, horses, motor vehicles, length and state of track, are given each year.

The Transport Commission took over a well-established system of statistics that had previously been looked after by the Ministry of Transport and the four main line railways. Before nationalization there were two publications, *Railway Statistics*, a monthly, and *Railway Returns*, an annual. Both were interrupted by the war, but summary annual returns of railway operation were produced after the war by the Ministry of Transport for the period 1938 to 1944, 1945, 1946, and 1947.

This series of statistics goes back to the early 1920's when the four main line railways were established. There are less complete statistics, published by the Board of Trade, back to the early days of railway operation and the first attempts at statutory control.

Road transport

Statistics of road transport are neither as comprehensive nor as detailed as for the railways. Most of them arise from the workings

[1] For a detailed description of statistics on road and rail transport and a bibliography of sources see F. A. A. Menzler, 'Rail and Road', in *The Sources and Nature of the Statistics of the United Kingdom*, ed. M. G. Kendall (Oliver and Boyd, 1952), vol. I, pp. 279–302.

[2] Summaries are given in the *Monthly Digest of Statistics* and *Annual Abstract of Statistics*. This is often a more convenient source, especially since comparative figures are given back to 1938, whereas the Transport Commission's publications usually give comparative figures for only one previous year.

of some administrative control, such as the issue of licences for road transport operation, or from taxation, such as the tax on motor vehicles of all kinds. Nearly all the statistics refer to the number and type of vehicles in use; there is only the sketchiest information about traffic on the roads and the volume and type of freight carried.[1]

The taxation of all motor vehicles enables the Ministry of Transport to enumerate in detail the motor vehicles in use, classified by type of vehicle and area. The licences are issued on a quarterly basis by County Boroughs and Counties, and an analysis is published each quarter for the country as a whole of the licences current, new registrations during the quarter, and the receipts from taxation. Once a year, for the quarter ended 30 September, the census is given in great detail, both by type of vehicle and by licensing authority.[2] These statistics provide the main basis for analysing the use of motor vehicles in this country and are regularly published and discussed by the Society of Motor Manufacturers and Traders in their *Monthly Statistical Review* and in the annual *Motor Industry of Great Britain*.

The operation of the Road Fund, an anachronism of British public finance, yields statistics of expenditure on the roads and the mileage of public highway in Great Britain, and these are published every year in the annual report of the Fund. Information about buses and coaches is obtained by the Ministry of Transport from all operators under the Road Traffic Act of 1930. A summary of these statistics is published annually by the Ministry of Transport.[3] The statutory returns do not apply to the London Transport Executive, but separate tables on the operations of London Transport are included in this annual publication.

The British Road Federation try to bring together some of the most important statistics on road transport in their annual publication *Basic Road Statistics*. The main advantage of this

---

[1] For an analysis of road goods transport on the basis of a sample enquiry, see K. F. Glover and D. N. Miller, 'The Outlines of the Road Goods Transport Industry', *Journal of the Royal Statistical Society*, series A, vol. 117, pt. 3 (1954), pp. 297–330.

[2] *Mechanically Propelled Road Vehicles: Census of Vehicles for which licences were current at any time during the quarter ended 30 September*, 1953 (H.M.S.O., 1954).

[3] *Public Road Passenger Transport Statistics, Great Britain* (H.M.S.O.).

publication is that an attempt is made to give a continuous set of annual figures from the beginning of the century, but only the most important figures are included and then only in summary form. The Transport Commission's monthly *Transport Statistics* and annual reports cover the operation of passenger and goods vehicles owned by the Commission, but since road transport was denationalized these are only a small section of the whole road transport industry.

Shipping [1]

Statistics of shipping are of two kinds. Those dealing with the size and type of ships in the fleet, and those dealing with operations, particularly the goods carried in the overseas trade of this country. Figures of the merchant shipping fleet arise from the registration of all shipping by statute and the information kept by Lloyd's and the Chamber of Shipping. The published statistics analyse the ships in the fleet in great detail by size, age and type. This is done annually by both Lloyd's [2] and the Chamber of Shipping. [3] Summary tables are given in the *Annual Abstract of Statistics*.

The *Trade and Navigation Accounts*, both monthly and annual, include information on the shipping engaged in foreign trade with the United Kingdom. Figures of total shipping entered and cleared from British ports are given each month, together with an analysis of their nationality and main trading areas.

There is often confusion between the different units of measurement that are used in analysis of the merchant fleet and shipping operations. The three common units of measurement are 'gross registered tonnage', 'net registered tonnage', and 'dead weight tonnage'. The first two are measures of the ship's capacity in

[1] For a detailed analysis and bibliography of shipping statistics see M. G. Kendall, 'Merchant Shipping', in *The Sources and Nature of the Statistics of the United Kingdom*, ed. M. G. Kendall (Oliver and Boyd, 1952), vol. I, pp. 267–78, and 'The United Kingdom Mercantile Marine and its Contribution to the Balance of Payments', *Journal of the Royal Statistical Society*, Series A, vol. CXIII, pt. I (1950), pp. 9–36.

[2] *Lloyd's Register of Shipping*, *Extract from Appendix*, 1954 (1954), Section 6, Statistical Tables.

[3] *Chamber of Shipping of the United Kingdom*, *Annual Report* 1953–1954 (Witherby, London. 1954), pp. 149–56.

volume,[1] the third of weight of cargo carried. 'Gross tonnage' measures the volume of enclosed space in the ship and is usually used in this country for figures of shipbuilding and the analysis of the fleet by type, size and age.[2] 'Net tonnage' is the gross tonnage less the space used for machinery, the ship's company and ship's stores. Port dues are usually charged on the ship's net tonnage, and the Board of Trade's figures of entrances and clearances given in the *Trade and Navigation Accounts* are in these terms. 'Dead weight tonnage' measures, in weight, the amount of cargo that a ship can carry when the vessel is down to its load-line. The actual dead weight tonnage carried may, of course, vary from voyage to voyage. The distinction between these three measures of shipping is most important in making international comparisons, for the United Kingdom practice, outlined here, does not apply uniformly to other countries.

Air transport

Statistics of air transport are being extended year by year as the traffic increases. Statistics of air traffic and operation are published each month in a press statement by the Ministry of Transport and Civil Aviation,[3] and a summary of these figures is included in the *Monthly Digest of Statistics* and *Annual Abstract of Statistics*. The statistics cover the two Airways Corporations and private companies operating scheduled flights. The operations of the two corporations are analysed in greater detail in their annual reports.

The Ministry also collects and publishes statistics of the traffic handled at United Kingdom aerodromes, and these cover foreign as well as British companies.[4] The British Independent Air Transport Association publishes information in its *Annual Report* about the traffic handled by its members.

[1] 100 cubic feet being taken as equal to 1 ton.
[2] The statutory registration is in gross tonnage.
[3] *Operating and Traffic Statistics of the United Kingdom Airways Corporations and their Associates.*
[4] *Summary of Activity at Aerodromes in the United Kingdom and Channel Islands.*

CHAPTER VI

FOREIGN TRADE

FOREIGN trade statistics cover the economic transactions between residents of the United Kingdom and residents of other countries. As with other statistics, many of the figures about foreign trade result from administrative regulation and control and reflect the changing form and operation of such control.

Until recent years Government administrative control over foreign trade was confined in the main to goods leaving and coming into the country, and official statistics therefore referred only to the trade in such goods, or as it is sometimes called, the *merchandise trade* or *visible trade*. From the economic point of view, other transactions between the United Kingdom and overseas countries, although not recorded so well statistically, are just as important as the trade in goods or merchandise. Such transactions include trade in shipping, insurance, banking and other services, tourist payments and receipts, incomes from investment overseas and payments to foreigners holding investments in the United Kingdom. These and other transactions of this kind are often referred to as the *non-merchandise trade* or *invisible items of trade*.

If we bring together statistics of both merchandise and non-merchandise trade, we see the total payments that the United Kingdom makes for goods and services imported from overseas and the total receipts that the United Kingdom obtains from goods and services exported. Such statements, which attempt to cover all transactions with overseas countries, are usually referred to as *balance of payments* statistics. Since balance of payments statistics cover all items of trade, they can only be compiled for periods for which there are figures of non-merchandise as well as merchandise trade. For this reason it is only in recent years that regular and detailed statistics of the balance of payments have been compiled.

Even now, while statistics of merchandise trade are published every month, statistics of non-merchandise trade and the balance of payments are available only for half-yearly periods.

MERCHANDISE TRADE STATISTICS[1]

Figures of United Kingdom merchandise imports, exports, and
re-exports are compiled and published regularly for monthly and
annual periods. The figures for each month are announced first
in summary form, giving just the main totals of imports and exports, in a press statement and in the *Board of Trade Journal*
about two and a half weeks after the end of the month. About a
week later, the monthly *Accounts relating to Trade and Navigation
of the United Kingdom* are published, giving figures of trade in
some detail. At the same time there is usually an article in the
Board of Trade Journal analysing and commenting on the most
important changes which the accounts reveal.

The main analysis in the monthly accounts is by commodities
and groups of commodities, with the chief countries of import and
export under the important headings. Total figures are also
given of the United Kingdom's import, export, and re-export
trade with each country of the world. The basis of the commodity classification used is that laid down for importers and
exporters in the Import and Export Lists. This list is revised
and republished every year, but there are usually only minor
revisions in the list from one year to the next. The monthly
account does not give the full detailed figures obtained from
traders by the Customs and Excise, but this detail can usually be
obtained for particular items of trade by special arrangement.[2]

Since January 1954 the arrangement and grouping of commodities into categories in the trade accounts has been based on
the Standard International Trade Classification laid down by the
United Nations Statistics Commission. The use of this classification makes the international comparison of trade statistics easier
but involves a substantial break in the continuity of the British
statistics, for the new classification is substantially different from
that used by the United Kingdom before 1954.[3] But the import

[1] For a detailed discussion of statistics of merchandise trade, see A.
Maizels, 'Overseas Trade', in *The Sources and Nature of the Statistics of
the United Kingdom*, ed. M. G. Kendall (Oliver and Boyd, 1952), vol. I,
pp. 17–34.

[2] On payment of a fee.

[3] See 'January Trade Figures and New Classification of United Kingdom Trade', *Board of Trade Journal*, 20 February 1954, p. 366. Annual
figures back to 1935 for the four main groups of imports and exports are
given on the new basis in the *Report on Overseas Trade*.

and export lists, and therefore the figures of trade for individual commodities, is not affected by this change; the break is only in the arrangement of the tables and in the figures of trade by groups of commodities.[1]

Figures are given in the monthly accounts not only for the current month but also for the corresponding months of the two previous years; also cumulative figures for the year so far, again with the two previous years.[2] The cumulative figures given in the December return thus relate to the calendar year January to December, and this is the most useful source for annual figures until the *Annual Statement of Trade* appears.

The monthly *Trade and Navigation Accounts* give the basic detailed figures of United Kingdom merchandise imports and exports, but the information is not presented in a form convenient for picking out the most important features of changes in British foreign trade month by month. This is now done in a monthly publication called the *Report on Overseas Trade*,[3] which the Board of Trade started in 1950. This gives a summary of the figures of trade for the main commodities, countries, and the main trading areas of the world, for the current month with comparative figures for earlier periods. The main figures of the

[1] For example, before January 1954 trade was classified under five main headings and total figures given for each as well as for sub-groups. The headings used were food, drink and tobacco; raw materials and articles mainly unmanufactured; articles wholly or mainly manufactured; animals not for food; and parcel post. The main headings used now are food, beverages and tobacco; basic materials; mineral fuels and lubricants; manufactured goods; and miscellaneous.

[2] This means that figures on the basis of the new classification, introduced in 1954, are available for 1953 and 1952.

[3] This monthly report appears about a month later than the monthly *Trade and Navigation Accounts*, that is, about seven weeks after the end of the month to which it relates.

The difference in the description of the *Trade and Navigation Accounts* and the *Report on Overseas Trade* may confuse. The *Trade and Navigation Accounts* are described by the month to which they relate, while the *Report on Overseas Trade* is described by the month in which it is published. Thus the *Trade and Navigation Accounts* published in March 1953 giving figures for February 1953 is entitled *Account for February, 1953*; but the *Report on Overseas Trade* issued in March 1953 which gives figures up to January 1953, is entitled *Report on Overseas Trade, March* 1953.

138

volume and prices [1] of British exports and imports are also given. Some of the summary tables from the *Report on Overseas Trade* are given in the *Monthly Digest of Statistics*. The Digest also includes tables showing total imports and exports of the most important commodities by quantity month by month over the previous twelve months with comparative figures for previous years and for 1938. These are a most useful set of tables, for although the figures could be got from the monthly accounts, this would involve the long and laborious job of extraction from a large number of separate issues.

After an interval of rather over a year the *Annual Statement of the Trade of the United Kingdom* is published. This is in four volumes: Volume I gives all the aggregates of trade, first by commodity and then by country including figures of retained imports. Volume II gives figures of imports and re-exports by commodity with details for principal countries. Volume III gives similar figures for exports, and Volume IV gives trade with each country analysed by main commodities. [2] The figures for imports and exports given in Volumes I, II and III use the full classification of the Import and Export List, and thus give considerably more detail than the *Trade and Navigation Accounts*. The analysis of trade by country and commodity included in Volume IV is not done in the *Accounts*, but there is a special annual tabulation, from *Accounts* data, entitled *Trade of the United Kingdom with Selected Countries*, published in April each year. [3] The *Annual Statements* also include revisions to the figures, and for this reason may not agree with the figures in the December trade return for the year concerned. All the tables in the *Annual Statement* give comparative figures for four previous years. A series of annual figures going back to pre-war is given for the most important items in the *Annual Abstract of Statistics*.

There is a great deal of historical statistical information about foreign trade, for Governments have always found it convenient to raise a substantial part of their revenue by taxing imports or

[1] See pp. 145–54.

[2] A supplement to Volume IV, now published every three years, gives particulars of trade by ports. The last issue of this supplement, published in 1953, gives figures for 1949, 1950 and 1951.

[3] However, some of this analysis is now done in the *Report on Overseas Trade*.

exports. Statistics for the United Kingdom broadly on a comparable basis with those published at present, although not as detailed, extend back to the middle of the nineteenth century, and there is much useful information for earlier periods.[1]

SOME PROBLEMS IN USING MERCHANDISE TRADE STATISTICS

General and special trade and the 'trade balance'

In using figures of imports and exports it is important to know whether they relate to total imports and total exports, or whether they refer more narrowly to imports for domestic use only and exports of goods of domestic origin only. Figures on the first basis are usually referred to as statistics of 'general trade'; and those on the second basis as statistics of 'special trade'. In the United Kingdom trade statistics most of the figures given are for total imports (whether for domestic consumption or later re-export), for exports of the produce and manufacture of the United Kingdom, and for re-exports.[2] If re-exports are deducted from total imports we arrive at figures of 'retained imports'. Figures of 'retained imports', which are given in the *Annual Statement of Trade*, however, are not quite the same as figures of 'imports for domestic consumption'. First, because goods re-exported in any one month or year may not have been imported during the same period. Indeed, occasionally the re-exports in a period may exceed the total imports during the period, thus giving a minus quantity for 'retained imports'. Secondly, the value of re-exports will normally exceed the value of the same goods at the time they were imported because of merchanting, transport, insurance and other charges arising in this country.

If we deduct the value of total imports from the value of exports plus re-exports we get figures of the *balance of merchandise trade*. Such figures can be worked out either for total trade or for

[1] For a description of the historical material see A. Maizels, 'Overseas Trade', in *The Sources and Nature of the Statistics of the United Kingdom*, ed. M. G. Kendall (Oliver and Boyd, 1952), vol. I, pp. 17–34, and Werne Schlote, *British Overseas Trade from 1700 to the 1930's*, trans. W. O. Henderson and W. H. Chaloner (Blackwell, 1952).

[2] Re-exports are goods exported in the same (or essentially the same) condition in which they were imported, while exports are goods which have been transformed by processing or manufacture in this country, or which have been grown or produced here.

trade with individual countries or groups of countries, and are now given regularly in the monthly *Report on Overseas Trade*. These figures should not be confused with the *balance of payments*. They relate to the trade in goods only, and even for transactions in goods they do not measure at all accurately the difference between what we pay out and what we receive for imports and exports.[1] But even now balance of payments statistics are available only once every six months and then only after a considerable interval, whereas the balance of trade can be worked out promptly every month. Inevitably, therefore, great use is made of the monthly balance of trade figures, and commentators often draw conclusions from the trade figures about what is probably happening to the balance of payments. This is very dangerous.

Coverage of the figures

In general the trade returns cover all merchandise imported into and exported from the country. There are, however, important categories of merchandise which are excluded, and some traded goods are left out because they are not considered to be merchandise imports or exports.[2] Monetary items, of which the most important is gold, are excluded as not being merchandise, and so are ships' stores and bunkers. Examples of merchandise items excluded are fissionable material and precious stones; the first, for defence reasons, the second because it is difficult to get reasonably accurate figures. Another important group of items excluded is equipment for the armed forces imported from the United States under the Mutual Defence Assistance agreement. There have been changes in the particular items excluded from the returns and these must not be overlooked when figures from different returns are being used for comparative purposes.

Some of the goods which are excluded from the trade returns enter into the payments transactions of the United Kingdom,[3] and an allowance has to be made for them, if only on a rough

[1] The reasons for this are explained in later paragraphs.

[2] A detailed explanation of the coverage of the trade figures is included in 'Notes' at the front of every month's *Trade and Navigation Accounts*, and in the 'Introductory Notes' to each volume of the *Annual Statement of Trade*.

[3] For an estimate of the value of the goods excluded from the returns see Maizels, *op. cit.*, p. 19.

basis, in the figures for merchandise included in the balance of payments estimates. This is one reason why the figures which are given in the trade returns differ from the figures for imports and exports given in the balance of payments statements.

Period to which the figures relate

The statistics published in the trade returns are based on the declarations made by importers and exporters to the local Customs and Excise officers who then send them on to the Statistical Office, Customs and Excise. In general, the documents received by the Statistical Office during any month are used as the basis of the trade figures for that month. The Statistical Office takes no account of the dates on which the goods arrived or left the country, but is merely concerned with the date on which it receives the documents; for example, all documents received in January will be counted as 'January trade' and included in the January *Trade and Navigation Accounts*.

Importers are required by law to make their returns within fourteen days after the arrival of the goods, but the returns may also be sent in before the goods actually arrive. For exports subject to licence, the returns·have to be made before the goods are shipped, but in other cases exporters are allowed seven days after shipment within which to make the returns. There is then an interval between the receipt and examination of the returns by the local Customs office and their despatch to the Statistical Office. It follows that the figures published for a month do not refer at all precisely to the trade which actually took place during that month. And the figures of trade from one month to the next may fluctuate because of changes in the rate at which returns are made and forwarded to the Statistical Office, rather than because of fluctuations in the actual trade which is taking place. For this reason it is unwise to attach great importance to short-period changes in the trade figures from one month to the next.

The figures relate to calendar months and reflect differences in the lengths of months and in the number of working days in the month. When the trade figures are first announced and discussed in the *Board of Trade Journal* the number of working days in the month is usually given, and comparisons of exports with earlier periods are often made on the basis of trade per working day. But this is only done for total trade and not for trade by commodities or countries.

The imports and exports that are recorded in the trade accounts for any period do not tell us what has to be paid for imports or what is received for exports during that period. For payment may have to be made for imports before they arrive and may not be received for exports until after they have left. This is another reason why figures for merchandise exports and imports in the trade accounts will differ from the figures for merchandise payments and receipts in the balance of payments statements.[1]

Valuation of imports and exports

The value of imports given in the trade returns is traditionally related to the value put on the goods when they are assessed for *ad valorem* customs duty. In the case of the United Kingdom this is the c.i.f. value of the goods at the port of landing, that is, the value that the goods have when they arrive in this country, including the freight, insurance and other charges involved in bringing them here.[2] Exports are recorded at the value that they have at the port of departure from the United Kingdom, that is, free on board (f.o.b.) value.[3]

The f.o.b. value for exports is also appropriate for balance of payments figures, but the c.i.f. value is not appropriate for

---

[1] The balance of payments figures in principle relate to time of transfer of ownership (credit or debit) rather than actual payments. In general it is assumed that imports are transferred to British ownership when they leave the foreign port, and that exports are transferred to foreign ownership when they arrive at the country of destination. The figures in the balance of payments, therefore, in general relate to an earlier period than the trade accounts for imports and to a later period for exports. The difference between the two sets of figures on this account alone may be quite substantial if imports or exports are rising or falling. (See p. 165.)

[2] But excluding duty here.

[3] Imports and exports by parcel post not charged to customs duty are included under one general heading (Class V) and are valued by applying an average value to the number of parcels. This was based on a sample analysis taken before the war with allowance for changes in the general price level. During 1952 a new sample was taken and revised estimates of the average values of parcels have been used since January 1953. These average values are considerably higher than those used previously. For example, parcel post exports in January 1953 were £3 million higher than they would have been on the earlier basis of valuation, and imports £0·7 million higher. The figures for 1952 are also to be revised on the new basis, but the revision is not being taken any further back (see *Board of Trade Journal*, 21 February 1953, p. 36).

valuing imports. For this value includes the shipping, insurance and other costs of bringing the goods to this country, and some of the payments for these services may in fact be made to companies in this country and not to residents of other countries. Where this happens the payments should not appear at all in the balance of payments. And payments that are made to other countries are better included under the appropriate headings of invisible items rather than as part of the payments for merchandise imports. In the balance of payments figures, therefore, merchandise imports are shown at their f.o.b. value. And so we have yet another reason why the figures for merchandise trade in the trade accounts are different from those in the balance of payments.

The monthly balance of trade [1] figures published by the Board of Trade are arrived at from the published trade account figures, that is, by subtracting imports c.i.f. from exports and re-exports f.o.b. Some commentators try to adjust the import figures to a f.o.b. basis before calculating the balance of trade. This is often done by assuming that the margin between c.i.f. and f.o.b. value is roughly 10–12 per cent.[2]

The British system of valuing imports c.i.f. and exports f.o.b., is by no means universal, and this must be remembered in comparing United Kingdom trade figures with those for other countries. There is a wide variety of systems of valuation and there have been important changes over time.[3]

Trade by countries

There are four main systems in use for classifying trade by country:

	Import	Export
(1)	Original production	Ultimate consumption
(2)	Purchase	Sale
(3)	Shipment	Shipment
(4)	Consignment	Consignment

[1] See p. 140.

[2] In fact, of course, the difference between c.i.f. and f.o.b. values may vary substantially with changes in the pattern of import trade, and fluctuations in freight, insurance and other charges.

[3] For a detailed discussion of the methods of valuation used by different countries, see N. M. Petruzzelli, *Some Technical Aspects of Foreign Trade Statistics, with Special Reference to Valuation* (Catholic University of America Press, 1946).

Many items of trade would be classified under the same country whichever of these four was used; but in some cases the country would be different for each of the four. Take, for example, United Kingdom goods which are sold to a firm in Germany which sends on all or part of them for consumption in Yugoslavia, and suppose that the goods are consigned to a firm of forwarding agents in Antwerp. If the country of 'ultimate consumption' were used for classifying exports, the trade returns would show these goods as exports to Yugoslavia; if the country of 'sale' were the criterion, as exports to Germany; and if the 'consignment' basis were used, as exports to Belgium.

The United Kingdom trade returns use consignment as the basis for classifying both imports and exports. The country of consignment is defined as 'the country from which (or to which) the goods were originally despatched, with or without breaking bulk in the course of transport, but without any commercial transaction in an intermediate country'. The great advantage of the consignment basis is its simplicity; the importer or exporter always knows the country of consignment, but he might often be unable to give the information for the other classifications.

This basis of classification must be remembered when using the trade figures by countries, especially for continental countries where all trade has to pass through some third country. For example, a substantial part of British goods which are eventually used in Switzerland may originally be consigned to Germany and therefore shown in the United Kingdom returns as exports to Germany. Similarly an appreciable part of our exports to China will be shown as exports to Hong-Kong, and of exports to Burma, Siam, and Indonesia as exports to Malaya (where they are consigned in the first place to Singapore). This point is of great importance if the trade return figures are used for market research, or if the figures of imports, exports and production are used to estimate total consumption in any market.

THE VOLUME OR QUANTUM OF MERCHANDISE TRADE

All the figures of the value of imports and exports published in the monthly and annual returns are based on current values and these figures reflect changes in prices as well as changes in the quantities of trade. In making annual or monthly comparisons of trade one usually wants to distinguish between changes in quantity and changes in price. For particular commodities this can be done quite simply by looking at the figures of quantity as well as the figures of value. If one wanted to see, for example, how far the fall in the value of exports of cotton piece goods in 1952, compared with 1951, was due to a fall in quantity, one would examine the figures of square yards of cotton piece goods exported.

In considering the movement of groups of commodities, say all textiles, or of trade as a whole, one is faced with the problem of combining the different percentage changes in the quantities of trade for a range of commodities. This can be done by averaging the percentage changes, and giving the change for each commodity a 'weight' representing the importance of the commodity in imports or exports. If we are comparing two years, say, 1954 and 1950, and we give the percentage change in the quantity of each commodity a weight represented by the value of trade in that commodity in the year 1950, then we have a base-year weighted index of the volume of trade in 1954 compared with 1950. Alternatively, this index can be thought of as a measure of the percentage change in trade between 1954 and 1950, valuing the quantities of trade in both years at the average values of 1950, and so eliminating the effect of price changes.[1] In the first

[1] These are merely two different ways of thinking of what is in effect the same index.

Taking

q_{50} and q_{54} as the quantity of each commodity exported in 1950 and 1954 respectively

v_{50} and v_{54} as the value of each commodity exported in 1950 and 1954 respectively

then $\dfrac{v_{50}}{q_{50}}$ or p_{50} and $\dfrac{v_{54}}{q_{54}}$ or p_{54} equals the average value of each commodity exported in 1950 and 1954 respectively.

Then the first formulation of the index for the volume of exports in 1954 (1950 = 100) would be

$$\Sigma\left(\frac{q_{54}}{q_{50}}\right)v_{50} \times 100 \Big/ \Sigma v_{50}.$$

and the second formulation would be

$$\Sigma\left(q_{54}\frac{v_{50}}{q_{50}}\right) \times 100 \Big/ \Sigma\left(q_{50}.\frac{v_{50}}{q_{50}}\right).$$

Both of these are the same as

$$\Sigma q_{54}p_{50} \times 100 \Big/ \Sigma v_{50}.$$

formulation we think of the index as a weighted average of the ratios of the individual quantities in the two years; in the other as the ratio of the trade in the two years, each valued at the average values or prices of the first year.

As with other index numbers, either the base or the current year's values or prices can be used as weights. If relative prices have altered, then the two index numbers will give different results,[1] and one cannot say that one is more correct than the other. But in practice an index of the volume of trade with fixed base-weights has certain advantages. Using current-year values as weights means that the weights change from year to year [2] and fluctuations in such a series of indices reflect changes in the pattern of trade and relative prices as well as changes in quantities. If base-year weights are used this complication does not arise, for the weights are the same from year to year. A base-year weighted index is also easier to calculate than a current-year weighted one. But if the base year with which comparisons are made is many years away, the relative prices and weighting of commodities in the base year may be so different from the current position as to make the recent figures quite misleading. For this reason, where base-year weighting is used, the base year is changed at frequent intervals so that there is a series of index numbers with different years as base.

The Board of Trade calculates and publishes regularly in the *Board of Trade Journal* a quarterly index number of this type for the volume of imports and exports in total and for the main groups of commodities.[3] A summary of the figures is given in the *Monthly Digest of Statistics* and the *Report on Overseas Trade*. A

[1] If there is an inverse correlation between quantity and price movements (that is, if quantities fall relatively where relative prices rise, and rise where prices fall) then a base-year-weighted index will show a greater rise or a smaller fall in volume than a current-year-weighted index. But if there is no such correlation one cannot say in general what the relation between the movements of the two sets of indices will be.

[2] Or if the index is calculated quarterly or monthly, from quarter to quarter or month to month.

[3] For a detailed description and explanation of the volume index, see the special note *Volume Index Numbers of Imports and Exports, Change of Base Year*. This can be obtained from the Statistics Division of the Board of Trade. The indices have been recalculated on the new commodity classification annually for 1950, 1951, and 1952, and quarterly from the beginning of 1953.

monthly figure of the volume of total exports only has also been published in recent years. The indices are base-year weighted and calculated from the value and quantity figures published in the *Trade and Navigation Accounts*.[1] The present index compares the volume of trade with the average for 1950 and is based on the average values for that year. This base was introduced in November 1952 for the figures for the third quarter of that year, and at the same time figures on the new base were given for the year 1951 and quarterly for 1952.[2]

The revisions of the base over the last twenty years have been as follows[3]:

	Base year
November 1952–	1950
June 1947–November 1952	1947
May 1946–June 1947	1938
March 1937–May 1946	1935
June 1932–March 1937	1930

These changes of base make it impossible to compare changes in the volume of imports and exports over a long series of years directly from the published figures. For the Board of Trade publishes the index numbers only back to the base year being used at the time[4] and does not link the differently based indices

---

[1] For some items—those headings shown in the *Accounts* in terms of value only and those for which the *Accounts* headings are so wide as to make the values per unit misleading indicators of price changes (or what amounts to the same thing, the figures of quantity misleading indicators of the change in volume)—the method of direct revaluation at average values of the base year cannot be used. In these cases estimates of the value at base year prices are made each quarter by assuming that the price change compared with the base year for the item concerned is the same as that for a similar item or group of items. This method is used for about 25 per cent of total exports and about 3 per cent of imports.

[2] See *Board of Trade Journal*, 15 November 1952, pp. 921–8.

[3] The following articles in the *Board of Trade Journal* explain the revision of the base on each occasion:

24 June 1950, pp. 1312–16; introduction of 1947 as base.

4 and 11 May 1946, pp. 522–4 and 557–60; introduction of 1938 as base.

4 March 1937, pp. 295–303; introduction of 1935 as base.

21 January 1932, pp. 80–8; introduction of 1930 as base.

[4] This statement is true only for the full detail of the volume indices as published each quarter in the *Board of Trade Journal*. Indices on the

to give a continuous run of figures. But very often it is just such a continuous series of figures that are wanted. These can, however, be worked out without difficulty, since at each change of base the Board of Trade calculates the figure for a short period both on the new and the old weighting system. Thus when the most recent change to 1950 as a base was made in November 1952, volume figures for 1947, 1951 and 1952 were given on the new base of 1950 as well as on the old base of 1947. It is thus possible to link the two sets of figures arithmetically and calculate a continuous run of figures from 1947 onwards with either 1947 or 1950 as 100. If one wants to go further back still, this index would have to be linked to the earlier one based on 1938 and so on. For a continuous series from 1930 indices on five different bases would have to be linked together.

There is one major difficulty in linking together indices in this way. For each overlapping period there are always two bases of comparison, the old and the new weights, and they may differ from each other. Sometimes when the change in the relative movement of average values and quantities is substantial, the difference between the two indices may be very wide. This is so in comparing the volume of export trade before and after the war. If the export trade of 1947 is revalued at the average values of 1938, it is 1 per cent less than in 1938; but if the export trade of 1938 is revalued at the average value of trade in 1947, the 1947 trade is 11 per cent greater. Thus on the basis of 1947 weighting the volume of trade between the two years increased by 11 per cent, but on 1938 weighting the volume actually fell by 1 per cent.

There is no way of satisfactorily overcoming this difficulty, which is a common feature of all index numbers. One index cannot be said to be more accurate than the other, and although the difficulty is usually met in practice by taking an average of the two indices as the basis for linking, this does not in a true sense give the correct figure.[1] Indeed, where there are wide differences in the results obtained with current-year and base-year weighting this should be recognized as making accurate and precise comparisons over the period impossible. Linking by an average of

present base (1950) have been calculated back to 1947 for the four or five major groups of imports and exports and are published in the *Annual Abstract of Statistics*.

[1] The geometric average is usually taken, giving a result in accordance with Fisher's 'ideal index'.

the two indices conceals rather than reveals the true nature of the change.

The calculations of the volume or quantum of import and export trade published by the Board of Trade relate to trade as a whole and to the main groups of commodities. There is no difficulty in principle in doing similar calculations for the volume of trade with particular countries or groups of countries, but official figures of the volume of trade by countries are published only for the sterling area and the dollar area.[1]

INDEX NUMBERS OF THE AVERAGE VALUE OR PRICE OF IMPORTS AND EXPORTS

One method of arriving at indices of the change in the average value of trade is to derive them from indices of the change of volume and total value. Since any change in the total value of trade is a compound of the change in volume or quantum and the change in price, if we know the change in any two, we can derive the change in the third. If we know the change in total value and have calculated the change in volume in the way just explained, we can derive figures of the change in price by dividing the change in total value by the change in volume.

Such figures are calculated and published quarterly, together with the indices of the volume of exports and imports, in the *Board of Trade Journal*. These indices, which for reasons which will be explained later,[2] are called index numbers of 'average values', are usually given only for the current quarter. If a detailed continuous series over a number of years is required, many issues of the *Board of Trade Journal* have to be consulted. They are published for the same categories of commodities as for the volume indices. But figures for groups of these commodity categories can be calculated without difficulty.[3] Indices for the

[1] These figures were first published in August 1953 and the series was given back to 1947, see *Board of Trade Journal*, 1 August, 1953, pp. 220-1, for an explanation of the method used in calculating these index numbers.

[2] See p. 152.

[3] Suppose, for example, one wanted figures of the price of exports of textiles as a whole. The published figures show separate figures for cotton, wool, silk and artificial silk and other textiles. One would first combine the published volume indices for these four groups into a single

four or five main groups of imports and exports are given for a run of years in the *Annual Abstract of Statistics*.

An index of prices or average values derived in this way is a weighted index, the basis of weighting depending on the weighting used in the volume index from which it is derived. If the volume index used in the calculation is base-year weighted, the resultant price or average value index will be weighted by the current year's or quarter's trade.[1]

The Board of Trade index numbers of volume are base-year weighted. In consequence the indices of average value derived by dividing the change in total value by these indices of volume are weighted by the value of each commodity in the current period. The weights will therefore change every quarter with the change in the 'current period'. If there is a substantial difference in the distribution of trade in two quarters, this may account for part of the movement of the indices of average values over the period. The distribution of British import trade changes appreciably over short periods and it is unwise to use current-year-weighted indices for such periods.

The obvious way of overcoming this difficulty is to calculate indices with fixed base-period weights instead of changing current-period weights. This is done in a series of monthly

textile index, weighting the individual volume indices by the value of exports in the base period (1950). Then calculate an index of the change in the value of exports of all textiles compared with 1950. Divide this by the calculated index of volume, and the result multiplied by 100 would be an index of the average value of textile exports with 1950 as 100.

[1] Using the same nomenclature as on p. 146, and comparing 1954 and 1950,

(a) the change in *total value* is

$$\Sigma q_{54} p_{54} \times 100 \Big/ \Sigma q_{50} p_{50},$$

(b) the change in volume using base year (1950) weighting is

$$\Sigma q_{54} p_{50} \times 100 \Big/ \Sigma q_{50} p_{50},$$

and

(c) the change in average value derived from (a) and (b) is

$$\frac{\Sigma q_{54} p_{54}}{\Sigma q_{50} p_{50}} \times 100 \Big/ \frac{\Sigma q_{54} p_{50}}{\Sigma q_{50} p_{50}} = \Sigma q_{54} p_{54} \times 100 \Big/ \Sigma q_{54} p_{50}$$

$$= \Sigma v_{54} \times 100 \Big/ \Sigma \left(\frac{p_{50}}{p_{54}}\right) v_{54}.$$

This is an index with current-year weights.

indices of import and export prices which the Board of Trade started in 1946.[1] These indices also differ from the quarterly 'average value' indices, in being calculated directly instead of being derived from indices of value and indices of volume. Thus the percentage change in average value compared with a base period is calculated for each commodity; and these individual percentage changes are then combined by a fixed set of weights to give indices for groups of commodities and for import and export trade as a whole.[2] These indices are published in the *Board of Trade Journal*, the *Report on Overseas Trade* and the *Monthly Digest of Statistics*. They are, however, not given in as great detail as the quarterly derived indices of average values, only four categories being given for imports and five for exports.

Since the monthly 'price' indices are based on fixed weights they are not influenced by the changing composition of trade, but if in fact the pattern of trade is changing substantially they may become unrealistic and of little value if the same set of fixed weights are used over a series of years. The present practice of the Board of Trade is to change the weights used in calculating these index numbers each year. The fixed weights used are the trade of the previous year. In March of each year, when the new index is first published, figures are given monthly for two previous years. Thus in March 1954 indices were first published with 1953 trade as weights and 1953 as base, and monthly figures were given back to the beginning of 1952.[3] There are overlapping periods, therefore, between successive index numbers and these could be used as links to calculate a continuous series over a period of years. This is not done by the Board of Trade, since these price index numbers are constructed especially for

[1] For a detailed discussion and explanation of these price index numbers see 'Import and Export Prices, New Index Numbers', *Board of Trade Journal*, 13 April 1946, pp. 417–21; 'Import and Export Prices and the Terms of Trade', *Board of Trade Journal*, 4 August 1951, pp. 225–8.

[2] Using the same notation as in earlier footnotes, but taking o to represent the base year and 1 to represent the current year, the index is therefore

$$\Sigma\left(\frac{p_1}{p_0}\right)v_0 \times 100 \Big/ \Sigma v_0 \quad \text{or} \quad \Sigma p_1 q_0 \times 100 \Big/ \Sigma p_0 q_0.$$

[3] The figures were given back to the beginning of 1953 in the *Board of Trade Journal*, but figures for each month in 1952 were also given in the *Monthly Digest of Statistics* and the *Report on Overseas Trade*.

short-period comparisons. It is apparently the Board of Trade view that comparisons over longer periods of years should be based on the quarterly and annual, currently based, average value series.[1]

The monthly fixed-weight index numbers are called 'price' indices in order to distinguish them from the current-weighted quarterly index numbers derived from the volume figures, which are called 'average value' indices. This is, however, a confusing way of drawing the distinction between the two index numbers, for both are based on the average values derived from the figures of quantity and value given in the monthly *Trade and Navigation Accounts*. Certainly the monthly index is not a 'price' index in the normally understood sense; it is not based on prices being currently quoted for goods imported or exported.

It is important to keep this in mind in interpreting the figures. The goods actually imported or exported in any month may have been bought some months or even years earlier,[2] and current changes in prices may be reflected in the index numbers only after a considerable and varying time-lag. Furthermore, the average values derived from the *Trade and Navigation Accounts* refer to the categories of goods shown in those accounts, not to specified and closely defined particular grades of goods as is usual in actual price quotations. It is true that in calculating the monthly 'price' index the Board of Trade has taken great care in the selection of items included in the index to try, as far as possible, to include only average values which behave like a true price.[3] But even the most closely defined categories in the monthly trade accounts include a wide range of qualities, and a change in the average value of the goods in the category may reflect a change in the qualities and types included, as well as a change in the price of a standard quality.

The Board of Trade's use of only those average values which seem to behave like true prices and the fact that average values cannot be calculated for some items because quantities are not

[1] This may account for the omission of these import and export price indices from the *Annual Abstract of Statistics*.

[2] For example, in the case of some engineering exports for large construction contracts overseas, the price of the contract may have been fixed a year or two before the goods are actually exported from this country.

[3] See 'Import and Export Prices, New Index Numbers', *Board of Trade Journal*, 13 April 1946, pp. 417–21.

given, restrict the coverage of the indices. This limitation is most serious for exports, where less than 50 per cent of trade is covered by the average value figures used in the 'price' indexes; for imports the coverage is 70 per cent.[1]

Since the average value figures on which the index numbers are based are taken from the *Trade and Navigation Accounts*, they measure changes in the value of goods as defined in those accounts. These are the c.i.f. value for imports and the f.o.b. value for exports. Changes in the index for imports therefore reflect fluctuations in shipping freights, insurance rates and other charges as well as variations in the price of the goods themselves. To a substantial extent these payments are not overseas payments but payments to British shipping, insurance and banking companies.

THE TERMS OF TRADE

If the price of imports rises relatively to the price of exports, a larger volume of exports is needed to purchase the same volume of imports, or if we continue to export the same volume we can buy only a reduced volume of imports. Thus the relative movements of import and export prices are of great economic significance, and are called the 'terms of trade'.[2] The terms of trade do not compare the absolute level of prices of imports and exports at any particular time; indeed, there is no meaningful sense in which one can say that import prices are higher or lower than export prices at a certain date. The comparison is between the movement of import prices and the movement of export prices over a period of time. Thus when we say that the terms of trade moved adversely or against the United Kingdom in 1951, we mean that during that year import prices rose proportionately more than export prices. Or when we say that the terms of trade moved in the United Kingdom's favour in 1953, we mean that export prices rose more (or fell less) than import prices during that year.

The comparison between the movement of import and export

[1] These figures were given when the monthly index was first introduced in 1946. No later figures of the coverage have been published.

[2] For a fuller discussion of this and alternative measures of the terms of trade, see E. Devons, 'Statistics of the United Kingdom Terms of Trade', *The Manchester School*, vol. XXII (1954), pp. 258–75.

prices can be expressed either as the ratio of the import price index to the export price index; or the other way round, as the ratio of the export price index to the import price index. With the first measure, if import prices rise more, or fall less, than export prices, the ratio rises. We then refer to a rise in the ratio as an 'adverse' movement in the terms of trade and a fall as a 'favourable' movement.[1] If we use the ratio of export prices to import prices then the reverse is true; a rise in the ratio is a 'favourable' movement and a fall an 'adverse' movement.

It does not matter which of the two ratios is used, since one is merely the reciprocal of the other, as long as the basis is clearly stated. The first is more convenient if we are interested in measuring the changing volume of exports needed for an unchanged volume of imports; the second, if we are interested in measuring the changing volume of imports that can be obtained for an unchanged volume of exports. For the two ratios of import prices to export prices, and export prices to import prices, give us just these two measures.[2]

Since import and export price index numbers for the United Kingdom are available for merchandise commodity trade only, the terms of trade can only be calculated at present for this part of our foreign trade. The calculation can be done either on the

[1] The 'adverse' movement may in fact be due to favourable economic changes in the United Kingdom. Thus the fall in export prices relatively to import prices may be due to increased productivity in United Kingdom export industries leading to lower prices. (See Devons, *op. cit.*, pp. 265–6.)

[2] Suppose, for example, that import prices rise from one year to the next by 20 per cent and export prices rise by 10 per cent. The volume of imports bought in the first year would cost 20 per cent more in the second year, and if export prices had not changed at all the volume of exports would have to be 20 per cent higher in the second year than in the first (or 120 in the second year, taking the first as 100) to buy these imports. But export prices have increased by 10 per cent, so to buy this unchanged volume of imports the volume of exports must be $120/110 . 100 = 109$ in the second year (again taking the first year as 100). This is the same as the terms of trade expressed as the ratio of the import price index to the export price index. Similarly, the same volume of exports in the second year as the first would buy $110/120 . 100 = 92$ volume of imports (with the first year as 100) in the second year. This is the same as the terms of trade expressed as the ratio of the export price index to the import price index.

basis of the monthly 'price' index numbers, or the quarterly and annual average value index numbers. Figures are published on both bases; it is apparently intended that those based on the monthly price index numbers should be used for short-term comparisons, and those based on the average value index number for comparisons over longer periods. The monthly figures were calculated and published for the first time in August 1951 [1] with figures back to January 1949. They can, of course, be calculated without difficulty for earlier periods for which monthly price indices are available.[2] The index is changed to a new base every year together with the price index numbers. The annual figures of the terms of trade published in the *Annual Abstract of Statistics* [3] are calculated from the figures of average value indices derived from the annual volume and value indices. Those in the latest *Annual Abstract* are based on 1950. Figures are given in the *Annual Abstract* for 1935 to 1938 and for each year from 1947, but a longer series, giving figures for 1913 and for each year from 1919 to 1938 as well as for post-war years, was given in the *Board of Trade Journal*, 4 August 1951.[4] But there have been big changes in the composition of United Kingdom trade over this period, and comparisons between two widely separated years, say 1913 and 1947, are not of much value.

The terms of trade indices published in the *Board of Trade Journal* and *Annual Abstract of Statistics* are expressed as the ratio of the import price index to the export price index. [5]

Since these indices are based on the 'price' and average value indices derived from the *Trade and Navigation Accounts*, they are subject to all the limitations and qualifications of those index numbers. They refer to merchandise trade only, to the average

[1] See *Board of Trade Journal*, 4 August 1951, pp. 225–8.

[2] That is, monthly from January 1945.

[3] See *Annual Abstract of Statistics No.* 91, 1954 (H.M.S.O., 1954), Table 217, p. 191.

[4] Both series involve linking together successive indices on different bases. Since there are two index numbers for the overlapping periods when the base is changed, presumably the links have been based on a geometric average of the new and old index at each change of base.

[5] With the ratio in the base period taken as 100. It is common in other countries and in international publications to express the terms of trade the other way round as the ratio of export prices to import prices.

value of goods when they enter or leave the country, not to prices for contracts being made currently, and to the c.i.f. value of imports and the f.o.b. value of exports.

NON-MERCHANDISE TRADE AND THE BALANCE OF PAYMENTS

Although statistics about non-merchandise trade have increased in recent years, they are still meagre compared with those for merchandise trade. The main items of the United Kingdom's non-merchandise trade are shipping, tourism, interest and profits on overseas investment, banking and insurance services, and military expenditure. There are other items of payments and receipts, but each is relatively small and to list them all completely would take many pages.

There is no statistical information about any of the non-merchandise items comparable in detail with that available in the *Trade and Navigation Accounts* about merchandise trade. The regular statistics available are published in Balance of Payments White Papers, which cover both merchandise and non-merchandise trade and the discussion here will, therefore, be confined to the explanation and interpretation of statistics included in those statements.[1]

Statements of the balance of payments attempt to set out for the country as a whole the payments that are made for goods and services bought from overseas and the receipts from goods and

---

[1] For some items there is additional information apart from that published in balance of payments statistics. The British Travel and Holidays Association publishes some information on tourism, and the Board of Trade's external migration figures yield some statistics on the number of people leaving or coming to this country on short visits. There is an annual article in the *Board of Trade Journal* on British Tourist Statistics (see *Board of Trade Journal*, 20 March 1954, pp. 574–5). Before the war Sir Robert Kindersley published every year an article in the *Economic Journal* on 'Overseas Investments' which gave figures for income received over a limited field (for the last article in this series see *Economic Journal*, vol. XLIX (1939), pp. 678–95. A similar analysis has been continued by the Bank of England in an annual series entitled *United Kingdom Overseas Investment*. There have been detailed enquiries for particular years on other items, but no regular statistical series. On shipping, for example, see M. G. Kendall, 'The U.K. Mercantile Marine and its Contribution to the Balance of Payments', *Journal of the Royal Statistical Society*, series A, vol. CXIII, pt. I (1950).

services sold abroad. They thus cover, as already explained, both merchandise and non-merchandise trade; and if possible include not only current transactions, but also transactions on capital account.[1] Detailed statements of the balance of payments of the United Kingdom have been issued for the first time in the post-war period, reflecting both the increased importance of problems of the balance of payments and the greater information available to the Treasury through its control of overseas payments and receipts. In the pre-war period when overseas transactions were substantially free from control, balance of payments figures were much more meagre and based on hazardous estimates.

Statistics are issued in a series of Treasury Balance of Payments White Papers at half-yearly intervals about four months after the period to which they relate and form a series going back to 1946. The coverage and detail has been gradually extended with every issue, and the statements now include a mass of information about the United Kingdom's international financial transactions.

The statements now give information about the United Kingdom's balance of payments not only with the rest of the world as a whole, but also with each of the main currency regions.[2] There are also tables analysing the United Kingdom's gold and dollar deficit or surplus; the United Kingdom's transactions with the European Payments Union; and figures of the United Kingdom's gold and dollar reserves and sterling liabilities.

The figures included in these statements are based on estimates which may be substantially revised as later information becomes available.[3] This is especially true of the items of invisible trade and the transactions on capital account. Revised figures for earlier periods are given in the latest returns.

For the inter-war years annual estimates of the balance of payments were published in the *Board of Trade Journal*. But they gave only the broadest summary, even of the items on current account,[4] and there was no information about capital transactions

---

[1] For the meaning and significance of this distinction see p. 162.

[2] The dollar area; other western hemisphere; O.E.E.C. countries; rest of sterling area; non-territorial organizations.

[3] The revisions are sometimes due to changes in definition, but it is often impossible to distinguish these from statistical changes.

[4] Apart from merchandise and silver bullion figures were given for: net shipping income; net income from overseas investments; net receipts from insurance, commissions, etc.; net income from other sources.

or payments by regions. This series of estimates extends from 1923 to 1938,[1] together with comparable figures for 1913. A little more detail is given for the year 1938 in the early issues of the post-war series of statements.[2] There is not space to discuss here the basis and reliability of these inter-war estimates, but experience of errors and revisions in balance of payments figures in the post-war period when so much more information has been available, would lead to the conclusion that the pre-war figures are at best very rough estimates and should be used with the greatest caution.

There are no official figures for the period before the First World War.[3] But there are the well-known annual estimates of C. K. Hobson[4] for the period 1870–1913. These have recently been criticized and revised by A. K. Cairncross.[5] The basis used in these calculations and the reliability of the results is not very different from that of the official Board of Trade estimates for the inter-war years.

PROBLEMS IN INTERPRETING BALANCE OF PAYMENTS STATISTICS

The present balance of payments statistics are most complex and intricate. Not only has one to be a specialist in the subject, but one has also to be in the confidence of the authors, to be able to use the published figures without fear of slipping into error. The subject is intrinsically difficult, but additional problems have been created for the user by the ever-changing definitions and form of presentation used in the published statements. It is not possible in an introductory study of British statistics to explain all these intricacies and difficulties, and the discussion here will be limited

[1] Figures for 1936, 1937 and 1938 were given in the *Board of Trade Journal*, 23 February 1939. All the figures for previous years, i.e. for 1913 and 1923–1935 are given in *Statistical Abstract for the United Kingdom, January* 1937 (Cmd. 5353, H.M.S.O., 1937), p. 418.

[2] The figures for 1938 were given for the last time in *United Kingdom Balance of Payments* 1946–1949, no. 2 (Cmd. 7928, H.M.S.O., 1950).

[3] Except for the year 1913.

[4] C. K. Hobson, *The Export of Capital* (Constable, 1914), pp. 164–205.

[5] A. K. Cairncross, *Home and Foreign Investment*, 1870–1913 (Cambridge, 1953), pp. 170–81.

to some of the more important points that need to be kept in mind in using these figures.[1]

The balance of payments as a statement of debits and credits

Since the balance of payments is designed to show what we pay and what we receive in our international transactions, it divides all items into debits and credits. For current items of trade this distinction is fairly clear and straightforward: imports of goods, payments for shipping services to overseas shipping companies, the expenditure of United Kingdom tourist overseas, Government expenditure overseas, payment of profits, interest and dividends on shares and other investments in the United Kingdom held by people overseas, as well as payments for other miscellaneous services, are all debits; exports of goods, receipts for shipping services provided to other countries by United Kingdom shipping companies, receipts of profits, interest and dividends on overseas investments, the expenditure of tourists in the United Kingdom, the expenditure of foreign Governments in the United Kingdom and payments for British insurance, banking and other miscellaneous services, are all credits. The difference between the total of credits and debits on current account gives us the balance of current transactions. If credits exceed debits, this is shown as a figure with a plus, and is called a *favourable* balance; if debits exceed credits, as a figure with a minus, and is called an *unfavourable* or *adverse* balance.

All credits and debits are not shown separately in the statistics; for some categories a net figure only is given of the excess of payments over receipts.[2] Take, for example, the entry for migrants'

[1] For a fuller discussion see R. G. D. Allen, 'Official Papers: Statistics of the Balance of Payments', *Economic Journal*, vol. LXI (1951), pp. 179–96. There is also a useful general introduction to each of the recent White Papers explaining the basis and meaning of the statistics in general terms, and explanatory notes to the tables at the end dealing with detailed points of definition. But these latter notes are by no means easy to follow.

[2] This means that it is only the difference between the total figures of credits and debits which is significant, not the absolute level of the total figures themselves.

In *United Kingdom Balance of Payments*, 1946 to 1954 (Cmd. 9291, H.M.S.O., 1954) net figures are given in this way for: migrants' funds legacies, and private gifts; and 'other' credit items.

funds, legacies, and private gifts shown in the British figures. This is shown as a 'net' item under debits; the figure thus tells us the excess of payments over receipts that we make under this heading. It is the general practice to show a 'net' item under debits, if payments exceed receipts for that item, and under credits if receipts exceed payments. But payments may exceed receipts in one year, and receipts exceed payments in another. In these circumstances, the practice is to classify the net item according to the normal position and then show the abnormal entries with a minus. Thus in most recent years funds taken out by British emigrants, legacies to people overseas and gifts sent overseas, exceed funds brought in by immigrants into this country, legacies and gifts received here from overseas. The 'net' item for this category is, therefore, shown under debits. But, exceptionally, in 1946 and in 1950 we received more than we paid out, and the net figure for that year is shown with a minus, a minus debit being the same as a credit.

With non-current or capital items the treatment, although in principle the same as for current items, is more difficult to follow and often leads to confusion. Capital items, as we shall see later,[1] refer to the sale and purchase of overseas assets, including gold and foreign exchange. Now the sale of overseas assets, borrowing, or the sale of gold and foreign exchange means that sums are paid to this country; and the purchase of overseas assets, overseas investment, lending, or the purchase of gold and foreign exchange, results in payments by this country. In terms of receipts and payments, therefore, the first group are credits, or plus items, the second are debits, or minus items.[2] Thus if the United Kingdom sells reserves of gold and foreign exchange, this is shown as plus; if she buys gold and foreign exchange, as minus.

The items shown in the capital account are only a summary of the large number of transactions that take place, the net figure

[1] Pp. 162–4.

[2] This is the practice in the current White Papers. In earlier issues up to and including that for 1951 (Cmd. 8505), exactly the opposite convention was used; the sale of overseas assets etc. being shown as minus, and the purchase of overseas assets etc. as plus.

The current items are grouped together as credits and debits, but the capital items are not grouped in this way, but according to the nature of the transactions, and each figure is therefore prefixed by a plus or minus according to whether the transactions result in a net receipt or a payment.

given being the balance of payments over receipts or the balance of receipts over payments for a particular group of transactions. The interpretation of some of the items requires careful thought. Take, for example, the figure for the change in sterling liabilities.[1] Our sterling liabilities represent deposits in British banks and other short-term sterling assets, for example Treasury bills, held by overseas countries. An increase in these liabilities means that we owe these countries more, that is, that we are borrowing; a decrease that we are paying off our debts and owe them less. When these countries 'buy' bank deposits or Treasury bills in this country they pay us; when they reduce their deposits or sell Treasury bills, we pay them. An increase in liabilities, in terms of payments and receipts, is, therefore, a plus figure and a decrease a minus figure. The figure entered in the balance of payments statement is the net result of an increase in liabilities to some countries and a decrease in liabilities to others.[2] In using the figures for any item in the capital account, the exact meaning of the figures should be worked out, as has been done here for sterling liabilities.

The distinction between current and capital items

One of the purposes of balance of payments statements is to show whether the country is living within its current income, and how the deficiency, if any, is met from gifts, grants, borrowing, sales of overseas assets and the use of reserves of foreign exchange. For this purpose, therefore, a distinction is made between current items of income and expenditure and changes in the overseas capital assets of the country. If the payment or receipt corresponds to a change in this country's overseas debt or assets position, it is included in the capital account, and for this purpose changes in holdings of gold and foreign exchange are treated as changes in overseas assets and shown in the capital account.[3] In the

[1] *United Kingdom Balance of Payments* 1946 *to* 1954 (Cmd. 9291, H.M.S.O., 1954), Tables 3–8, item 33.

[2] Details of sterling liabilities to the main areas of the world are given in Table 14 of *United Kingdom Balance of Payments*, 1946 *to* 1954 (Cmd. 9291, H.M.S.O., 1954). The difference between the total liabilities for all areas for successive dates corresponds to the entry for the 'change in sterling liabilities' in Tables 3–8.

[3] Changes in capital assets due to changes in market valuation or physical destruction, etc., are, however, not included in the capital

official White Papers the capital account is called the 'Investment and Financing Account'. Other transactions—imports [1] and exports, shipping services, current military expenditure, tourism, insurance, banking and other services, and income from overseas investment—are all classified as 'current' items.

Gifts and grants received or made by this country do not easily fit into this division between current and capital items, and there are no firm theoretical principles on which they can be classified. The British statements adopt an arbitrary practice of treating private gifts, relief, grants to Colonial Governments, post-war settlements, military expenditure and defence aid from the United States as current items, but E.R.P. grants and Australian and New Zealand gifts to this country as capital items. One must keep this arbitrary classification in mind in interpreting the figures of the balance of payments on current account. [2]

If all items—current items, capital items and gifts and grants— are taken into account, then the payments must add up in total to exactly the same figure as the receipts. For what is not paid for out of current overseas income must be paid for from sales of overseas assets, borrowing, running down reserves, or gifts and grants; or if current income is more than enough to pay for current expenditure, the excess must be used for purchase of overseas assets, lending, increasing reserves, or gifts and grants. If, therefore, we group all the items into two categories, current and capital, including gifts and grants, a surplus or deficit of payments on one must be exactly balanced by a deficit or surplus on the other of exactly the same amount. [3]

In practice, however, there will be an exact balance only if we

account. The capital account cannot be used, therefore, for making reliable calculations of the cumulative change in our total holding of overseas assets.

[1] The fact that imports and exports are counted as current items in the balance of payments does not mean that all items imported or exported are for current consumption. Imports may, for example, include items of machinery which will be used for capital investment in the United Kingdom.

[2] The statements now give figures of the current account balance, both excluding and including Defence Aid; but there are other items of gifts and grants in the current account which it would be useful to know separately, so as to calculate the balance 'net' of these.

[3] On the present practice in the Balance of Payments a plus on current account will be balanced by a minus of exactly the same figure on the investment and financing account.

have completely accurate and comprehensive statistics about all items. But an exact balance may be shown in the statistics if we assume that all error and incompleteness is in a single item, and then derive this by difference on the assumption that both sides of the balance add up to exactly the same total. This implies that all the other items are accurate and that the main error is in the figure derived by difference. This is the practice in the British statistics. The item 'other capital transactions (net)'[1] is treated as the balancing item in the whole set of accounts.

The relation between the balance on current account and the change in gold and dollar reserves

As has already been explained the 'Investment and Financing Account' covers a large group of capital transactions as well as the receipt and payment of certain grants treated as capital. It is only the net movement of all these in total which will be equal to the balance on current account. After allowing for gifts and grants, this will correspond to overseas investment or disinvestment over the period only if these terms are used in the widest sense to cover all foreign assets, debts, borrowing, and so on, including gold and foreign exchange reserves. Clearly within this total individual items may move in opposite directions. There may be an increase in investment in particular projects overseas—using investment in a much narrower sense than above —and at the same time a decrease in other forms of assets, for example an increase in liabilities to the rest of the sterling area or a reduction in gold and foreign exchange reserves. There is no simple and straightforward connection between the various items on the capital account. All we can say is that if we take them all together and allow for gifts and grants, the net balance must be the same as that for the current account. It is presumably because the items on the capital account necessarily include many transactions, apart from investment in the narrow sense, that the term 'Investment and Financing Account' rather than 'Capital Account' is now used in the British statements.

Another important point to keep in mind in interpreting the figures in the capital account, is the United Kingdom's position as banker for the whole sterling area, holding the central reserves

[1] Item 31, Tables 3–8, in *United Kingdom Balance of Payments*, 1946 *to* 1954 (Cmd. 9291, H.M.S.O., 1954).

of gold and foreign exchange. The United Kingdom's balance of payments will reflect the transactions of the rest of the sterling area with the non-sterling world. For example, if the rest of the sterling area is on balance a net receiver of dollars in its transactions with the dollar area, the dollars are usually sold to the United Kingdom in exchange for sterling deposits in London. In the United Kingdom's balance of payments this would be reflected in an increase in the United Kingdom's holding of dollars and in a corresponding increase in the United Kingdom's sterling liabilities to the rest of the sterling area.

Since the change in 'gold and dollar reserves' is merely one item among many in the 'Investment and Financing Account', there is no reason why it should fluctuate in the same way as the figure of the total of the capital account; and movements in one should not be taken as an indication of movements in the other.[1] Figures of the gold and dollar reserves are now published regularly every month, as well as being given in the half-yearly statements on the balance of payments.

Merchandise trade in the Balance of Payments White Papers and in the Trade and Navigation Accounts

The figures given for merchandise trade in the balance of payments statements are different, often substantially different, from those in the *Trade and Navigation Accounts*.[2] There are many

[1] The following are the movements of the two items for 1949 to 1953 taken from United Kingdom Balance of Payments, 1946 to 1954 (Cmd. 9291, H.M.S.O., 1954), pp. 10–11.

Total Investment and Financing	1949	1950	1951	1952	1953
(+ decrease in assets – increase in assets)	− 31	− 300	+ 400	− 242	− 211
Gold and dollar reserves (+ drawings on (decrease in assets)	+ 3	− 575	+ 344	+ 175	− 240
− additions to (increase in assets))					

[2] None of the refinements discussed below were made in the balance of payments figures of merchandise trade in the inter-war years. The figures were taken straight from the *Trade and Navigation Accounts*. Imports were shown at the c.i.f. value and an allowance was made for this in the entries under the invisible items.

reasons for this, some of which have already been referred to in discussing the *Trade and Navigation Accounts* statistics.[1] The most important reasons for this difference are summarized in the following paragraphs.[2]

First, all figures of imports in the *Trade and Navigation Accounts* are c.i.f., and include shipping, insurance and other charges, many of which are paid to British concerns and are not, therefore, international transactions. The Balance of Payments White Papers value imports f.o.b., and allow for any shipping or other service payments which are made to non-United Kingdom firms under the appropriate item of invisible trade.

Secondly, there are certain items of trade which are not included in the *Trade and Navigation Accounts* which have to be paid for or yield receipts to this country. An allowance is made for these in the balance of payments figures.

Lastly, the timing used in the Balance of Payments White Papers is different from that in the *Trade and Navigation Accounts*. Goods are included in the latter when they leave (exports) or reach (imports) this country. In principle the basis of the balance of payments is to relate the figures to the time of change of ownership. Generally it is assumed that imports are transferred to British ownership in the country of origin, usually at the time of shipment; and that exports are transferred to overseas ownership when they reach their destination. This means that in any period the import figures that appear in the Balance of Payments White Papers refer to some imports which will not appear in the *Trade and Navigation Accounts* until later, and the export figures in the Balance of Payments White Papers refer to some exports which appeared in the *Trade and Navigation Accounts* for an earlier period. So if imports and exports are rising, on these grounds alone imports would be much higher and exports much lower than in the *Trade and Navigation Accounts*.

The difference between the two sets of figures is not proportionately the same at different periods, and it is most dangerous to draw conclusions from one set about what is happening to the

[1] See pp. 141–4.
[2] A reconciliation of the merchandise trade figures in the Balance of Payments with those in the Trade and Navigation Accounts is now regularly included in the White Paper. See, for example, *United Kingdom Balance of Payments 1946 to 1954*. (Cmd. 9291, H.M.S.O., 1954), pp. 36–7.

other.[1] This is, however, a great temptation at present when the state of the balance of payments commands such attention. For the *Trade and Navigation Accounts* are available once a month and the balance of payments statistics only once every six months.

[1] The following figures show the visible trade balance from the *Trade and Navigation Accounts* and the Balance of Payments White Papers. (All figures are in £ million, and are negative, that is, imports exceed exports.)

	1949	1950	1951	1952	1953
Trade and Navigation Accounts	431	352	1193	749	658
Balance of Payments White Papers	137	126	733	125	211

PRICES

STATISTICS of prices have a wide variety of uses. As we have seen, where figures of output, trade or sales are given in value, price indices are needed if we want to estimate changes in volume. To measure changes in real incomes, we must have appropriate measures of price changes to apply to figures of money incomes. Any attempt to analyse statistically the forces affecting the demand or supply for a commodity or group of commodities must depend on adequate information about the movement of prices. The business man is interested in the actual and expected movement of the prices of the raw materials and fuel he buys, and of the products he sells. And the interrelation between price movements in different sectors of the economy and the effects of such movements on fluctuations in business activity is an important subject in economic research.

Price statistics are of two kinds. There are first the basic data of the actual prices of individual commodities or services; and second, price index numbers which set out to measure the average movement in prices for groups of commodities and services. Most of the published statistics of prices are in the form of index numbers and in this chapter we shall be concerned mainly with explaining what index numbers there are, how they are constructed, and with discussing some of the problems that arise in using them.

There are two main groups of price index numbers; those which measure changes in the prices of goods bought and sold by manufacturers, merchants, and distributors, and those which measure changes in the prices of goods and services bought by the general public or final consumers. The first group are usually referred to as *index numbers of wholesale prices*; the second as *index numbers of retail prices* or *index numbers of the cost of living*. The term 'wholesale prices' may be misleading. It does not refer to prices charged by wholesalers as normally understood in the distributive trades, but to the prices at which goods are sold by merchants to producers or by producers to wholesalers or other buyers. Thus changes in the prices of raw cotton sold by cotton importers, cotton yarn sold by spinners, and cotton cloth sold by weavers are all included, if regular figures are available, in indices of wholesale prices.

INDEX NUMBERS OF WHOLESALE PRICES

It is easiest to get regular figures of prices for those commodities which are bought or sold on organized produce exchanges, for frequently keeping a record of the prices at which transactions take place is a feature of the working of the exchange. Such produce exchanges also usually lay down detailed, precise specifications for the different grades and types of the commodity in which trading takes place, and this makes it easier to ensure that a series of price quotations over a period of time refers to the same grade and type.

Because of the important price information yielded by organized produce markets, historically regular price statistics first became available for the main internationally traded foodstuffs and raw materials, such as wheat, maize, cotton, rubber and tin, for which organized exchanges were set up. The first indices of prices compiled in the nineteenth century relied heavily on the price information yielded by these exchanges. But the price movements of such commodities were not typical of price movements as a whole, and the main development in wholesale price index numbers in recent years has been to collect information about a wider range of commodities and particularly to include prices of manufactured products in the indices. This extension has involved the special collection of price information from manufacturers and traders.

The current Board of Trade index numbers

The most important current index numbers of wholesale prices are those compiled by the Board of Trade and published each month in the *Board of Trade Journal*. These were started in 1951 and measure price changes compared with June 1949. This new series of index numbers marks a major change in the statistical analysis of price information in this country.[1] Until this

[1] For a detailed discussion of the reasons for the change as well as a description of the basis of the new indices, see J. Stafford, 'Indices of

series was started, most attempts at measuring wholesale prices were designed to measure the movement of wholesale prices as a whole in a single index number, with subsidiary group indices. This reflected the view frequently put forward in monetary theory in the nineteenth century that changes in the volume or velocity of the circulation of money had certain general influences on all prices, and that it should be possible to measure this general influence, as distinct from the factors that affected the price of particular commodities, by an index averaging the movement of all prices. But this view of the relation between changes in money and the 'general price level' no longer finds much support among economists.[1] It is now felt that price indices should measure changes for groups of commodities that have certain common economic characteristics, and that little significance can be attached to the average price movement for all commodities as a whole. The Board of Trade's new series follows this view. Separate indices are given for individual commodities and groups of commodities but no single index of the general level of wholesale prices is calculated.

The index numbers are published in four main groups. The basic detailed series for particular commodities or narrow groups of commodities is given in two separate tables: the first covers goods produced in the United Kingdom, mainly manufactures; the second covers goods wholly or partly imported, mainly raw materials.[2] The indices for home-produced goods are given in the order used in the Standard Industrial Classification. Some of the indices refer to the single commodities of specified types and grade, for example, 'sulphuric acid, R.O.V., 94/95 per cent'; others to groups of commodities, for example, 'china and earthenware'. Some of the actual prices used are given as annual averages, but most of the information published is in the form of index numbers.

Then there are two general sets of index numbers: the first

Wholesale Prices', *Journal of the Royal Statistical Society*, series A, vol. XCIV, pt. IV (1951), pp. 447–67.

Shorter descriptions of the new indices are given in *Board of Trade Journal*, 19 May 1951, pp. 1050–1, and *ibid.* 16 June 1951, pp. 1253–8.

[1] For a detailed criticism of the earlier view, see J. M. Keynes, *A Treatise on Money* (Macmillan, 1933), vol. I, Chapter 6.

[2] These two tables are Tables 3(a) and 3(b) respectively in the monthly article in the *Board of Trade Journal*.

measures the average change in prices of materials used in particular industries and in industry as a whole; the second measures the change in prices of the output of major groups of industrial products. An example in the first group is the index for 'materials used in the textile industries'; an example in the second group is the index for the output of 'clothing and footwear'.

The Board of Trade is still at the stage of building up the detailed statistics needed to compile these price index numbers, and the number and scope of the indices has gradually been extended since the new series was first started in 1951. But it may be some time before indices are published for some important sections of industry. At the end of 1954, there were no detailed or group indices for any part of the output of the engineering, vehicle, or food, drink and tobacco industries. Until some of these major gaps are filled the new set of index numbers cannot be used to provide a general picture of price changes throughout the British economy.

All the index numbers are weighted arithmetic averages. For the output indices the weights used are the sales of the products included, and for the indices of materials used, the value of purchases. Although the base of the index is June 1949, the weights relate to 1948.[1] The indices are thus not the simple aggregate type, but measure the change of prices of the pattern of 1948 expenditure relative to the position in June 1949.[2] Although this difference in base and weighting period is in theory not defensible statistically and makes the index a little difficult to explain precisely and yet simply, the two periods are not far apart and it is unlikely that the use of June 1949 for weighting as well as for the base period would have made any appreciable difference to the figures.

---

[1] The detailed information in the Census of Production for 1948 being the main basis for estimating the weights.

[2] If q_{48} = quantity of goods purchased or sold in 1948

p_{48} = price in 1948

p_{49} = price in June 1949

p_x = the price in year x.

q_x = quantity of goods purchased or sold in a later year x

Then the index number for the year x on the basis used by the Board of Trade would be

$$\Sigma\left(\frac{p_x}{p_{49}}\right)q_{48}p_{48} \times 100 \Big/ \Sigma q_{48}p_{48}.$$

Although all the indices compare prices with the level in June 1949, the period for which information is available varies a good deal. For some commodities and groups the new indices have been compiled monthly back to January 1945, for others, because of lack of information, the indices cannot be taken back earlier than the beginning of 1952. In the monthly article in the *Board of Trade Journal* figures are now given for each of the previous twelve months as well as for the current one, but twice a year there is a review over a longer period with some charts and textual comment on the most important price movements.

The old series of index numbers

The new series of wholesale price indices was intended to replace completely the wholesale price index previously published by the Board of Trade, but for the time being the main groups [1] of the old index continue to be calculated and published. [2] The Board of Trade has given warning that in no circumstances will publication continue beyond the end of 1955.

As explained earlier, until the new series was published most indices of wholesale prices were designed to measure the general level of prices in a single index, with separate figures for sub-groups and individual commodities. The old wholesale price index is of this type. In its latest version it is an unweighted [3] geometric average of changes in the prices of about 200 commodities compared with 1930. [4] In addition to the total index, there were eleven main industrial indices, and indices for basic materials, building materials, intermediate products and manufactured articles. These indices have been severely criticized. [5]

[1] The main groups are: intermediate products; iron and steel; total food and tobacco; cereals; meat, fish and eggs; other food and tobacco. The index for 'all articles' is also given.

[2] This is the result of representations by firms who have contracts with price clauses linked to movements in the old wholesale price index.

[3] It is, however, effectively a weighted index since the number of quotations included for particular commodities or groups is related to their importance.

[4] For a detailed description of the index see 'Wholesale Prices, 1930–1934, Board of Trade Index Number, a new compilation', *Board of Trade Journal*, 24 January 1935.

[5] See R. G. D. Allen, 'Wholesale Prices, 1938–1948', *Economic Journal*, vol. LIX (June 1949), pp. 137–53, and J. Stafford, 'Indices of

The meaning and usefulness of the industrial group indices is especially questionable. The group index for 'cotton', for example, included the price of raw cotton, cotton yarn and cotton cloth. It is difficult to discover any significance in an index measuring the average of these three together or for what purpose such an average might be used. It is certainly of little use in analysing the fortunes of the cotton industry, for it does not measure fluctuations in the prices of materials used by that industry nor of the prices of the goods it sells, but an average of the two together, an average which has little, if any, economic or business significance. Similar criticism applies to the indices for other industrial groups.

Other important objections to the old index numbers were that the implied weighting gave some very queer results, and that the index for 'manufactured articles' in fact included singularly few final manufactured products. These and other strictures tend to discredit the indices altogether. But for the period before 1949 they represent the main statistical information about the movement of wholesale prices. It is unlikely that the basic price information for the period can now be much improved or extended, but it might be possible to regroup the original data in indices of more value and significance. But even if such regrouping were possible, the old indices would not be comparable with the new series which are based on much more extensive data.

The latest version of the old series of wholesale price index numbers was introduced in 1935 with 1930 as base. It was a modification of an earlier index, also published by the Board of Trade, which compared prices with 1913.[1] The earlier version covered fewer price series, combined them in eight industrial groups instead of eleven, and did not give indices for 'basic materials', 'intermediate products', and 'manufactured goods'. The implied weighting was based on the Census of Production for 1907. This index, first published in 1921, in its turn replaced an earlier official index, started in 1903, which compared prices with the level in 1871. The detailed figures for this index number

Wholesale Prices', *Journal of the Royal Statistical Society*, series A, vol. xciv, pt. IV (1951), pp. 447–67.

[1] For a detailed description of this index, see A. W. Flux, 'The Measurement of Price Changes', *Journal of the Royal Statistical Society*, vol. LXXXIV, pt. II (1921), pp. 167–215.

for each year from 1871 to 1920 are given in the *Nineteenth Abstract of Labour Statistics*.[1] But this index was hardly a whole-sale price index in the sense in which we now use the term, for of the 47 quotations used, 35 were average values of imports and 4 average values of exports, all calculated from the figures in the *Trade and Navigation Accounts*.

Other index numbers

In addition to the official indices compiled by the Board of Trade there are a large number of price indices published by private organizations and research workers. Perhaps the Sauer-beck, or *Statist*, index is the best known of these, mainly because it is available continuously on the same basis over a longer period of years than any other price index. The index, which compares prices with the average of 1867–77, is currently published every month in *The Statist*; and every year there is an article in the *Journal of the Royal Statistical Society*[2] giving annual figures and the series in some detail back to 1846. The actual price quota-tions used in the index are also given. The index is an unweighted arithmetic average of about 45 items, all either basic materials for industry or foodstuffs.[3] The index, therefore, measures primary commodity prices, and since it has included practically the same quotations since it was first started, it takes little account of the changing relative importance of the consumption of these commodities in the United Kingdom.

Until recently *The Economist* compiled and published three index numbers: an index of wholesale prices, a sensitive price index, and a commodity price indicator. The wholesale price index has a long history. It was first started in the 1860's with 1845–50 as base, and has been substantially revised with changes of base at frequent intervals.[4] In the most recent version it was

[1] Cmd. 3140, H.M.S.O., 1928, p. 128.

[2] See, for example, 'Wholesale Prices in 1951' by the Editor of *The Statist*, *Journal of the Royal Statistical Society*, series A, vol. CXV, pt. III (1952), pp. 430–4.

[3] The main items are: flour, barley, oats, wheat, maize, potatoes, and rice; beef, mutton, pork, bacon, and butter; sugar, coffee, and tea; iron ore, copper, tin, lead, and coal; cotton, flax, jute, wool, and silk; hides, leather, tallow, oils, soda, nitrate, petroleum, indigo, and timber.

[4] For a history and summary of this index number see *The Economist*, 19 and 26 August and 18 November 1911, and 15 December 1928.

given fortnightly for five main groups [1] with 1927 = 100, and for the total with 1913 = 100 as well. The sensitive price index was started in 1940 and compared prices with 1935. [2] It was based on a few commodities which were supposed to be particularly sensitive to international trading conditions. The commodity price indicator was started in 1952 as a measure of world, as distinct from British, movements in prices. [3]

These three indices were published in the *Records and Statistics* supplement to *The Economist*, but since that supplement was discontinued in June 1953 only the commodity price indicator is published once a month in *The Economist* itself.

Index numbers of prices are also compiled by *The Times* and Reuters, [4] and Moody's daily index for the United States is frequently quoted in the British financial press. Indeed, the superfluity of such index numbers may cause confusion. They are all, as are the Sauerbeck and *Economist* indices, based mainly on prices of the chief primary foodstuffs and raw materials. The difference between them is largely accidental, reflecting differences in the technical methods of computation and the particular price quotations used.

Agricultural prices

All these indices discussed above, including those of the Board of Trade, are general price indices, even though they give figures for groups of commodities or particular industries. There are in addition indices which refer to particular sectors of the economy only. Of these the most important and best known are those for agricultural products and shipping freights.

A great deal of information about prices of agricultural products has been collected and published for many years by the Ministry of Agriculture and Fisheries. Price information is published in great detail in *Agricultural Statistics, Part II*. [5] Price index numbers are also calculated for agricultural output as a

[1] Cereals and meat; other foods; textiles; minerals; and miscellaneous.
[2] For a detailed explanation of the index see *The Economist*, 26 October 1940, pp. 522–3.
[3] For a detailed explanation of the index see *The Economist*, 19 July 1952, pp. 182–5, and *Records and Statistics* for the same date, p. 47.
[4] Quoted in the *Financial Times*.
[5] In the series for England and Wales and Scotland (see p. 116).

whole and for its main constituents, and for feeding-stuffs and fertilizers. The calculation of price indices for agricultural output raises some very difficult and intricate problems: particularly, how to deal with seasonal variations, with the large range of qualities especially in fruit and vegetables, and with Government subsidies. It is beyond the scope of this book to discuss at length the way in which the Ministry of Agriculture deals with these problems and the special cautions that are necessary in interpreting the figures. There is room here only for a brief description of the index numbers.[1]

All the indices relate to the produce of England and Wales only.[2] The comparison is with average prices in 1927–9, but the individual indices are combined by weighted arithmetic averages, with moving weights based on the distribution of output in the latest five years.[3] In principle the indices measure the prices the farmers receive for their output, and the prices they pay for feeding-stuffs and fertilizers. The first set of prices may be quite different from the prices at which the products are sold by the Ministry of Food or the marketing boards. Some of the payments that the farmers receive are not related to output or sales, but are based on the acreage cultivated, as in the case of wheat and potatoes. Separate indices are calculated including and excluding these special acreage payments.

All these indices and the detailed figures of prices are published in full detail only in the much delayed *Agricultural Statistics*. More recent annual figures are given in the *Annual Abstract of Statistics*, and monthly figures for output and fertilizer prices in the *Monthly Digest of Statistics* and *Agriculture*, the journal of the Ministry of Agriculture; the indices given in these three publica-

[1] For a detailed explanation of the basis of the present index see G. T. Houghton, 'A new Index of Agricultural Prices', *Journal of the Royal Statistical Society*, vol. CI, pt. II (1938), pp. 275–316 and *Ministry of Agriculture and Fisheries, Index Number of Agricultural Prices*, 1938 (H.M.S.O., 1938). For a briefer description see D. K. Britton and K. E. Hunt, *Agriculture*, especially pp. 57–60, in *The Sources and Nature of the Statistics of the United Kingdom*, ed. M. G. Kendall (Oliver and Boyd, 1952), vol. I, pp. 35–74.

[2] Although price information is published for Scotland, there are no price indices for output as a whole or the main constituents of output.

[3] Strictly, the output over the latest five years valued at the prices of 1927–9. Fixed weights, based on estimated annual consumption in 1936–8, are used in the index of fertilizer prices.

tions include acreage payments. *Agriculture* gives the original indices with 1927–9 = 100; in the *Monthly Digest* and *Annual Abstract* they are recalculated with the average of 1936, 1937 and 1938 = 100.

Shipping freights

Index numbers of tramp shipping freights are compiled by the Chamber of Shipping and are published each month in the *Monthly Digest of Statistics*. The present indices compare the level of freights with the average in 1952 and separate figures are given for voyage and time charter. The index for voyage charter is a weighted arithmetic average, the weights being based on freights earned in 1951. The index for time charter is based on fixtures for ships of 8000 tons deadweight and over.[1] These indices, first published in the *Monthly Digest of Statistics* in the middle of 1953, replaced an earlier index for voyage charter only. Comparison was with 1948, but the weights used were based on freights in 1935.[2] This index was a modified version of the pre-war index with 1935 as base, also calculated by the Chamber of Shipping and published regularly in *The Statist*.[3] Freight indices were also published before the war by *Lloyd's List*, *The Economist* and the *Manchester Guardian*.

Import and export prices

The Board of Trade publishes each quarter indices of the average value of imports and exports and each month indices of the price of imports and exports. The basis of these indices are discussed in detail in Chapter VI.[4] The most important points to keep in mind when using these figures together with figures of

[1] For details of the method of construction of the indices see 'Tramp Shipping Freights, Report of the Freight Index Committee' compiled by the Chamber of Shipping of the United Kingdom.

[2] For a detailed description of the index, see M. G. Kendall, 'The United Kingdom Mercantile Marine and its Contribution to the Balance of Payments', *Journal of the Royal Statistical Society*, series A, vol. CXIII, pt. I (1950), pp. 18–22.

[3] For a detailed description of this index as well as for annual figures from 1869 to 1936, see L. Isserlis, 'Tramp Shipping Cargoes, and Freights', *Journal of the Royal Statistical Society*, vol. CI, pt. I (1938), pp. 53–146.

[4] See pp. 150–4.

wholesale prices, are that they are based on the average value of goods traded and not on actual price quotations; also, they refer to the time when the goods are actually imported or exported and not to current contracts.

INDEX NUMBERS OF RETAIL PRICES

Index numbers of retail prices and the cost of living are among the most widely discussed of all statistics. This is because they set out to measure changes in the prices of the goods and services which the general public buys, and are used in comparison with figures of money incomes to measure changes in the real standard of living. Arguments about the effect of price changes on the standard of living figure prominently in wage negotiations; issues of economic policy are frequently considered in terms of their effect on the price index; and one of the most powerful arguments used in support of a Government is its capacity to keep prices from rising. Statistics of changes in retail prices are regularly bandied about in political argument and debate. Their accuracy has often been attacked, and in consequence the Government has instigated a series of enquiries into the reliability of the official indices, and we know much more about how these indices are compiled than we do about most official statistics.

There are three main recurrent themes in the discussion about these index numbers. First, what prices should they measure? Secondly, how should the movement in the individual prices be combined to give group indices and a total index? In other words, what weights should be used in the index? And thirdly, what year should be used as a basis for comparison? Sensible answers cannot be given to these questions unless we decide to which group of people in the community we wish the indices to relate. If we want an index which measures the effect of price changes on the very rich we will have to include quite different commodities from those we would include if we want an index which measures the effect of price changes on the very poor. And the relative importance, or weight, to be attached to the various groups of commodities, will differ in the two indices. Of course, if all prices are moving up or down in exactly the same proportion it does not matter which commodities we choose or how we weight them, since the average would always be the same. The problem of what commodities to include and how to weight them assumes greatest importance, therefore, in periods such as the last fifteen years, when there are great disparate price movements and big shifts in the patterns of expenditure of different classes in the community.

The first attempts at measuring prices paid by final consumers were confined to goods bought by wage-earners. When the first indices were calculated the standard of living of wage-earners was very much lower than now and at the time was only sufficient to provide a minimum level of existence. It was for this reason that such price index numbers were called *cost-of-living index numbers*.

As incomes rise we can either continue to measure the price of this minimum standard, or the prices of the things which wage-earners actually buy with their higher incomes. If we do the latter, the index no longer measures the minimum cost of living. In an attempt, not altogether successful, to make this clear, it is now customary to call indices which measure the changes in the prices of goods on which incomes are actually spent, *retail price indices*.

The measurement of retail prices raises further problems. When standards of living are only sufficient to cover minimum needs, consumer expenditure is largely governed by physical needs for food, shelter and clothing, and there is little room for variation in expenditure according to individual taste and idiosyncrasy. In such circumstances there is little difference between the expenditure of one consumer and another among the working class, and an index which measures the change in the average of prices for them all together will also measure the change in prices as it affects each and every one of them. But as incomes increase and people can afford more than the bare minimum, choice plays a much more important role; there may be substantial differences in the way in which people use their 'surplus'. Some may spend more on entertainment and holidays, some on better housing, and some on more food or clothing. If there is wide variation in expenditure habits, and if prices have not been changing uniformly, an index number which measures the average movement of retail prices for the group as a whole may not in fact be at all relevant for individuals within the group. If, for example, the expenditure pattern of large families is very different from that of small families, of the man who earns £12 per week from the man who earns £7, of those who live in a large city from those who live in a small industrial town or in the country, then a single index which attempts to measure the average for all of them together may be statistically correct, in the sense that it measures the average accurately, but may not be of much significance. For the extent of the price movement affecting most people may be very different from that shown by the index, because their pattern of expenditure is very different from that assumed in the index. For some people prices may have gone up much more than the average, for others much less; there may be very few for whom the statistical average is relevant. Thus when there are big variations in price changes an index of average retail prices will only be significant and useful if the group to which it refers is homogeneous in its expenditure habits.

It is only if these general problems of constructing retail price indices are appreciated that the recent and continuing controversy about the meaning of the official indices can be understood.

The interim index of retail prices

The present retail price index, called the 'interim index of retail prices', measures the change in prices compared with January 1952.[1] The figures are published each month in the *Ministry of Labour Gazette* for nine groups of commodities and services,[2] and at quarterly intervals [3] in greater detail for some of the groups.[4] The index is based on a large number of price quotations covering both a wide range of commodities and services, and villages, towns and cities of different sizes. None of the actual prices used are published, but there are notes each

[1] The methods of calculation, prices covered, and weights used in the index are described in great detail in *Interim Index of Retail Prices; Method of Construction and Calculation (Revised Edition)* (H.M.S.O., 1952). The index is based on the recommendations of the Cost of Living Advisory Committee (see *Report on the Working of the Interim Index of Retail Prices* (Cmd. 8481, H.M.S.O., 1952)).

[2] Food; rent and rates; clothing; fuel and light; household durable goods; miscellaneous goods; services; alcoholic drink; and tobacco.

[3] January, April, July and October.

[4] The additional detail is given for food (7 sub-groups); clothing (7); fuel and light (2); household durable goods (4); miscellaneous goods (2); and services (3).

month in the *Ministry of Labour Gazette* about the main price changes during the month that affect the index.

In principle the index is confined to prices paid by wage-earners and small salary earners, the price material being collected from retailers who fall under the broad description of those catering for working-class households. Estimates of working-class expenditure on various items in 1950, with allowance for price, but not quantity, changes between 1950 and January 1952 are used as weights in calculating the group and total indices. This gives the same index as one based on 1950 and weighted by expenditure in that year and then recalculated arithmetically with January 1952 as 100.[1] So the index measures the changing cost since January 1952 of the collection of goods and services estimated to have been bought by working-class households in 1950.

The estimates of expenditure used for the weights are mainly from the calculations made for the National Income Blue Book. These figures refer to total expenditure of all consumers, not merely to expenditure of consumers in the wage-earning and low-salary group. They have therefore to be adjusted on a rough basis before they can be used in weighting the price index.

It is largely because the expenditure figures used for weighting

---

[1] If p_{50}, p_{J52}, p_{53} are taken as prices in 1950, January 1952, and 1953 and q_{50}, q_{J52}, q_{53} are taken as the corresponding quantities then the official index for 1953 is

$$\Sigma\left(\frac{p_{53}}{p_{J52}}\right)q_{50}p_{J52} \times 100 \Big/ \Sigma q_{50}p_{J52} \quad \text{or} \quad \Sigma q_{50}p_{53} \times 100 \Big/ \Sigma q_{50}p_{J52}. \quad (1)$$

An index for 1953 with 1950 base and weights would be

$$\Sigma\left(\frac{p_{53}}{p_{50}}\right)q_{50}p_{50} \times 100 \Big/ \Sigma q_{50}p_{50} \quad \text{or} \quad \Sigma q_{50}p_{53} \times 100 \Big/ \Sigma q_{50}p_{50}. \quad (2)$$

An index for January 1952 with 1950 base and weights would be

$$\Sigma\left(\frac{p_{J52}}{p_{50}}\right)q_{50}p_{50} \times 100 \Big/ \Sigma q_{50}p_{50} \quad \text{or} \quad \Sigma q_{50}p_{J52} \times 100 \Big/ \Sigma q_{50}p_{50}. \quad (3)$$

Therefore (2), the index for 1953 with 1950 as base and weights, reworked with January 1952 = 100 would be (2) divided by (3), that is

$$\frac{\Sigma q_{50}p_{53}}{\Sigma q_{50}p_{50}} \times \frac{\Sigma q_{50}p_{50}}{\Sigma q_{50}p_{J52}} \times 100 \quad \text{or} \quad \frac{\Sigma q_{50}p_{53}}{\Sigma q_{50}p_{J52}} \times 100,$$

which is the same as (1) above.

are a rough estimate that the index is called an 'interim' index. A precise and accurate check on the weights used will not be possible until the post-war survey of consumers' expenditure in 1953 is analysed.[1] The main purpose of this enquiry is to provide a firm and up-to-date basis for a new revised index of retail prices.[2]

The present index, which follows closely the recommendations of the Cost of Living Advisory Committee, replaced an earlier index based on June 1947 = 100.[3] This was also called the 'interim index of retail prices'. The main differences between this index and the current index is the basis of weighting.[4] The June 1947 index was weighted on estimates of working-class expenditure calculated from the budget enquiries taken for the years 1937–8. Since June 1947 was taken as 100, these were adjusted for estimated price changes between 1937–8 and June 1947.[5] The index thus measured the change compared with June 1947 of the collection of goods and services bought by working-class households in 1937–8.

When the interim index was published with June 1947 = 100, it was frequently attacked on the grounds that the distribution of consumption had changed greatly since 1937–8, and it was argued that the index was bound to be inaccurate as a measure of what was really happening to prices in the post-war period. It was also frequently suggested that since out-of-date weights were used, the index underestimated the extent of the rise in retail prices. But the mere fact that the weighting was out of date would not by

[1] See *Ministry of Labour Gazette*, January 1953, pp. 8–9.

[2] See *Interim Report of the Cost of Living Advisory Committee* (Cmd. 8328, H.M.S.O., 1951).

[3] The basis of this earlier index as well as the current one is explained in detail in *Interim Index of Retail Prices: Method of Construction and Calculation (Revised Edition)* (H.M.S.O., 1952).

[4] There were also some changes in the range and treatment of price quotations. Of these the most important was the extension of the rent figures in the 1952 index to include the rents of working-class houses built since 1947, and the different formula for measuring price changes when the strength of beer was altered.

[5] An index weighted by 1937–8 patterns of expenditure but recalculated arithmetically with June 1947 = 100 by implication used as weights 1937–8 quantities and June 1947 prices. In the same way the current interim index uses as weights 1950 quantities and January 1952 prices (see p. 181, n. 1).

itself necessarily mean that the index underweighted those items which had risen most in price and overweighted those which had risen least in price. As the Advisory Committee showed in its report, such information as was available led to the conclusion that the contrary was the case; that with more up-to-date weighting the index would have shown a rather smaller rise in prices between 1947 and 1951.[1] Notwithstanding this demonstration that the old interim index did not have a downward bias, the Committee recommended that the more up-to-date weighting system now used should be adopted. This was because the use of pre-war weights tended to discredit the index, even though it made little difference to the final result; and because the lack of substantial bias between 1947 and 1951 was itself no guarantee that there would be no bias in later years.

The change in weighting and the use of January 1952 instead of June 1947 as the basis of comparison broke the continuity of the interim index figures. There are monthly figures from June 1947 to January 1952 with June 1947 = 100, and from January 1952 onwards with January 1952 = 100. But the overlap of one month makes it possible to link the two indices together to give a continuous series from June 1947 onwards. Such a linked series is calculated and published by the Ministry of Labour, but for the total index only and not for the separate group indices.[2]

The cost-of-living index

The interim index of retail prices replaced the cost-of-living index in 1947. The cost-of-living index, instituted in the early stages of the First World War, was designed to measure the percentage increase month by month in the cost of maintaining the standard of living among working-class households in July 1914.[3]

[1] The upward bias in the index due to using out-of-date weights was, however, offset by the downward bias in the rent index.

[2] Linked indices can of course be calculated in the same way for individual groups. But a total index derived from such linked indices, whether weighted by the old or revised system of weights, would not give the same figures as those obtained by linking the totals themselves.

[3] For a detailed explanation of this index see *The Cost of Living Index Number: Method of Compilation* (H.M.S.O., 1944). The weaknesses of this index as a measure of price changes after the Second World War and the reasons for discontinuing it are discussed in *Interim Report of the Cost of Living Advisory Committee* (Cmd. 7077, H.M.S.O., 1947).

As explained earlier, because the working-class standard of 1914 was considered to be very little more than a minimum standard necessary for reasonable living, it was thought of as measuring the changing cost of living, and quickly became known as the *cost-of-living index number*.

The cost-of-living index gives the only official information of price changes affecting wage-earners for the period from 1914 to 1947. The index was heavily criticized in later years both on the grounds that it covered too narrow a range of commodities and services, excluding many goods commonly bought by working-class households, and because it used weights based on out-of-date habits of expenditure.[1] There is no doubt about the validity of these criticisms and the consumer budget inquiry of 1937–8 was taken mainly to provide the basis for a revised and more up-to-date index number. But the outbreak of the war prevented this.

Although the cost-of-living index number was out of date in many respects even in the inter-war years, it does not follow from this that a more up-to-date and complete index would have given different figures for the general movement of retail prices. Indeed, reweighting the groups in the index by 1937–8 instead of 1914 expenditure, and allowing for price movements of some of the more important items not included in the index, makes very little difference to the comparison of the general level of retail prices in 1937–8 and 1914.[2]

For the period of the Second World War and the post-war years the position is quite different. The items which were most heavily weighted in the index, such as food, rose least in price, whereas items which were either underweighted or were not included at all, such as alcoholic drink, increased most in price.

Indeed, after 1942 one of the Government's main aims in tax and subsidy policy was to try to keep the index stable. Items included or heavily weighted in the index were subsidized while others were heavily taxed. The index may have continued to measure accurately the cost of the 1914 standard but it bore little

[1] The weighting of food expenditure was based on a Board of Trade Inquiry in 1904, of rents on an Inquiry made in 1912, and of other items on miscellaneous, but not very reliable, estimates of working-class expenditure in 1914.

[2] See A. L. Bowley, 'Earnings and Prices, 1904, 1914, 1937/38', *Review of Economic Studies*, vol. VIII (1941), pp. 129–42.

relation to changes in the prices of the things on which people were actually spending their money. For some of the items most heavily subsidized, such as food and utility clothing, were also rationed; while increased sums were spent on other items, such as beer and tobacco, which were heavily taxed, and yet not adequately covered in the index. As a measure of the general level of retail prices, therefore, the index clearly had a very substantial downward bias after 1942.[1] The index, which showed practically no rise in retail prices between 1942 and June 1947, was discredited long before it was discontinued.

Other estimates of working-class retail prices, 1938–47

The official cost-of-living index is such a bad measure of retail price changes after 1941 that it should not be linked to the interim index to provide a continuous series back to the pre-war period. But there are good unofficial estimates covering this period which are specially designed to provide such a link.

R. G. D. Allen has estimated the change in retail prices for each year from 1939 to 1947 [2] by applying the weights used in the interim index to estimates of price changes derived from the National Income Blue Book.[3] This method assumes that the movement of prices for individual commodities was not very different for working class families and the community as a whole. Dudley Seers has made similar calculations [4] using in addition the price figures which must, by implication, have been used in calculating the weights for the interim index.[5] Allen's and

[1] It was this experience that led so many to conclude, quite wrongly, that all indices based on an out-of-date weighting system will have a downward bias.

[2] See R. G. D. Allen, 'Retail Prices', *London and Cambridge Economic Service Bulletin*, vol. xxv (III) (11 August 1947), pp. 74–6, and vol. XXVI (I) (18 February 1948), pp. 18–19; *idem*, 'Prices', *Bulletin*, vol. XXVII (I) (February 1949), pp. 15–17.

[3] See p. 188.

[4] See D. Seers, *Changes in the Cost of Living and the Distribution of Income since* 1938, and *The Levelling of Income since* 1938 (Oxford, Basil Blackwell, 1949).

[5] The weights used in the interim index were estimated expenditure in 1937–8 at the prices of June 1947. Estimates must therefore have been used of price changes between 1937–8 and June 1947, but these estimates were never published. They can, however, be worked out by comparing the weights used in the interim index (distribution of 1937–8 expenditure

Seers' estimates give approximately the same result for June 1947 compared with 1938. The difference between these estimates and the official cost-of-living figure is very substantial after 1941.[1] Allen's estimates have been used by the London and Cambridge Economic Service to link the cost-of-living index for 1914 to 1938 with the interim index from June 1947, thus giving a continuous series back to 1913, which is published in their *Bulletin*.

One of the issues that has been frequently raised in the controversy over the accuracy of the official retail price indices over the last few years, is whether one can expect a single index to measure adequately what is happening to retail prices. Clearly during the war and post-war period any index appropriate to working-class expenditure, however accurate, would not have been significant for other classes in the community. It has been suggested earlier that even an index confined to working-class expenditure might not be significant if there are wide variations in expenditure and, therefore, in the impact of price changes on different groups within the working class. There is no doubt that there are such variations, depending not only on family size and the level of wages, but also on social habits.

One possible remedy for this difficulty is to have more than one index. It has been suggested that there should be separate indices for middle-class households and salary-earners, and for different regions of the country. These suggestions were considered by the Cost of Living Advisory Committee,[2] but they recommended 'that only one official index of retail prices should be published monthly',[3] mainly because 'there would be real danger of confusion if two or more official monthly indices were published'.

The enquiry into household expenditure which was taken for 1953 covered a sample of households in the population without limitation as to income, and particulars were obtained about in-

[1] at June 1947 prices), with the actual distribution of expenditure shown in the 1937–8 budgets (distribution of 1937–8 expenditure at 1937–8 prices).

		1939	1940	1941	1942	1943	1944	1945	1946	1947
Official cost-of-living index	1938 =100	101	117½	127	128	127	128½	130	130	130
Allen's estimate of working-class price index		102	119	130	139	143	146	148	150	161

[2] *Interim Report of the Cost of Living Advisory Committee* (Cmd. 8328, H.M.S.O., 1951).

[3] *Ibid.* para. 15, p. 5.

come as well as expenditure. When the results are analysed and published there will, therefore, be much more information than at present about the relation between income, type of household, and distribution of expenditure. Even if only one retail price index is published officially, it may be possible for others to calculate subsidiary indices when the full results of this budget inquiry are published.

Retail food prices

A series of price indices for food expenditure has been started by the National Food Survey Committee and published in its *Annual Reports* since 1950.[1] The price indices refer to urban working-class households only. These indices are compiled in a different way from most price indices. The price data used are not based on actual price quotations, but on the 'average value' per unit of quantity bought in each of 88 food groups. These average values are obtained from the sample surveys taken by the Committee, the sample in 1950 covering 3334 urban working class households. The individual price changes are combined by the Ideal Fisher index formula.[2] The base year is 1945 and the total index is given for each year back to 1942.

The main advantage of this index is that the price information used in its compilation is given in full detail. Since the report analyses expenditure within the sample according to type of household, it is possible from the information given to calculate subsidiary price indices for different types of households, even though this is not done in the report itself. But since the data used are average values of quantities bought, and not price quotations for particular grades, they may be affected by the changing proportions of different qualities bought from year to year.[3] The index is also very much out of date when first published. The latest indices given in the *Annual Report* issued in 1953, for example, were for 1951. This index has not been

---

[1] *Domestic Food Consumption and Expenditure*, 1950. *Annual Report of the National Food Survey Committee* (H.M.S.O., 1952), pp. 122–5.

[2] That is, for each year the geometric average of base-weighted and current-year-weighted indices.

[3] This is met to some extent by the great detail for which average values are worked out. There are, for example, fifteen separate items for meat and six for fish; but only one for cheese, shell eggs, and tea.

published long enough for one to draw any significant comparisons between it and the food group in the interim retail price index.

The general level of consumer prices

The interim index of retail prices, the cost-of-living index, and the index of food prices refer only to working-class expenditure and there are no official estimates of price changes for other classes of the community. Indices of price changes for consumers as a whole can, however, be derived from the official estimates of consumers' expenditure given every year in the National Income Blue Book and each quarter in the *Monthly Digest of Statistics*. Two sets of figures are given: first, consumers' expenditure at current prices, and secondly, expenditure revalued at the prices of some base year, that is, the volume or quantum of expenditure at unchanged prices. By comparing these two sets of figures we can arrive at price indices of consumer expenditure. These price indices differ from the interim price index in two respects: first, they relate to national consumption as a whole, and secondly, they are weighted by the distribution of current expenditure in the latest year.[1]

These derived price indices, with $1948 = 100$, are now given in

[1] A price index derived from a base-year-weighted volume index and a current value index will be weighted by current expenditure.

If p_{48}, p_{51} = prices in 1948 and 1951

q_{48}, q_{51} = quantities consumed in 1948 and 1951,

the index of the volume of expenditure in 1951 ($1948 = 100$) as calculated in the Blue Book is

$$\frac{\Sigma q_{51} p_{48}}{\Sigma q_{48} p_{48}} \times 100. \qquad (1)$$

The index of value in 1951 is

$$\frac{\Sigma q_{51} p_{51}}{\Sigma q_{48} p_{48}} \times 100, \qquad (2)$$

and the index of price is (2) divided by (1), that is

$$\frac{\Sigma q_{51} p_{51}}{\Sigma q_{48} p_{48}} \times 100 \bigg/ \frac{\Sigma q_{51} p_{48}}{\Sigma q_{48} p_{48}} = \frac{\Sigma q_{51} p_{51}}{\Sigma q_{51} p_{48}} \times 100,$$

or

$$\Sigma q_{51} p_{51} \bigg/ \Sigma \left(\frac{p_{48}}{p_{51}}\right) q_{51} p_{51}. \qquad (3)$$

the National Income Blue Book for each year back to 1946. For 1948 and earlier years similar figures were given in the earlier White Papers with 1938 = 100. It is thus possible to calculate a continuous linked series back to 1938.[1] The Blue Books and White Papers provide annual figures only, but quarterly figures can be derived from the tables in the *Monthly Digest of Statistics*.

Real wages, earnings and incomes

If changes in money wages, earnings or other incomes are compared with changes in prices, we can obtain indices of the change in real wages, earnings or income. This is done by taking the quotient of changes in money incomes and changes in prices, expressed in comparison with some base period as 100.[2] The meaning, significance and reliability of such figures of real income depend on the figures of money income and prices from which they are derived. Some of the crude comparisons which are frequently made are quite misleading. Thus, for example, the wage-rate index is often divided by figures of retail prices derived from the interim index and the cost-of-living index, and the result used as if it measured changes in the real income and standard of living of the working-class family. To derive measures of changes in real standards from figures of money incomes and prices is not as easy as this. One has to take account of the movement in earnings in relation to rates, the effects of taxation, benefits received from the State,[3] changes in the composition of the family, as well as the relevance of the available price index to

[1] Price indices were given in the White Papers for 1942 and 1943, not given for 1944, 1945 and 1946, and have been given regularly each year since 1947. They can, however, easily be calculated for the missing years from the figures of actual and revalued consumption given in each of the White Papers for those years.

[2] If, for example, money wage rates in year x are 10 per cent above year y and prices have increased by 5 per cent between the two years, then taking real wage rates in year x as 100, real wage rates in year y would be

$$\frac{110}{105} \times 100 = 104 \cdot 8$$

[3] One of the debatable points is whether one should take account of services in kind, for example, education and National Health Service, as well as money benefits.

the expenditure of the group being considered. To get any significant results, painstaking detailed research is necessary, and even then with the present state of statistical information the results are hazardous estimates, to be used with great caution.[1]

[1] For a courageous attempt to compare the real incomes of various groups in the community in 1938 and 1949, see D. Seers, *The Levelling of Incomes since* 1938 (Oxford, Basil Blackwell, 1949), pp. 47–73.

CHAPTER VIII

INCOMES

THERE are many ways of analysing incomes statistically. We can classify incomes by type—wages, salaries, rent, interest and profit —and calculate the rate of payment to each, the total amount going to each, or the share of each in the total national income. Thus for wages we have figures of changes in the standard rates of wages, of average wages actually earned by each worker, of the total amount paid out in wages (the wage-bill), and of the share of wages in total national income.

Many of the terms used in the statistics of incomes by type— wages, rent, interest, profit—are the same as those used in economic theory. But although the same terms are used they frequently have quite a different meaning, and this often leads to confusion. Many of the statistics, as we shall see, are a by-product of income tax collection, and they reflect the categories and rules laid down in income tax law and administration, not the conclusions of theoretical economic analysis.[1]

Incomes can be classified according to the industry or occupation in which they arise. This gives us a measure of the contribution which each industry makes to the total national income or product.[2] If the information is available, the incomes arising in each industry can also be analysed by type of income.

Yet another way of analysing incomes statistically is by the size of income received by individuals or families. This gives us figures of the distribution of incomes by income ranges. Such figures usually lump together the income received from all sources, but there are some statistics of income distribution which give details of type of income for each income range.

Figures of incomes, whether analysed by type, by industry, or by size ranges, can be calculated either before or after taking into account what is paid in taxation. For many purposes we may wish to allow for the effect of changes in prices on the real value of incomes. If we want to do this, we must measure the change in

---

[1] See Chapter IX, pp. 218 ff.   [2] See Chapter IX, pp. 222 ff.

the prices of the goods and services on which the incomes are spent, and we can then make an estimate of the change in 'real' incomes as distinct from the change in 'money' incomes.[1]

Clearly, if confusion is to be avoided, it is important that statistics of income should be described in precise terms. For example, it would not be much use giving a set of figures merely described as showing the percentage change in wages over a series of years. Before we could use such figures we would need to know whether they were based on the total wage-bill, the share of wages in the national income, standard wage-rates or actual average earnings; whether they were before or after deducting tax payments and national insurance contributions; and whether they measured 'money' wages or 'real' wages.

THE MAIN SOURCES OF INCOME STATISTICS

There are four main sources of information about incomes. First, there is the mass of information about rates of pay agreed between employers and workers through employers' associations and trade unions or fixed by statutory authorities. This deals mainly with minimum wage rates. Secondly, there are the special enquiries on actual wage and salary earnings, of which the most important are those now undertaken by the Ministry of Labour, and by the Board of Trade in the Census of Production and the Census of Distribution. Thirdly, the Board of Inland Revenue, in assessing individuals and firms for income tax, collects a great deal of information about incomes, most of which is published in the Board's *Annual Reports*. This is the most comprehensive information and deals with wages, salaries, rent, interest and profits. Lastly, there are the published accounts of public enterprises, nationalized industries and public companies, which contain important information on their income and profits.

In recent years the information from all these sources has been used to make estimates of the main categories of income and of the total national income of the country. These estimates are published every year in the Blue Book on *National Income and Expenditure* which is discussed in a later chapter.[2] We shall, however, refer to some of these figures here as we discuss the various statistics of income.

In most statistics of income a distinction is made between the

[1] See Chapter VI, p. 189.   [2] See Chapter IX.

wage earner and salary earner and between wages and salaries.[1] There are no precise and logical criteria for making such a distinction; indeed, it is doubtful whether much economic significance can be attached to such a division, although it may be of political or social importance. But whatever the basis used for dividing employees into these two categories, there are bound to be difficult problems of allocation on the borderline, which have to be dealt with quite arbitrarily.

The present practice is to follow, as far as possible, the division used in the Census of Production between 'operatives' and 'administrative, technical and clerical employees'; the first category being treated as wage earners and the second as salary earners. On this definition, managers, superintendents, works foremen; research, experimental, development and technical and design employees (other than operatives); draughtsmen and tracers; and travellers and office employees, are all treated as salary earners: and all other classes of employees, that is, broadly speaking, all manual workers, are treated as wage earners.

But this division is not a very useful guide in deciding how to classify some occupations. Shop assistants are one of the borderline cases. In the Blue Book on National Income and Expenditure they are now treated as wage earners; but before 1952 they were treated as salary earners.

WAGE-RATES

Most of the information about wage-rates arises from collective agreements between employers and trade unions and the regulations of statutory wage-fixing authorities. These are usually complex, detailed documents which cannot easily be understood without knowledge of the production processes and the labour organization of the trade concerned. A summary of the main changes in these rates is published every month in the *Ministry of Labour Gazette*, and the current rates are given in some detail for workers on time-rates only in the annual publication of the Ministry of Labour entitled *Time Rates of Wages and Hours of*

[1] For a detailed discussion of the distinction between wages and salaries see A. L. Chapman and R. Knight, *Wages and Salaries in the United Kingdom*, 1920–1938 (Cambridge, 1953), No. 5 of Studies in the National Income and Expenditure of the United Kingdom (General Editor, Richard Stone), pp. 13–16.

Labour.[1] A summary for the more important industries used to be given in the *Abstract of Labour Statistics*, but this has not been issued since 1937.

The Ministry of Labour uses the information it receives about wage agreements to make monthly estimates of the changes in the weekly wage-bill implied by the changes in rates. These estimates are published in the *Ministry of Labour Gazette* each month for the main groups of industries. They are not very useful and are certainly not a reliable guide to the effect of changes in wage-rates on the wage-bill of the country as a whole.[2]

INDICES OF WAGE-RATES

Current indices of wage-rates

If the monthly information about changes in wage-rates in various trades and occupations can be expressed as a series of percentage changes compared with the rates in some base period, and if we then average these percentage changes, using an appropriate set of weights, we have a wage-rate index. Such an index measures the average change in wage-rates for the industries and occupations covered by it. Changes in time-rates per hour, per shift, or per week, whether percentage or flat-rate changes,[3] can easily be expressed as percentage changes compared with the base date, since the base rate will also be so much per unit of time. With piece-rates, percentage changes also present no difficulty; but flat-rate increases can only be expressed as percentage changes if they are related to figures of normal weekly piece-rate earnings.

In combining the percentage changes in rates to arrive at the average change, one wants to give each change its due importance in influencing wages. The appropriate weighting therefore is the total wage-bill[4] of the workers covered by each rate. As with

[1] Annual publication began in 1946. Before that date there were issues in 1893, 1900, 1906, 1912, 1913, 1915, 1920 and 1929.

[2] For a more detailed explanation of the reasons for this see R. B. Ainsworth, 'Labour Statistics', in *The Sources and Nature of the Statistics of the United Kingdom*, ed. M. G. Kendall (Oliver and Boyd, 1952), vol. I, pp. 81–2.

[3] 'Flat-rate' changes are expressed in terms of a sum of money, so many pence or shillings per hour, per shift, or per week.

[4] See p. 205.

other index numbers, there is the choice of base-year or current-year weighting. For the usual reasons of convenience and availability of information, base-year weighting is usually used, with the base year revised at intervals.

An official wage-rate index of this type is compiled each month and published in the *Ministry of Labour Gazette* and the *Monthly Digest of Statistics*. The index, which measures changes in rates per week, is based on the rates agreed by trade unions or laid down by wage-fixing authorities, and covers about 80 industries. The only important groups of wage-earners apparently not represented in the index are domestic servants and workers in commerce and finance.[1] The comparison is with June 1947, although the weights used are estimated wage-bills in 1946. Separate figures are shown for males, females and juveniles, but no figures for individual industries or group of industries. It is clear that figures for individual industries are available in the Ministry of Labour, for the note outlining the basis of the index explains[2] that percentages are first worked out for each industry and are then combined, using wage-bills as weights, to give the totals.

The index compiled by A. L. Bowley and published in the *London and Cambridge Economic Service Bulletin*[3] until March 1954 used to give figures for individual industries as well as the average for all industries. Although the total index has now been discontinued, percentage changes in rates for a series of occupations[4] are still given, and they provide a useful supplement to the official total index.

Rather more information about changes in wage-rates is published by the International Labour Organization than is published

[1] Clerical, technical and administrative workers are, in any case, excluded from the index, since in the Ministry of Labour classification they are part of the salariat.

[2] See *Ministry of Labour Gazette*, February 1948, p. 41.

[3] See p. 6.

[4] The occupations given are:

> *Men:* Bricklayers, building labourers; engineering fitters, engineering labourers; shipbuilding; dock labourers; railwaymen; compositors; labourers and trams in local authorities; lorry drivers; agriculture.
>
> *Men and women:* Cotton; wool.
>
> *Women:* Bootmaking; tailoring and shirts; confectionery.

in any official source in this country. The following tables for the United Kingdom were included in the *Statistical Yearbook* for 1951–2.[1]

(1) Index of wage-rates per hour for all manual workers (agricultural, mining, manufacturing, construction, commerce and transport).
Figures for 1937, 1938, 1939, 1946 (1946 = 100).
Figures for 1947, 1948, 1949, 1950, 1951 (1948 = 100).

(2) Index of wage-rates in mining, manufacturing, construction, commerce and transport: (*a*) per hour, (*b*) per week, separately for males, females and total (including juveniles).
Figures for 1937, 1938, 1939, 1946 (1946 = 100).
Figures for 1947, 1948, 1949, 1950, 1951 (1948 = 100).

(3) Similar figures to (2) above, but for manufacturing only.

Comparable information for earlier periods is given in previous issues of the *Yearbook*.[2] Presumably all these statistics are supplied to the International Labour Office by the Ministry of Labour and why these are not published in this country is something of a mystery. Certainly they give useful additional information, especially on the movement of wage-rates per hour.[3] Indeed, now that there is no *Abstract of Labour Statistics*, the summary of wage-rate and earnings information given in the International Labour Office *Yearbook* is much better than anything available in United Kingdom publications, including the *Annual Abstract of Statistics*.

Indices of wage-rates for earlier periods

The current official wage-rate index compares changes with the level in June 1947 and only gives figures back to that month. But the Bowley index is available continuously back to 1920 and

[1] *Yearbook of Labour Statistics* 1951–52 (Geneva, 1952), Table 16, p. 146 and Table 17, p. 155.
[2] See, for example, *Yearbook of Labour Statistics*, 1949–50 (Geneva, 1951), Table 16, p. 149 and Table 17, p. 165.
[3] An index of hourly rates and of normal hours per week from 1937 to 1949, also not published in the United Kingdom, is given in another I.L.O. publication, *Wages and Payroll Statistics* (Geneva, 1949), Table IV, p. 176.

can be linked to an earlier one, which it replaced, back to 1914. The index covered a much narrower range of industries than the present official index.[1] It was originally published with 1924 = 100 and weighted by 1924 wage-bills, but after February 1949 was arithmetically recalculated and published with 1938 = 100.

The present official index, which gives figures back to June 1947, replaced an earlier one which compared changes in rates with September 1939. This index was first published in the *Monthly Digest of Statistics* and only later, from March 1946, in the *Ministry of Labour Gazette*. It has, however, been published on a monthly basis back to January 1935 in the *Annual Abstract of Statistics*.[2] The main apparent differences between this index and the current one are: first, a smaller range of industries and occupations is included;[3] second, it is weighted by estimates of pre-war wage-bills; and third, it gives only a single figure whereas the current index gives separate figures for males, females and juveniles.

For the inter-war years an index was published quarterly in the *Ministry of Labour Gazette* comparing rates with the average in 1924. This index was first published in February 1936 and continued until the end of 1939.[4] It is available back to the beginning of 1920.[5] As in the later index, there was only a single figure for all industries, and shop assistants, clerks, domestic servants, and Government employees were not covered. This index in turn replaced one comparing rates with the average for 1914. This was published annually in the *Ministry of Labour Gazette* until 1935,[6] and the series was included in tables in the annual *Abstract*

[1] For a detailed explanation of the index, see A. L. Bowley, *A New Index of Wages* (London and Cambridge Economic Service, Special Memorandum No. 12, January 1929).

[2] See *Annual Abstract of Statistics*, No. 84, 1935–1946 (H.M.S.O., 1948), Table 140, p. 118.

[3] Retail distribution, catering and entertainments are the most important industries not included in this index but covered in the current one.

[4] *Ministry of Labour Gazette Quarterly Supplement*, February 1940.

[5] See *Abstract of Labour Statistics of the United Kingdom* 1919–1933 (Cmd. 4625, H.M.S.O., 1934), p. 88, for figures from January 1920 to December 1933.

[6] In the series of articles entitled 'Relative Levels of Rates of Wages at August 1914 and December (of current year)'. See, for example, *Ministry of Labour Gazette*, March 1935, pp. 86–8.

of Labour Statistics.[1] The index was also given in the *Abstract* as part of a Table showing changes in rates for individual occupations and industries, and a very clear picture can thus be obtained of the coverage of the index. This suggests that there is little difference in coverage between this index and the later one based on 1924 = 100. All these indices relate to rates per week; but in the annual article in the *Ministry of Labour Gazette* comparing rates with 1914, useful rough estimates were given of changes in rates per hour as well as in rates per week.

E. C. Ramsbottom, the Director of Statistics at the Ministry of Labour published a much more detailed and reliable index for the inter-war years in a paper to the Royal Statistical Society.[2] As he explained in his paper, Ramsbottom was trying out his new index on the Royal Statistical Society before publishing it officially as a Ministry of Labour index. Unfortunately, although it was favourably received, it was never officially published by the Ministry of Labour because of the outbreak of the war. Ramsbottom's index was originally calculated for the period 1920–35, but figures were given later for 1936, 1937 and 1938.[3] The index is based on a much wider range of occupations and industries than the Ministry of Labour's official index at the time.[4] But the main distinguishing feature of Ramsbottom's index was the separate indices given for a large number of individual industries throughout the period, and a detailed list of the occupational rates which had been included in the index. In fact the movement in the total shown by this comprehensive index was not very different from the Ministry of Labour's and Bowley's indices.

[1] The *Abstract of Labour Statistics of the United Kingdom*, 1919–1933, Cmd. 4625, H.M.S.O., 1934, gives this index for each year from 1920.

[2] E. C. Ramsbottom, 'Wage-Rates in the United Kingdom, 1921–1934', *Journal of the Royal Statistical Society*, vol. XCVIII, pt. IV (1935), pp. 639–94. The discussion of Mr. Ramsbottom's paper, in which most of the experts on this subject took part, is well worth reading. All the problems that arise in calculating wage-rate indices are raised in this discussion.

[3] E. C. Ramsbottom, 'Wage Rates in the United Kingdom, 1934–1937', *Journal of the Royal Statistical Society*, vol. CI, pt. I (1938), p. 202, and 'Wage Rates in the United Kingdom, 1938', *Journal of the Royal Statistical Society*, vol. CII, pt. II (1939), p. 289.

[4] There is evidence that the coverage of the official index published after the war with September 1939 = 100 was the same as Mr. Ramsbottom's index.

Thus there are several indices for the inter-war years. These have not been sorted out in any official publication to give a continuous run of figures from 1914 onwards. But such linking together is done by the London and Cambridge Economic Service, which publishes an index with 1938 = 100, giving annual figures back to 1913 and monthly figures for recent years. This index is calculated by linking together three indices: the current official index back to June 1947, the earlier official index for the period August 1939 to June 1947, and Bowley's index for the period 1913 to 1939.[1]

In the period before 1914 an official index was published comparing rates with the average for 1900, and calculated annually back to 1880.[2] This was based on a very narrow range of industries[3] and only a few occupations in each industry. This was inevitable; wage-rate indices must perforce be based on agreed trade union rates and statutory minima, and in the period before 1914 trade union collective bargaining and wage legislation covered a much smaller part of industry than they do today.

The index is a peculiar hybrid. Some of the rates used are per hour, some per shift, and some per week. In view of this it is not possible to say exactly what the index measures.[4] Professor Bowley has also done a great deal of research on the movement of wage-rates during this period; the main results are given in his *Wages and Income in the United Kingdom since 1860.*[5]

WAGE EARNINGS

The two main sources of statistics of actual wage earnings are the

[1] See 'The Wage Rate Index: A Technical Note', *London and Cambridge Economic Service Bulletin*, March 1954, p. viii, in *The Times Review of Industry*, March 1954.

[2] See *Nineteenth Abstract of Labour Statistics of the United Kingdom* (Cmd. 3140, H.M.S.O., 1928), p. 97, which gives the complete run of figures for 1880–1914.

[3] Building, coal-mining, engineering, textiles and agriculture.

[4] For a severe criticism of the index on these grounds, see J. W. F. Rowe, *Wages in Practice and Theory* (Routledge, 1928), pp. 4–8.

[5] See A. L. Bowley, *Wages and Income in the United Kingdom since 1860* (Cambridge, 1937), especially pp. 1–11. Revised figures for this period have recently been published by E. H. Phelps Brown with S. V. Hopkins, 'The Course of Wage Rates in Five Countries, 1860–1939', *Oxford Economic Papers*, vol. 2, no. 2, (1950), pp. 226–96.

inquiries made by the Ministry of Labour and the Censuses of Production and of Distribution.

The Ministry of Labour now collects figures on a voluntary basis from a large sample of firms in industry of the number of workpeople employed, the total wages paid, and the total number of hours worked. On the basis of these inquiries, statistics are published twice a year showing average earnings per week and per hour and average hours worked, for men, women, youths and girls, in a large range of industries.[1] The figures now relate to a single week in October and April each year, and are published in the *Ministry of Labour Gazette* for the following March and September.

The figures are of limited value. They are averages for industries as a whole and give no information about the dispersion of earnings, earnings in particular occupations within each industry, or variations in earnings according to skill.[2] Since each industry covers a wide range of occupations, grades and skills, the averages for industries should not be used to compare the absolute level of earnings in one industry with another. The danger of using them in this way can be seen from looking at the figures for each of the four groups given—men, women, boys and girls— in relation to the average for all workers. Take, for example average weekly earnings for all workers in national government service and in cotton-weaving in October 1953;[3] these are given as 148s. 9d. and 136s. 4d. respectively. Yet for each of the four separate categories earnings in national government service are much lower than in cotton-weaving.

Average Wage Earnings in a Week in October 1952

	Men	Youths	Women	Girls
National government service	156s. 5d.	73s. 0d.	108s. 1d.	62s. 4d.
Cotton-weaving	178s. 11d.	87s. 7d.	118s. 0d.	81s. 7d.

[1] Important figures of the percentage of workers paid under systems of payments by results have also been collected and published for April 1947, October 1947, October 1949, October 1951, and October 1953, in connection with these inquiries. (See *Ministry of Labour Gazette*, October 1947, April 1948, March 1950, April 1952, and April 1954.)

[2] For estimates of average earnings by regions see P. Deane, 'Regional Variations in United Kingdom Incomes from Employment', *Journal of the Royal Statistical Society*, series A, vol. CXVI, pt. II (1953), pp. 123-39.

[3] See *Ministry of Labour Gazette*, March, 1953, pp. 81-2.

Comparing the average for all workers and comparing the separate categories give very different impressions because the four categories—men, women, youths and girls—are combined in very dissimilar proportions in the two industries; over half the labour force in cotton-weaving are women, while well over 80 per cent of those in national government service are men. Differences between each of these four categories may also be affected by varying proportions of skilled, semi-skilled and unskilled workers employed, so that a higher average figure for all men in one industry than in another does not necessarily mean that, grade for grade, workers in the first one are paid more than in the second. Conclusions of this kind cannot be drawn without much more detailed statistics of earnings by grade and occupation.

The main uses of the statistics, therefore, are to give a general indication of the movement in earnings in different industries, rather than a comparison of absolute levels, and to make possible estimates of the total wage-bill.[1]

Many industries are excluded from these half-yearly inquiries, the most important ones being agriculture, coal-mining, railways, London Transport, road services, port transport (docks), shipping services, distribution, catering, entertainment, commerce and banking, and domestic service. One should not overlook the fact that the figure of average earnings for all industries given in the earnings inquiries does not cover these important sections of the economy. A great deal of information about average earnings in the first six of these is, however, available elsewhere, often in much greater detail than in the Ministry of Labour inquiries.[2] A summary of the figures for these industries is usually given in the article dealing with the half-yearly inquiry. But the figures for each of these industries are on a slightly different basis and none are strictly comparable with those in the main earnings tables. This is unfortunate and it is a pity that the Ministry of Labour has not found it possible to adjust the figures for these industries to bring them more into line with the general inquiries and so give the half-yearly tables a much wider and more representative coverage.[3]

It is important to remember that the figures refer to earnings in one week only in October and March. These months are

[1] See p. 205.   [2] For example, for coal-mining.
[3] This is important because in some of the industries excluded, there have been increases in earnings much above the average in recent years.

chosen so as to avoid the incidence of holidays and major sickness. The figures, therefore, relate in the main to a full week's work; and since every week in the year is not like this, they should not be multiplied by 52 to arrive at annual earnings figures.[1]

The current series of inquiries has been made since April 1947, but the continuity of the figures was affected when the Standard Industrial Classification was adopted in analysing the results from October 1948. No overlapping set of figures, on the new and old classifications, was given, thus making it difficult to assess precisely the effect of the change on the comparability of figures for individual industries before and after October 1948.[2]

The present series of inquiries replaced a previous similar series started in 1940, relating to earnings for a week in January and July of each year. Were it not for the change in industrial classification these inquiries would be comparable with the current ones. The change in classification rules out comparisons before and after 1948 for individual industries, but figures of totals for all workers and for broad industrial groups can probably be used as a continuous series since 1940 with safety.[3]

[1] Exactly what to multiply them by is one of the problems that arises in calculating the wage-bill (see p. 205).

[2] When the change was made the Ministry of Labour explained that 'one result of this (the adoption of the standard industrial classification) is that, as the compilation of figures of average earnings and hours on the new basis is not practicable for past dates, no precise comparison of the figures for industry groups derived from earlier enquiries is available'. (*Ministry of Labour Gazette*, March 1949, pp. 83–4). But there is no explanation why such compilation 'is not practicable for past dates'.

[3] At first the inquiries were taken and published at irregular intervals. Figures of hours worked, and therefore of hourly as well as weekly earnings, were not obtained until the inquiry for July 1943, and the tables for July 1946 gave weekly earnings for all employees only, without separate figures for men, women, youths and girls. The following is a full list of the inquiries taken between 1940 and 1947, when the current series started, together with the issues of the *Ministry of Labour Gazette* in which the results were published:

Date of inquiry	July 1940	July 1941	Jan. 1942	July 1942	Jan. 1943	July 1943
Date of publication in *Ministry of Labour Gazette*	March 1941	Nov. and Dec. 1941	June 1942	Dec. 1942	June 1943	Feb. 1944

Figures of average earnings can also be worked out from the Census of Production and of Distribution. The Census of Production [1] gives for each trade figures of the average number of workers employed and their remuneration during the year, showing separately operatives, and administrative, technical and clerical staff. This division corresponds to that between wage earners and salary earners, [2] so figures can be worked out of the average wage and the average salary earned. But only for the total of each group, since the figures of earnings are not analysed by either age or sex.

The Census of Distribution reports give figures for wages and salaries together. Average earnings figures which would be obtained by dividing such figures by the total numbers of employees, including part-time workers, would not be of much significance.

Before the war information about wage earnings appeared much less frequently, but in some respects was much more detailed. Inquiries similar to the current ones were taken by the Ministry of Labour in 1924, 1928, 1931, 1935 and 1938. [3] The 1938 inquiry was in much greater detail than any of the others or those taken since. The forms asked for earnings for each worker, not merely for the total wage-bill. This made it possible to work out dispersions of earnings in each industry, as well as mere averages. [4]

Date of inquiry	Jan. 1944	July 1944	Jan. 1945	July 1945	Jan. 1946	July 1946
Date of publication in *Ministry of Labour Gazette*	Aug. 1944	Feb. 1945	Aug. 1945	Feb. 1946	July 1946	Oct. 1946

Figures of average earnings from 1948 onwards, as well as for earlier periods, are given for broad industrial groups in the *Annual Abstract of Statistics No.* 90, 1953 (H.M.S.O., 1953), Table 131, p. 119.

[1] For the coverage of the Census of Production see Chapter IV, p. 81.

[2] See p. 193.

[3] See *Ministry of Labour Gazette* for June 1926–September 1927, October–December 1929, January–March 1933, and February–July 1937 for the results for 1924, 1928, 1931 and 1935. The results of the 1938 inquiry were published together with the figures for July 1940 in the *Ministry of Labour Gazette* for November and December 1940 and March 1941.

[4] Only the average figures of earnings have been officially published in the *Ministry of Labour Gazette*. Tables on the distribution of earnings, medians, quartiles and deciles, as well as interesting figures on time,

Information collected by the Ministry of Labour was also used in the Censuses of Production for 1924, 1930 and 1935.[1] The whole of the information on wage earnings for the inter-war period has been exhaustively and meticulously examined by the Department of Applied Economics, Cambridge.[2] This is a model piece of research in carefully piecing together a large variety of statistical sources and making the best estimates to fill the gaps. It is certain to be the standard work of reference on this subject for the inter-war period.

The most comprehensive and detailed earnings inquiry ever undertaken in this country was in 1906. A great deal of information was also obtained in an earlier inquiry, the first of its kind, in 1886. The 1906 inquiry[3] published in a series of volumes each covering a group of industries, gave figures of earnings by individual occupations within each industry, by intervals of 1/-, by areas, and even by individual towns. There were also tables about hours of work in relation to earnings. We may have progressed since 1906 in the frequency of earnings inquiries, but we are still very much behind in the detail, comprehensiveness and usefulness of the information obtained.

THE MOVEMENT OF WAGE-RATES AND THE MOVEMENT OF AVERAGE WAGE EARNINGS

The index of wage-rates measures changes in the standard rate of pay for a normal week; the figures of wage earnings give the actual earnings per week paid by employers. These two sets of figures may move quite closely together, but they may also

piece-rate and overtime earnings are given in R. B. Ainsworth, 'Earnings and Working Hours of Manual Wage-Earners in the United Kingdom, 1938', *Journal of the Royal Statistical Society*, series A, vol. CXII, pt. I (1949), pp. 35-66.

[1] These figures were collected on a voluntary basis and are not comprehensive. The coverage of the figures varied a great deal, being highest for coal-mining (97 per cent) and lowest for the timber trades (49 per cent).

[2] A. L. Chapman and R. Knight, *Wages and Salaries in the United Kingdom*, 1920-1938 (Cambridge, 1953), No. 5 of Studies in the National Income and Expenditure of the United Kingdom (general editor, Richard Stone).

[3] *Report of an Enquiry by the Board of Trade into Earnings and Hours of Labour of Workpeople of the United Kingdom*, 1906 (H.M.S.O., 1909).

diverge substantially.[1] One can best appreciate the reasons for such divergence by outlining some of the factors which may influence the average level of earnings, but which are not measured in the wage-rate index. Earnings are affected by changes in the amount of overtime or short time worked but no account is taken of this in the wage-rate index. If the standard working week is reduced, say from 48 to 44 hours, and the weekly rate of pay is left unchanged, this change would have no effect on the wage-rate index. But if the workers go on working 48 hours a week they will now get four hours' pay at overtime rates, and average earnings will go up. The rates on which the wage-rate index is based are usually the minima agreed in national bargaining and they take no account of local or factory agreements, bonuses or special incentive payments, all of which will influence the figures of average earnings. Earnings on piece-rate may increase, because of improved machinery, better methods of organization, or greater effort, even though there is no change in rates. Lastly, average earnings may increase because people move to the more highly paid occupations and industries or because of regrading and more rapid promotion. But since the wage-rate index uses a fixed set of weights in combining the changes in different industries into an average, it takes no account of such movements.

No official analysis is published of the contribution of each of these factors to the divergence between the movement of rates and earnings. The Ministry of Labour used to estimate the effect on average earnings of the changes in distribution of the labour force by industry, sex and age, but no such estimates have been published since 1948.[2]

THE WAGE-BILL

The wage-bill for any industry or group of industries is the total amount paid out in wages during a period, usually a year. The figures of wages paid out in all industries together, that is for the

[1] The evidence available suggests little divergence in the inter-war years, but a substantial difference since 1938. Average earnings of operatives covered by the Ministry of Labour's inquiries were 323 in October 1954, while the wage-rate index for the same group of industries was 232 (October 1938 = 100).

[2] The factors leading to the divergence between rates and earnings have been analysed from time to time in articles in the London and Cambridge Economic Service.

country as a whole, is often referred to as the 'national wage-bill'.

The wage-bill for particular industries can be obtained either directly from returns of wages paid during the year or by multiplying estimates of average earnings per worker by the average number of operatives employed. Figures of total wages paid during the year are given in the Census of Production.[1] For the industries covered by the Ministry of Labour inquiries and others for which similar data are available, the wage-bills can also be worked out by multiplying average earnings by the number of operatives employed. But the Ministry of Labour's figures relate to only two weeks in the year, one in March and one in October, and in using them to calculate average earnings for the whole year, holidays, short time, overtime, sickness, and absenteeism must all be taken into account.

Figures of the national wage-bill, and of the wage-bills of the major groups of industry, are now published regularly in the Blue Book on *National Income and Expenditure*.[2] The analysis for manufacturing industry, based on the Census of Production, is more detailed than for the rest of the economy. There is not sufficient information to distinguish wages from salaries in distribution, insurance, banking and finance and other services, and for these groups a single figure is given of wages and salaries together. These figures are referred to as 'income from employment'. Detailed estimates of the wage-bills in the inter-war years are given in the Cambridge study,[3] and the most useful series for the period before 1914 is that made by Bowley.[4]

WAGES AFTER TAX AND REAL WAGES

When there are substantial changes in the taxes paid on wage incomes, as in recent years, crude figures of money wage-rates and

[1] The Census of Distribution does not distinguish between wages and salaries. The information obtained by the Board of Inland Revenue under P.A.Y.E. also covers wages and salaries together.

[2] See, for example, *National Income and Expenditure*, 1946–1952 (H.M.S.O., 1953), Tables 11 and 12, pp. 18–21.

Estimates of regional wages-bills by industries in 1948 are given by Deane, 'Regional Variations in United Kingdom Incomes from Employment', *Journal of the Royal Statistical Society*, series A, vol. CXVI, pt. I (1953), p. 126.

[3] Chapman and Knight, *Wages and Salaries in the United Kingdom*, 1920–1935 (Cambridge, 1953).

[4] Bowley, *Wages and Income in the United Kingdom since 1860* (Cambridge, 1937), pp. 76–7.

money earnings cannot be used as a measure of changes in what the worker has available to spend. There are no published figures of wage-bills, wage-rates or wage earnings after tax,[1] but individual firms must have a great deal of information from the records that are kept in administering P.A.Y.E.

All the figures so far discussed are of money wage-rates, wage-bills or earnings. If we want to measure changes in 'real' wage-rates or 'real' earnings or the 'real' wages-bills, we must allow for changes in prices. Here the problem is to get a price index which measures adequately the prices of the goods and services on which wages are spent.[2]

SALARY-RATES AND THE SALARY-BILL

It has already been suggested that the distinction between wages and salaries is in many respects arbitrary.[3] On the present definition used in statistics in this country the salariat is a much less homogeneous group than the wage earners. The salariat includes, for example, clerical workers of the most junior grade as well as the most senior and highly paid administrative staff in business. Since salaried workers comprise a highly heterogeneous group with wide variations in incomes, little significance can be attached to figures of the average salary earned in particular industries or in industry as a whole.

There are much fewer published statistics about salaries than about wages. There is no index of salary-rates. It is true that there is a great deal of information about salary-rates in particular occupations[4] and it would be an interesting and useful piece of research to try to bring all this together; but it has not yet been done.[5] A useful private inquiry into clerical salaries has been

[1] Figures of wage-bills after tax used to be given in the Blue Book (see *National Income and Expenditure*, 1946–1951 (H.M.S.O., 1953), Table 14, p. 26), but since the issue for 1952 only a single figure has been given for all employee income after tax, that is, wages and salaries, pay in cash and kind of the Forces and Employers' insurance and pension contributions.

[2] See Chapter VII, pp. 189–90.

[3] See pp. 192–3.

[4] The information relates mainly to the public services, national and local; there is little about salary rates in private business or the nationalized industries.

[5] An attempt has been made to calculate a salary index for teachers. See F. Conway, 'An Index of Teachers' Salaries', *Bulletin of the Oxford University Institute of Statistics,* vol. xv, nos. 6 and 7 (1953), pp. 237–48.

taken at intervals over the last ten years by the Office Management Association,[1] and salary-bills are given in the Census of Production. But these two together cover only a small part of the salariat. No doubt estimates can also be made by the official statisticians for salaried workers in central and local government, the armed forces and certain public authorities.

The remaining source of information about salaries is the Board of Inland Revenue. Before 1943–4, incomes taxed under Schedule E were divided into incomes assessed annually and incomes assessed half-yearly.[2] This corresponded roughly to the distinction between salaried workers and manual wage-earners.[3] But since P.A.Y.E. was introduced for all employees in 1943–4 no distinction has been made between different categories of workers. The Board of Inland Revenue now publishes figures for all employees together in some detail by industries [4] and for 1949–50 by counties.[5] These figures can be used to estimate the wage- and salary-bill together, both in total and for groups of industries.[6]

Figures of the annual salary-bill are now given regularly in the Blue Book on *National Income and Expenditure* for the same groups of industries as are given for the wage-bill.[7]

[1] Surveys were made in 1942, 1946, 1948, 1950 and 1952. The results of the 1952 inquiry, with comparative figures for earlier years, are published in *Clerical Salaries Analysis*, 1952 (Office Management Association, n.d.). This publication also includes a useful set of tables on salary scales of clerks in government departments and other large organizations (Section D, pp. 58–68).

[2] See, for example, *Report of the Commissioners of Inland Revenue for the year ended 31st March*, 1944 (Cmd. 6773, H.M.S.O., 1946), p. 24.

[3] On this basis shop assistants were classified as non-manual salaried workers. This accounts for the traditional treatment of shop assistants as salaried workers before 1952 (see p. 193).

[4] See, for example, *Report of the Commissioners of Inland Revenue for the year ended 31st March* 1953 (Cmd. 9030, H.M.S.O., 1954), Table 54, p. 73.

[5] *Report of the Commissioners of Inland Revenue for the year ended 31st March* 1952 (Cmd. 8726, H.M.S.O., 1953), Tables 90–185, pp. 98–145.

[6] The crude figures would have to be adjusted to take account of such factors as incomes below the income tax exemption limit and incomes in kind.

[7] See p. 206.

For the inter-war years daring, and often hazardous, estimates of salary bills have been made in the Cambridge study.[1]

OTHER INCOMES, RENT, INTEREST, PROFITS

The most important source of information about other incomes is the annual Blue Book on *National Income and Expenditure* and this is discussed in Chapter IX. In addition to the figures published in the National Income Blue Books, valuable analyses of non-wage and salary incomes are published in the annual reports of the Commissioners of Inland Revenue, and these analyses have been much extended in recent years. Beginning with the report for the year ended 31 March 1949 an analysis is given each year of assessments to income-tax under Schedule D[2] by main industrial trading groups, and in the first set of tables comparative figures were given for 1937–8, 1938–9, and 1939–40. Since these figures relate to income-tax assessments they are reckoned after the deduction of profits-tax.[3] The Standard Industrial Classification is used, but the analysis is necessarily in terms of financial units and not establishments. The figures are therefore not comparable with those in the Census of Production or the Ministry of Labour's publications, where the classification is on an establishment basis.

A more detailed analysis of the operating figures of companies,[4] also by industrial groups, was started for 1949–50, with comparative figures for 1938–9. These show turnover, the main items of costs, stock changes, trading profit, depreciation, losses, other income, and the distribution of income and taxation.[5] For a

[1] Chapman and Knight, *op. cit.*

[2] Schedule D covers business profits, professional income, interest and income from abroad (except income from British, Dominion and foreign government securities, where tax is deducted at the source) and various miscellaneous sources of income.

[3] There are other reasons why they do not agree with figures of profits shown in the National Income Blue Book. See *National Income and Expenditure,* 1946–1951 (H.M.S.O., 1952), p. 70, n 1.

[4] Excluding individual traders and partners, local authorities, nationalized industries and co-operative societies.

[5] See, for example, *Inland Revenue Report, year ended 31st March 1953* (Cmd. 9030, H.M.S.O., 1954).

sample of these for 1949–50[1] and 1950–1[2] there is a similar analysis of outgoings by ratio of profit to turnover. These tables now give a valuable new mass of information about company operation which has hardly yet been used in economic analysis or research.

The published accounts and balance sheets of public companies give important information about a large section of business. But they have been largely ignored by economists and statisticians as a source of material for economic and statistical analysis. This may be because an expert knowledge of accounting and company law is necessary to interpret them correctly. *The Economist* attempts to bring this information together in a usable form. Summaries of company results are compiled every week and each quarter there is a more elaborate analysis of company balance sheets, profits and earnings.[3] *The Economist* has been publishing statistics based on company reports for many years, and the provisions of the Companies Act, 1948, requiring much fuller and more satisfactory company accounts, have made possible a much more elaborate and reliable analysis than anything which could be done previously. Similar information is published by the *Financial Times*.

THE DISTRIBUTION OF INCOMES

The statistics of incomes that we have discussed so far relate to income by type or form of payment. But an individual may receive incomes from many different sources and if we are interested in the distribution of incomes by size, we must have

[1] *Inland Revenue Report, year ended 31st March* 1951 (Cmd. 8436, H.M.S.O., 1952), Tables 68–83, pp. 74–89.

[2] *Inland Revenue Report, year ended 31st March* 1952 (Cmd. 8726, H.M.S.O., 1953), Tables 67–81, pp. 71–85.

[3] For a description of the basis of the current analysis see *The Economist*, 22 January 1949, pp. 152–3 and *Records of Statistics* supplement for the same date, pp. 90–1. While the *Records and Statistics Supplement to The Economist* was published the weekly company results and quarterly analysis were included in that supplement, but there was usually a quarterly article discussing the figures in *The Economist* itself. Since the publication of the supplement stopped at the end of June 1953, the quarterly analysis is given in *The Economist* itself (the issue for 1 August 1953, for example, pp. 351–2, gives figures for April–June 1953), but the weekly summaries of company results are not now published.

figures of total incomes of individuals from whatever source they come. Here again the main information is from assessments of income for income-tax, for the rate of tax is related to the size of income and the taxing authorities have therefore to obtain from each individual subject to tax figures of his income from all sources.

A summary of income distribution by size of income is now given in the National Income Blue Book [1] and more detailed figures are given in the Board of Inland Revenue reports. The Blue Book figures are by ranges of income before tax, but the Board of Inland Revenue reports give a distribution by post-tax incomes as well. The Blue Book includes estimates of personal incomes below the taxation exemption limits, and allocates certain transfer incomes to income ranges, but these are excluded from the Board of Inland Revenue tables. The Board of Inland Revenue also analyses incomes by family circumstances, and gives an analysis of earned and investment income for incomes of £2000 and over. [2]

Much more detailed information about the distribution of income is available for 1949–50 from the sample analysis undertaken by the Board of Inland Revenue for that year. This gives very extensive information by type of income, family circumstances and county. [3] The previous detailed income analysis, less elaborate than the recent one, was taken for 1937–8. [4]

The interpretation and analysis of the figures of income distribution given in the Board of Inland Revenue reports is difficult. Only the main points to be borne in mind are mentioned here. [5] The figures cover only income assessed to tax on

[1] For some unstated reason no figures were given in the National Income Blue Book for 1946–51.

[2] That is, above the sur-tax limit.

[3] *Inland Revenue Report, year ended 31st March* 1951 (Cmd. 8436, H.M.S.O., 1952), Tables 90–109, pp. 97–116 and Tables 111–15, pp. 118–127; and *Inland Revenue Report, year ended 31st March* 1952 (Cmd. 8726, H.M.S.O., 1953), Tables 90–185, pp. 93–145.

[4] *Inland Revenue Report, year ended 31st March* 1940 (Cmd. 6769, H.M.S.O., 1946), Tables 21–22, pp. 32–39.

[5] For a detailed analysis of some of the figures see: The following series of articles by E. C. Rhodes in *Economica*: 'The inequality of incomes in the United Kingdom', vol. XIX, no. 74 (1952), pp. 168–75; 'The distribution of incomes and the burden of estate duties in the United Kingdom', vol. XVIII, no. 71 (1951), pp. 270–7; 'Distribution

individuals. The income excluded therefore consists of two parts; that which is not subject to tax and that which, although subject to tax, cannot be allocated to individual income ranges. The main items in the first category are interest on National Savings Certificates, dividends paid by co-operative societies, allowances of the armed forces, incomes in kind, certain transfer incomes, the investment income of charities and incomes below the exemption limit.[1] In the second category the main items are the investment income of life assurance funds and the undistributed profits of companies.[2]

The figures are related to incomes as defined for income-tax purposes. Usually a man and his wife are assessed together, and their two incomes together would be counted as one. The figures cannot, however, be treated as 'family incomes' since they do not classify incomes by ranges including earnings of children and other members of the household. Some of the income ranges cover a heterogeneous group of people in different real economic circumstances and at different stages of their earning capacity. The lowest range from £135 to £150, for example, covers young people just starting their first job,[3] perhaps part-time workers, retired people with a small income, as well as married men with families working in the lowest grades of the worst-paid occupations.

The figures do not all relate to incomes in the same year. The basis is the incomes assessed during the year. Wages and salaries are assessed under Schedule E and tax is paid on earnings in the

of earned and investment income in the United Kingdom in 1937–38', vol. XVIII, no. 69 (1951), pp. 18–34; 'Distribution of incomes in the United Kingdom in 1938 and 1947', vol. XVII, no. 66 (1950), pp. 146–58. Also T. Barna, *Redistribution of Incomes through Public Finance in 1937* (Oxford, 1945), especially pp. 63–75. D. Seers, *The Cost of Living and The Distribution of Income since 1938* (Oxford, Basil Blackwell, 1949).

[1] The exemption limit was £125 from 1935–6 to 1940–1, £110 from 1941–2 to 1945–6, and £120 in 1946–7 to 1947–8, and £135 from 1948–9 to 1951–2. It was then superseded by the small income relief, giving an effective exemption limit of £155.

[2] Attempts have been made to impute undistributed profits to income ranges; see, for example, T. Barna, *op. cit.*, pp. 92–4.

[3] The preponderance of single males and females in this category can be seen in the figures derived from the census for 1949–50. See *Inland Revenue Report, year ended 31st March* 1951 (Cmd. 8436, H.M.S.O., 1952), Tables III–15, pp. 118–27.

current year under P.A.Y.E., but most other assessments are made on incomes in the previous year. The special census for 1949–50 therefore relates in the main to salaries, wages and dividends earned or received in 1949–50, but to profits and professional earnings in 1948–9.

In addition to the peculiarities in the figures resulting from the administration of income-tax one must allow for evasion and non-declaration of income. There is apparently a considerable deficiency in the declaration of income from interest and dividends which are taxed at the source; an omission of a substantial number of married women in employment; and probably, before recent legislation, substantial non-declaration of interest on small savings. The Board of Inland Revenue has attempted to allow for the first two of these deficiencies in its summary estimates of income distribution for 1949–50. But although these deficiencies presumably also affect estimates for earlier years, no revised estimates of the back figures have been published.

It is clear that many special features of the income figures must be taken into account if they are to be used without error. Indeed, here is a classic example of the way in which statistics derived from administration reflect all the quirks and peculiarities of that administration.

CHAPTER IX

NATIONAL INCOME AND EXPENDITURE

EARLY estimates of the national income were designed to measure the total income of the community as evidence of its changing productive capacity and standard of living. Although other useful information was collected in making the calculations, attention was concentrated on the final figures of total income. In recent years work on the national income has been progressively extended to throw light on many different aspects of the working of the economy, and the estimates are no longer primarily concerned with figures of the total income of the nation.

Official calculations of national income and expenditure were first made in this country during the Second World War and the results published in an annual series of White Papers. From 1941 to 1951 there was a single annual White Paper published at the time of the Budget, giving figures for the previous year and earlier years for comparison. Since 1952 a White Paper published in the spring has given preliminary estimates of the main figures only. This has been followed by a Blue Book in August with final figures in much more extensive detail.

The scope of the official calculations has been extended most remarkably since the first estimates were made. Year by year problems of definition are cleared up, tables are given in greater detail, new topics are dealt with and the accuracy of the figures improved as new sources of information become available. But these developments and improvements inevitably have certain drawbacks. They frequently mean substantial revision in the figures from one Blue Book to the next, not merely because the accuracy of the estimates has been improved but also because the coverage or meaning of particular terms or headings is altered. It is most dangerous, therefore, to use different Blue Books or White Papers to get a continuous series of figures over a period of years. Sometimes it is possible after careful scrutiny of any difference in coverage and definition to adjust the figures taken from publications for different years to a comparable basis. But this is usually much too difficult and hazardous a task for the general user or beginner.

Fortunately the present series of Blue Books give a continuous run of figures for each year back to 1946,[1] and there are, therefore, revised figures on the basis of the definitions used in 1954 for each of the years from 1946 to 1953. Figures for 1938 on as nearly a comparable basis as possible with those given in the latest Blue Book have been published in the *Annual Abstract of Statistics*.[2]

The calculation and interpretation of national income and expenditure statistics raises many complicated theoretical and practical problems and there is now a very extensive literature on the subject. The Blue Books themselves contain much explanatory material and voluminous notes on the definition and meaning of particular items.[3]

It is well beyond the scope of this book to deal at all comprehensively with all these problems. Some of the simpler problems only will be discussed here, and an attempt made to explain broadly what the estimates are about, how they are made, how accurate and reliable they are, and in what sorts of ways they can be used.

NATIONAL INCOME

In national income statistics the economic activity of the nation is looked at from three different aspects: as income, as production and as expenditure. Alternatively the activities are portrayed in a set of social accounts, which aggregates the transactions of significant economic entities—for example, individuals, businesses,

[1] Or 1948 when the information is not available for earlier years.

[2] See *Annual Abstracts of Statistics, No.* 91, 1954 (H.M.S.O., 1954), Tables 282–97, pp. 246 ff.

[3] The explanation and notes are not all repeated in each Blue Book. The first of the series (1946–1951) has an 'Introduction' explaining the tables in general terms as well as 'Notes' at the end commenting on the definition and coverage of individual tables and items. In the second issue (1946–52), the 'Introduction' was omitted, but there was a fairly full but not comprehensive set of notes at the end. In the latest issue (1946–1953) fairly full notes are given for the 'Summary Tables', but there are only notes for the other tables where there is some special change worthy of comment. Attention is also drawn to any major revision in the estimates for earlier years. For a complete set of notes, therefore, one has to consult all the Blue Books so far issued.

and Government organizations—and shows the inter-relations between them.

We think of economic activity in terms of the incomes which are derived from it, when we discuss such questions as the distribution of income, the part of income that is taken in taxation, or the part that is saved. Figures on these subjects are frequently used in public discussion, and there is endless room for misunderstanding and confusion as well as for deliberate deception because of the various ways in which these terms may be defined.

Factor incomes and transfer payments

The first important distinction is between 'factor' incomes and 'transfer' incomes. Factor incomes are earned for performing some economic service which contributes to production, 'production' being used in a wide sense to cover services of all kinds, including service in the Armed Forces. Transfer incomes, on the other hand, are incomes for which there is no corresponding contribution to production. The most important transfer incomes are money payments under the various social insurance schemes and interest on the national debt.[1] If we want a total of incomes which corresponds to the total value of goods produced, we must, therefore, include only factor incomes. And if we want to see the proportions of incomes which go to the various 'factors of production'—labour, land, capital, and so on—it is the distribution of this total of factor incomes which is relevant. When the term 'national income' is used by itself, without qualification, it is usually meant in this sense of the total of incomes of factors of production.

Gross and net national incomes

Capital equipment is used in producing incomes. If we calculate the income of firms or the community as a whole before allowing for that part of income that needs to be set on one side

[1] The national debt was largely incurred during wars and the money raised spent on equipment and services which were fully used up in those wars. There is, therefore, no real capital in existence corresponding to the money debt.

to replace the capital used up in the process of production, we have 'gross income'. If we subtract depreciation, the term usually used for such an allowance, we have 'net income'.

There is, however, little accurate statistical information about the sums that should be set on one side for depreciation year by year to maintain capital intact. Practically the only general information is what the Board of Inland Revenue allows for depreciation in calculating 'net' incomes for tax purposes. One could subtract these taxation depreciation allowances from gross incomes and arrive at figures of net incomes and of the net national income, but it is doubtful whether such figures would have much significance. This is because there is a great deal of controversy as to whether the depreciation allowance for taxation purposes corresponds at all closely with what is really needed to replace used-up equipment, and also because the taxation provisions for such allowances have varied considerably from year to year recently. For these reasons nearly all the figures of incomes in the main body of the Blue Book are now given on a gross basis, that is before deducting depreciation.[1] It is important to keep this in mind in making calculations from the Blue Book of the share of the national income which goes to the various factors of production.

Incomes before and after allowing for stock appreciation

In years of falling or rising prices the figures of income, especially of profits, are affected by the way in which stocks and work in progress are valued. If prices are rising, the value of stocks and work in progress at the end of the year will be greater than at the beginning even if the volume of stocks has not changed. In general, accounting and taxation practice in this

[1] In the Blue Book for 1946–1951 and the White Papers for earlier years most of the income figures in the main tables were given 'net', not 'gross'.

Figures of depreciation are, however, given in the notes at the end of the Blue Book. See, for example, the Blue Book for 1946–1953, p. 88. An important point to note in using these figures is that depreciation for 'farmers' is on a current replacement basis, for 'public corporations' is what the corporations actually allow in their accounts, while for all the others, excluding Government trading, it is the depreciation allowance used by the Board of Inland Revenue for tax assessments.

country counts this rise as part of profits. But a mere increase in value as distinct from volume adds nothing to the real national income of the country. So if we want a true figure of national income we must deduct from the crude figures of incomes and profits this element of stock appreciation.

Unfortunately accurate estimates of stock appreciation or depreciation are very difficult to make. Figures are published in the Blue Book, but the warning is given that they are rough estimates and are open to a substantial margin of error. These figures are used to adjust the crude figures of total national income and expenditure to a basis which excludes the element of stock appreciation. But stock appreciation is not known in sufficient detail to make possible an adjustment of the individual constituents of total income and expenditure, so that most of the figures given in the Blue Book, apart from the national totals, are gross of stock appreciation or depreciation.

Distribution of incomes

The Blue Book gives a great deal of information about the distribution of the national income between factors, but the categories used reflect the peculiarities of the statistical sources rather than the usage of economic theory. As was explained in an earlier chapter, much of the information about incomes is obtained from income-tax statistics, and the analysis of incomes which is given in the Blue Book reflects income-tax law and practice. The main categories used are 'the income of employees'—wages, salaries, and the pay of the armed forces; [1] 'the income of self-employed persons'—farmers, professional persons, sole traders, and partnerships; 'the trading profits of corporate bodies'—companies, public corporations, and other public enterprises; [2] 'rent'; and 'net income from abroad'. None of these corresponds closely to the categories—labour, capital, land and enterprise—used in economic theory. The income of self-employed persons is a compound of labour income, interest and profit, and it is impossible to draw a meaningful distinction in the income of corporate bodies between true interest on

---

[1] Also employers' contributions to National insurance and to pension funds, which are treated in the Blue Book as part of factor incomes.

[2] Such as the trading activities of the central government.

capital, rent[1] and profit. The share of total national income received by each of these groups is often calculated and used in analysing the distribution of income. The peculiar coverage of each of these categories should be kept in mind in using such figures.

When we want to consider how incomes are distributed by size, we must include 'transfer' incomes as well as 'factor' incomes. Incomes then fall into three groups: first, the incomes of individuals; second, that part of the income of businesses which is not distributed to shareholders; and third, the income which public authorities receive from owning property or trading. In the Blue Book the first group of income is called 'personal income' and the second 'undistributed income'.[2] Both are derived from figures of factor incomes which include depreciation and stock appreciation, and they are, therefore, gross of these two items. It is not possible to distinguish between the business and personal incomes of farmers, professional persons and unincorporated businesses, so the whole of the incomes of these groups are included in 'personal' incomes. In other words the income of businesses in this group is treated as if it were all distributed and none of it retained in the business.[3]

Figures of the distribution of income by size of income, which are derived from income-tax statistics, are available for personal incomes only, and even for these exclude certain categories of income, such as interest on saving certificates and co-operative society dividends, which are not subject to tax. Private estimates have, however, been made of the distribution of incomes including such non-taxable income.[4]

---

[1] For example, where buildings are owned by the company an imputed rent is included in the company's income, but this is then counted as part of trading profit, not as rent. The imputed rent of owner-occupied houses, however, is included under 'rent'.

[2] In earlier official publications there used also to be a group called 'private income'—personal incomes plus the undistributed incomes of business—but this term has now dropped out of use.

[3] The category of 'personal' incomes also includes other incomes which are not in fact at the disposal of individuals. For example, the income of charities and educational institutions, and employers' contributions to superannuation and other pension funds.

[4] See Chapter VIII, pp. 210 ff., for a more detailed discussion of statistics of income distribution.

Proportion of incomes paid in taxes

Personal incomes are either spent on consumption, paid in taxation or saved; corporate incomes are either distributed as dividends and interest, paid in taxation, or saved. The Blue Book analyses the distribution of these two groups of income in this way.

In calculating what part of income goes to taxation, a distinction has to be drawn between the provision for taxation and actual tax payments during the year. This distinction is again a reflection of income-tax law and administration. Most businesses and professional persons, except those on a salary, are assessed for tax in any year on the income earned in the previous year. If the income in the current year is different from that of the previous year, the liability for tax arising out of the current year's income is different from what actually has to be paid to the Exchequer during the year. If income is higher in the current year than in the previous year, the liability is greater than the payment; if it is lower, the liability is less. The authors of the Blue Book assume that a prudent business will place to taxation reserve the difference between its liability for tax on current income [1] and the actual payments it has to make during the year. This difference between 'provisions for taxation' and 'payments' is shown as 'additions to tax reserves'.[2] We get different figures therefore for the proportion of income taken in taxation according to whether we include or exclude this item; and in years of rapidly rising or falling incomes the difference may be quite substantial.[3]

'Additions to tax reserves' are not part of Government income during the year since they are not paid to the Exchequer. But if we count them as taxation in the distribution of personal and corporate income, they will not appear as part of private savings. From the national point of view, however, they are available as savings for investment during the year and we must be careful not to overlook them when we come to add up all the

[1] After an adjustment for any excess or deficiency of provision in th previous year due to a change in the tax-rates.

[2] This will be negative when liabilities for tax on current income ar less than payments.

[3] In 1951, for example, provision for taxation was £1164 million out o undistributed corporate income of £2515 million; payment of taxatio was only £714 million.

various sources of saving to arrive at figures of total national savings.[1]

The figures of taxes paid by corporate businesses given in the Blue Book do not correspond to the figures of taxation paid out of profits which are now a regular feature of company accounts and the annual speeches of company chairmen. The figures which company chairmen quote usually refer to the amounts actually paid to the Exchequer,[2] including income-tax at the standard rate on interest and dividends distributed to shareholders. The figures of corporate tax in the Blue Book relate only to profits-tax and income-tax on undistributed income, the income-tax on interest and dividends paid on behalf of shareholders being shown as part of personal taxation.[3]

The proportion of personal income taken in taxation can be defined in many different ways. We can take taxes on income alone; we can include the payments made under the compulsory national insurance schemes;[4] and we can include the indirect taxation element[5] in consumers' expenditure. The Blue Book now shows each of these separately, but the figure of the proportion of personal income going to taxation[6] which is usually quoted includes all three. In the main tables on incomes the figures of personal and corporate income paid in taxation relate to taxes on income only. Similarly in arriving at the total of personal and corporate incomes, only transfers which are considered as income are included. Death duties and special contributions are treated as capital taxes, and refunds of excess profits tax, war damage compensation, war gratuities and pay credits are treated as transfers to capital accounts.[7]

[1] See p. 221.

[2] Or the provision for payment to the Exchequer.

[3] In the Blue Book for 1946–1953, figures of tax provisions by companies, including the tax paid on distributions made by the companies, are given in the Notes (see Blue Book, p. 84).

[4] Both employees' and employers' contributions, for employers' contributions are counted as part of gross wages and salaries.

[5] Net of subsidies.

[6] 26 per cent in 1952.

[7] The distinction between transfers to capital and transfers to income accounts is bound to be arbitrary to some extent. For example, repayment of income tax credits is treated as a transfer to income, although refunds of excess profits tax are treated as payments to capital.

Saving

If we subtract interest, dividends and provision for taxation from corporate income, we are left with a residual figure of corporate savings. And if we subtract consumers' expenditure and provision for taxation from personal income, we are left with a residual figure of personal savings. The income figures in the Blue Book with which we start are gross of depreciation and stock appreciation; so in both cases the residual figures of savings will include provision for these two items. But it is only after these have been subtracted that we get figures of true 'net' savings. However, as has been explained, the figures of depreciation and stock appreciation are only rough estimates and we cannot, at present, arrive at accurate figures of 'net' saving.

There is thus plenty of room for confusion in using the published figures of savings. For example, if we take corporate and personal savings [1] together in 1951, gross of depreciation and stock appreciation and including additions to tax and dividend reserves, we have a figure of £2109 million; if we deduct tax and dividend reserves, this is reduced to £1588 million; if we deduct the rough estimate for stock appreciation, this is reduced to £931 million; and if we deduct depreciation allowances as well, it is reduced to £191 million. We must also remember that for reasons given earlier,[2] none of these figures take account of taxes on capital or of transfers from the Government to capital account. If we include these, we would have yet another figure for private savings of £79 million. Clearly it is most dangerous to quote figures for private saving without explaining what is included.

NATIONAL PRODUCT

Relation between national product and national income

If we view economic activity as production, we can see the con-

---

[1] The addition of personal and corporate savings gives us figures of private saving. If we want figures of national saving, we must add to this the savings of the Government. Here we must construe 'Government' in the widest sense to cover not only the central government, but also local government, and the funds of such authorities as the National Insurance Funds which are not included in the central government budget.

Figure of saving for the three sectors together—persons, companies and Government, are now given regularly in the Blue Books.

[2] See p. 221.

tribution which each sector of the economy—industry, agriculture, distribution, and so on—makes to the total national output, and the interrelations between production in different sectors. The contribution that each sector makes to production is measured by the value that the sector adds to the goods and services that it buys from other sectors or from abroad. The 'value added' by each sector will be equal to the total of the wages, salaries, rent paid and the gross profit made. The total of the value added by each sector should therefore add up to the figures of the total incomes paid to factors of production, that is, to the national income at factor cost.

There are two important qualifications that have to be made to this statement. First, the total of factor payments includes net income received on property and investment held abroad. Unless we define production as including such income, the total value of production will not add up to the total of factor incomes. The present practice in the Blue Book is to call production excluding net income from abroad the 'domestic product', and production including income from abroad the 'national product'. Secondly, the total value of production will only be equal to the total national income if production is valued net of payments of indirect taxes and subsidies, that is, the value paid to the factors of production employed, or at factor cost.

Just as we can have incomes gross or net, before or after allowing for capital depreciation, so we can have 'national product', in total or for each industry, 'gross' or 'net'. All the product figures given in the Blue Book are 'gross'. Even the gross figures should exclude stock appreciation, but figures of stock appreciation are at present available only for production as a whole and not for individual industrial groups. The figures for the product of individual industries given in the Blue Book are, therefore, gross of stock appreciation and depreciation, and a single figure for stock appreciation is subtracted from the total in order to arrive at the 'gross national product' at factor cost.

Government contribution to the national product

There is often confusion and misunderstanding about the meaning of figures of the contribution of the Government to the national product. Public authorities contribute to production either by operating trading services or by providing services which are not sold commercially to the public, but are distributed on some other basis. Trading services, such as the Post Office, the trading operations of the Ministry of Food, local authority housing, and the nationalized industries, are all treated in the same way as other business enterprises, and the value of their product is included with other output in the appropriate industrial group. But services provided free, such as health, education, administration and defence, cannot be valued on a commercial basis. It is normally assumed in national income calculations that the value of such services is equal to what is spent on them. The contribution of the Government, as a producer, to this value is therefore that part of the cost which can be attributed to the wages and salaries of the Government employees who help in providing these services. The remainder of the cost is represented by goods and services bought from other industries and is included in the net product of those industries. Thus the contribution of public authorities to health and educational services consists of the salaries of teachers, doctors, nurses, and other staff. The cost of goods and services bought by public authorities from other industries to provide these services, such as books and furniture for schools or medical supplies for hospitals, is counted as part of the product of those other industries. Similarly the contribution of defence to the national product is largely the pay of the men in the armed forces; the value of the munitions produced for the armed forces being counted as part of the product of manufacturing industry.

Inter-industry relations

The value of the goods sold by any industry is equal to the value of the goods and services which it buys from other industries, or from overseas, plus the value which the industry itself adds in the process of production. The value of the goods the industry produces is also equal to the goods bought from it by other industries (including exports) or final consumers. If we have sufficiently detailed information about each industry's sales and purchases, we can portray statistically the inter-industry relations of the economy. Suppose we take a simple hypothetical case of an economy with three industries A, B, and C and no foreign trade. If we know the value of the output of each of the industries, what each purchases from the others, and the value added by each to production, we can draw up a single statistical statement of the relations between the three industries, as in the following table:

(Values in £ million)

Sales \ Purchase	A	B	C	Final buyers'	Total
A	—	5	5	10	20
B	6	—	3	6	15
C	2	3	—	8	13
Value added (payments to factors: wages, salaries, interest, profits, etc.)	12	7	5	24	—
Total	20	15	13		

Internal transactions within each industry are excluded, so this table presents a picture of the relations between the various industries, each considered as a single unit. In the horizontal rows the output of each industry is shown according to whom it is sold. So industry A's total output of £20 million is made up of sales of £5 million each to industries B and C and £10 million to final consumers. The vertical columns show what each industry purchases to produce its output. Thus industry A's output of £20 million is made up of purchases of £6 million of materials and services from industry B and £2 million from industry C, and £12 million paid in incomes to factors employed in production by A. The total of industry A's purchases including payments to factors is necessarily equal to the total of industry A's sales, for both are the same as the value of its output. Such a table is useful in showing the interdependence of the three industries, and what an expansion in the output of any one would imply in the output of the others.[1]

In practice an inter-industry table is much more complicated than this, not only because a division of the whole economy into three industries would not be very significant, but also because imports and exports, purchases and sales for capital investment,

[1] Assuming that the inter-industry relations are constant.

and indirect taxes and subsidies have to be fitted in. Such tables can only be compiled if there is detailed information about the goods and services bought by each industry. One of the main sources for this is the Census of Production, but the results of the Census are only available after a substantial interval, and detailed information about materials used has not been asked for in each Census. It is mainly for this reason that the tables on inter-industry transactions given in the 1953 and 1954 Blue Books relate to 1950. Tables for 1948 were given in the Blue Book for 1952, but there have been many changes in definition since then and the two sets of figures are not comparable.[1]

NATIONAL EXPENDITURE

Relation between national expenditure, national product and national income

When we are interested in the ways in which the national output is used—how much for consumption, for public services, and for investment, we view economic activity as expenditure. The total expenditure of the community, if defined appropriately, must add up to the total of what is produced—the national product, and the total of the income generated in producing it—the national income. To get this equality, national expenditure must be calculated at 'factor cost', that is, in terms of the payment made to factors of production as a result of the expenditure. The difference between expenditure defined in this way and the actual sums which are spent by consumers and other purchasers is the total of indirect taxes less subsidies, for indirect taxes raise prices above the level of payments to factors, and subsidies lower them below that level. If, therefore, we want to know what proportion of national resources is devoted to particular uses, we use figures of expenditure at 'factor cost'; but if we are interested in the ways in which people actually spend their money, it is expenditure at 'market prices' which is relevant.

All private expenditure, except that part going in indirect

[1] The Board of Trade, in collaboration with the Department of Applied Economics, Cambridge, are compiling a detailed input/output matrix for the year 1948. An unofficial analysis of inter-industry relations for Great Britain has been done for 1935 (see T. Barna, 'The Interdependence of the British Economy', *Journal of the Royal Statistical Society*, series A, vol. cxv, pt. I (1952), pp. 29–81).

taxation, results in payments to factors of production and exercises command over real resources. A large part of Government expenditure is not of this kind, but merely consists of money transfer payments which do not exercise any command over economic resources until the money is spent by the persons or institutions who receive it. The expenditure which corresponds to these payments is the expenditure undertaken by those who receive these transfers as income. When we are viewing national expenditure as a whole, therefore, we must exclude from Government expenditure that part which is merely transfer expenditure; that is, we must add to private expenditure on goods and services Government expenditure on goods and services only.

Expenditure at home, whether private or Government, is partly on goods produced at home and partly on imports.[1] Obversely some of the goods produced at home are not used here, but are exported. Total home expenditure will not, therefore, be equal to total national product, unless imports, which are not part of home production but are part of home expenditure, and exports, which are part of home production but not part of home expenditure, are exactly equal. If exports exceed imports, home expenditure will be less than home production; if imports exceed exports, home expenditure will be greater than home production. In both cases the deficiency or excess of home expenditure compared with home production will correspond to the difference between exports and imports. But this difference between exports and imports corresponds to the balance of payments on current account. If, therefore, we add this balance to domestic expenditure, we have a figure of national expenditure, which, if calculated at factor cost, is equal to national income and national product.

Current and capital expenditure

Expenditure can also be distinguished according to whether it is current or capital expenditure. With one exception—expenditure on new houses—the whole of the expenditure of final consumers is counted as current consumption during the period of the expenditure. Thus expenditure on motor-cars, refrigerators, furniture, radio and television sets, and other goods often classified as durable 'consumer goods', are counted as part of consumption when they are bought. Similarly no account is

[1] Including the 'import content' of home production.

taken of changes in stocks of non-durable consumer goods, such as food, which are held by final consumers. The same applies to the Government holdings of munitions, which are counted as consumed when they are purchased; any increase in stocks is therefore not counted as part of investment.

For private business expenditure the distinction between current and capital corresponds to the commercial and tax distinction between expenditure which is counted as a cost of current output, and that which is counted as adding to the value of the equipment or stocks at the disposal of the business. For Government expenditure the distinction is more difficult, since the Government's operations and methods of accounting, even in some of its trading activities, are not designed with any such distinction in mind. In distinguishing between current and capital expenditure in Government spending, the authors of the Blue Book have, therefore, to proceed by analogy with what is the practice in normal commercial operations. On the borderline these distinctions are inevitably arbitrary. However, when it is decided where to draw the line, the corresponding distinction must be made in exactly the same way in calculating the amount of Government saving, for expenditure made on capital account is by definition counted as saving, and we must, therefore, not count any such expenditure against current income when assessing the Government's current surplus or contribution to national saving.

Gross and net capital expenditure

We can count capital expenditure either gross or net, according to whether we deduct or do not deduct that part of the expenditure which is needed to replace capital used up in the process of production. This distinction corresponds to that between 'gross' and 'net' national income.[1] For reasons already explained,[2] the available information on depreciation is unsatisfactory and cannot be used as a basis for calculating reliable figures of net capital expenditure. All the capital expenditure figures in the current Blue Book are, therefore, calculated gross.

Capital expenditure is made up of three parts. Expenditure on plant, equipment and buildings—now known as 'fixed capital equipment', expenditure on additions to stocks and work in

[1] See pp. 216–17.   [2] See p. 217.

progress, and expenditure on investment or disinvestment overseas. It is only the first item, fixed capital equipment, which is counted gross, covering the whole of expenditure whether additional or for replacement; only the net change in stocks over the period is included in capital expenditure.

The value of the change in stocks over any period reflects changes in prices as well as changes in physical quantities. It is only that part of the change which is the value of the physical increase that we want to include in investment; the rest of the increase in value merely reflects stock appreciation.[1] Overseas capital investment or disinvestment should normally correspond to the surplus or deficit in the balance of payments on current account.[2]

Defined in this way, therefore, capital expenditure is equal to that part of the national product which is not consumed during the year, but is added to the stock of wealth. Fixed capital equipment, houses, the increase in the physical volume of stocks and work in progress, and investment overseas, are all parts of this stock of national wealth or capital. The total of capital expenditure, including overseas investment and the change in stocks, is referred to as 'total gross investment'; if overseas investment is excluded, the term 'gross domestic capital formation' is used, this being made up of 'fixed capital formation' and the 'value of the physical increase in stocks and work in progress'.

The figures of capital expenditure are often expressed as a percentage of total national expenditure and comparisons made with other countries and other years in an attempt to demonstrate that the United Kingdom's capital expenditure is either too high or too low. Sometimes the figure is compared with some percentage which is put forward as the right percentage[3] for the United Kingdom to invest in the interests of economic progress. We cannot stop to discuss the basis on which such comparisons are made. But it is worth while stressing again how easy it is, as with the figures of saving, to get different figures according to the definitions used. Thus one can have investment gross of stock appreciation including or excluding investment overseas; or

[1] See pp. 217–18.
[2] In the present British calculations overseas capital investment or disinvestment is only equal to the balance of payments on current account after allowing for capital grants.
[3] 20 per cent is the favourite.

fixed investment at home; or fixed investment in what is often called productive industry;[1] and all these can be either gross or net of depreciation. Those who want to emphasize the small percentage of resources devoted to investment may make their own estimate of 'true depreciation'. And any of these figures may be calculated as a percentage of national expenditure at market prices or factor cost, or of domestic expenditure. There is endless room for confusion and argument at cross purposes. It is certainly not uncommon to hear one person argue that investment in this country is now higher than it has been since before 1914 and another to argue that it has never been so low before.

One of the difficulties of interpreting the figures is that gross capital investment depends on the arbitrary distinction between current and capital expenditure. Take the change in the treatment of repair and maintenance of buildings as an example. Up to 1951 this was counted as capital expenditure and therefore included as part of gross fixed capital formation. In 1951 normal repair and maintenance was counted as an item of current cost and only 'excess' repair as capital expenditure. In 1952 this excess was also transferred to current costs, so that now only new building work is counted as capital. So in the 1952 Blue Book gross fixed capital formation in 1950 is shown as £1674 million compared with £2162 million given for that year in the 1950 White Paper.

The Blue Book is now the main source of information on capital expenditure. Most of the information given in it is not available in other published sources. More detailed information is available on Government expenditure, both central and local, in published accounts, but these are most complex and difficult to use.

Consumer expenditure

On consumer expenditure there are some useful sources giving more detailed statistics. There is the annual report of the National Food Survey Committee[2] which gives detailed figures both by physical quantities and value of domestic food consumption. The Social Survey has undertaken a large number of

[1] Usually fixed investment excluding housing and other public services, but sometimes investment in manufacturing industry only.
[2] *Domestic Food Consumption and Expenditure* (H.M.S.O.).

enquiries into particular items of expenditure, but these are usually for one date, not continuous series of figures. Similarly the budget inquiry undertaken by the Ministry of Labour will give us much more detail about the pattern of expenditure than is given in the Blue Books,[1] but it will provide us with an analysis for one year only.

Savings and investment

In a simple formulation of national income and expenditure, savings are by definition equal to investment, for savings are merely the difference between the total of income and what is spent on consumption, and investment is merely the difference between total expenditure on goods and services and what is spent on consumption. Since national income and expenditure, if appropriately defined, are equal, savings must be equal to investment. This equality of savings and investment is implicit in the figures given in the Blue Book, but both have to be carefully defined if this equality is to be preserved and confusion avoided. To see how they add up to the total of national savings we must consider the savings of persons, corporate bodies and public authorities together. If we take the savings of persons as equal to gross income less consumption and provision for taxation,[2] and the savings of corporate bodies as equal to their gross income less payments of interest and dividends and provision for taxation, then, when we come to add up the total of national savings, we must include an item for addition to tax reserves, since these reserves are not in fact paid to the Exchequer during the year and are not part of Government revenue. On the other hand, if we want the total of savings to equal gross investment in fixed capital and the value of the physical increase in stocks only, we must deduct that part of gross private savings which merely represents stock appreciation.

In arriving at the savings of public authorities we must define current expenditure to exclude those items which we have decided to include as part of capital investment. We must include not only central and local government savings but also the savings of extra-budgetary funds, such as the National Insurance Funds. In addition, we must take account of transfers to and from private capital accounts which are counted as part of

[1] See pp. 186–7.   [2] See p. 222.

the current revenue and expenditure of the central government. Thus gross national savings will be made up of the following items:

(1) Personal saving
(2) Company saving
(3) Public corporations surplus
(4) Public authorities surplus (central and local government and extra-budgetary funds)
(5) Tax and dividends reserves
(6) Transfers from Government accounts to private capital accounts
(7) *Less* taxes on capital
(8) *Less* provision for stock appreciation.

There is no obvious basis on which to divide these items between private and public saving. Grouping (1), (2), (7) and part [1] of (8) as private savings minimizes private savings and makes public savings relatively large; counting (1), (2), (3), (5), (6) and (7) as private savings does the reverse.

This total figure of savings will correspond to the gross capital formation, both domestic and overseas. If we deduct net borrowing and investment overseas, we have a figure of saving which corresponds to domestic gross capital formation.

Consumers' expenditure and the standard of living

The figures of consumers' expenditure given in the Blue Book are often used as a measure of changes in the standard of living. Apart from the problems of allowing accurately for changes in prices,[2] there are several points to bear in mind in using the figures for this purpose. First, it must be remembered that a substantial part of the services provided by the Government contributes to the standard of living. A change in consumers' expenditure may often reflect the provision by the Government, through taxation, of services previously bought by consumers out of personal income. For example, consumers' expenditure on 'other services'[3] includes private expenditure on medical

[1] Stock appreciation attributable to persons and corporate bodies.
[2] See pp. 189–90.
[3] See *National Income and Expenditure* 1946–1953 (H.M.S.O., 1954) p. 31, Table 19 (i), item 17.

services, which was much reduced after the introduction of the National Health Service in 1948.[1] But after 1948 public expenditure on health services increased by much more than private expenditure fell. It would clearly be most misleading to count such a transfer in expenditure as a fall in the standard of living.

An apparently simple way of dealing with this difficulty is to take current expenditure on goods and services of public authorities together with consumers' private expenditure as measuring the standard of living. But this would be misleading also, for the current expenditure of public authorities includes such items as expenditure on defence, general administrative services, services to industry, and what the Blue Book calls 'environmental services'.[2] Few would count the benefits derived from defence expenditure, necessary though it may be, as adding to the standard of living. And it can be argued that some of the other services mentioned above are not an addition to the consumer goods available but are part of their cost and have already been counted once. Perhaps the best compromise in the circumstances is to pick out those items of the current expenditure of public authorities on goods and services which would usually be acknowledged as contributing to the standard of living, and to add these to private consumers' expenditure. The most important items that might be added in this way are education and health services.

It is also necessary to take account of changes in population, and this is usually done by using figures of expenditure per head. This is acceptable over short periods, but over long periods we must not overlook the changing composition of the population, particularly the proportion of young to old and of large families to small. Clearly it would be useful if we could also work out expenditure per family; but this is practically impossible. All that we have, therefore, is an average per person which may conceal some divergent movements.

Because all goods, except houses, which are bought by final consumers, are counted as consumption when they are bought, the figures of consumers' expenditure are not a reliable indication

[1] Consumers' expenditure on 'other services' fell from £682 million in 1948 to £647 million in 1949; Government expenditure on health services increased from £240 million in 1948 to £410 million in 1949.

[2] Such as expenditure on roads, sewerage, and public lighting.

over short periods of the material well-being of the consumer. Suppose there is a burst of expenditure on durable consumer goods one year and then no expenditure in the following year. This would be shown in the Blue Book as a high figure for radios, washing machines, refrigerators, furniture, in the first year, and no expenditure on these in the second. But we should clearly be wrong in assuming that no one had any of these to use in the second year. On the contrary, in the year immediately after they were purchased they would probably all still be in use and yielding substantial benefits. In order to assess the changing situation of the consumer one would need to know the total stocks of such durable goods held by the consumer as well as the new ones that were purchased during the year.[1]

SOCIAL ACCOUNTS

One of the most important developments in national income statistics in recent years has been to portray the interrelations between the main sectors of the economy in a set of social accounts. In drawing up such accounts the economy is divided into significant economic groupings, such as individuals, productive enterprises and public authorities, and for each group an account is drawn up showing on one side the sources of the group's income and on the other side its main channels of expenditure. Thus the account for individuals, or the 'personal account' as it is usually called, would show on the income side the main sources of income—wages, salaries, dividends, insurance benefits, and other incomes, and on the expenditure side the main items of outlay—consumption, taxation and saving. In general, current items such as consumption are shown separately from capital items, and in the accounts for the United Kingdom transactions with overseas are also distinguished.

The two sides of any account should in principle add up to the same figure, for the total income of any group must also be the same as that group's expenditure, if borrowing or lending is included as an item of expenditure. But this equality will only be preserved if we have perfectly accurate statistics and if the concepts used in drawing up the accounts are consistent.

[1] For this reason the figures of the reduction in expenditure on durable consumer goods during the war exaggerate the hardship suffered by consumers.

In a set of accounts drawn up in this way, with each account showing separately transactions with each other account, we can trace every item twice, once on the receipts side and once on the expenditure side. Thus tax payments on the expenditure side of the current personal account would appear on the receipts side of the current account of public authorities; and payments of wages and salaries on the expenditure side of productive enterprises would appear on receipts side of the personal account.

The total of national income, product and expenditure can be built up from such a set of accounts. The accounts are, indeed, usually drawn up with this as one of the main objectives.

The social accounting method of portraying the details of national income, production and expenditure has many advantages. It shows in a revealing way the interrelations between the transactions of the various sectors of the economy. It ensures consistency in the treatment of different transactions and shows the implications for other parts of the system of any treatment proposed. Thus if we treat taxes on a provisions basis in the personal income account, this has clear implications for the treatment of tax reserves in the savings and investment account. These implications are brought to light much more readily in the accounting approach because we are forced by this method to trace every item on the payments side of the personal account to some item on the receipts side of another account; we soon discover that the 'tax reserves' element in personal taxation does not appear anywhere as Government receipts and realize that it must be treated as an item of receipts on the savings account.

If we have sufficient statistical information to estimate the two sides of each account directly, the difference in the totals of the two sides gives us a basis for assessing the reliability of the calculations; since in theory the payments and receipts side of each account should add up to the same total. Having made sure that any difference is not due to inconsistency in defining the two sets of transactions, we can then decide how to allocate the statistical discrepancy and adjust the individual figures so as to arrive at a consistent set of estimates. Similarly we can check the estimates for individual items by comparing the figures of receipts or payments on one account with the corresponding item of payments or receipts on other accounts.[1]

[1] Of course where the figures are derived from the same source this comparison provides no check. A comparison of payments of taxation in

If we cannot estimate both sides of the accounts directly we may be able to estimate some items as residuals. For example, if in the account of persons we can estimate all items on the receipts side but only consumption and taxation on the payments side, we can obtain the remaining item of expenditure (that is, saving) as a residual, by subtracting the estimated items of expenditure—consumption and taxation—from the total estimated receipts. Residuals arrived at in this way will, however, reflect the errors in the estimates from which they are derived.

The accounting form of presentation is now adopted for practically all the statistics given in the Blue Book. For the latest year the Blue Book brings together the figures for the individual sectors in a set of social accounts for the country as a whole, showing, wherever possible, each payment from one account as an identifiable receipt in another account. And most of the statistical tables which are not given in the payments and receipts form are an elaboration in greater detail of some items shown in one of the sector accounts.[1]

NATIONAL INCOME IN REAL TERMS

Nearly all the figures in the Blue Book are in current year prices. These are of great value in analysing the structure of the economy in a single year, tracing the changes in money flows from year to year, and in considering changes in the proportion of individual items to totals.[2] But for many purposes we want figures from which the effect of price changes has been eliminated. If we want to measure changes in the standard of living, for example, we are interested in figures of expenditure on goods and services of benefit to the consumer at unchanged prices. If we want to measure changes in the volume of national output and in productivity, we want figures of the national product not affected by fluctuations in prices.

the personal account with receipts of taxes on personal income in the Government account would not provide any statistical check if both figures are obtained from Government taxation statistics.

[1] Thus the tables of consumers' expenditure analyse in detail the single figure of 'consumers' expenditure' which appears as one item in the account of 'personal income and expenditure'.

[2] For example, personal expenditure as a percentage of personal income, or Government expenditure as a percentage of national expenditure.

For national product as a whole, two sets of figures at constant prices are given in the Blue Book. Both sets of figures relate to the gross domestic product at 1948 prices. 'Gross domestic product' is the total of national output before allowing for net property income from abroad.[1] The calculation is done in two ways: the first, by revaluing items of expenditure at 1948 prices; the second, by calculating indices of production for all industries and services.

On the first basis figures of expenditure at 1948 prices are given separately for private consumption, domestic capital formation, and public expenditure, and the addition of these before deducting imports and adding exports gives the total of domestic expenditure at unchanged prices. These figures are of great interest since they measure the total of real resources available for home use. When we add on exports and deduct imports, both at constant 1948 prices, we get the 'gross domestic product'.

The second method is in principle an extension of the index of industrial production.[2] The quantities of goods and services produced are compared year by year with 1948 and the percentage change in each is weighted by its 'gross product' in that year. This is in effect the same as measuring the percentage change in the value of output at the unchanged gross product prices of 1948.

In principle the two sets of calculations should give the same result. This would, however, only be true if either market prices or factor cost prices are used in both.

Expenditure figures are usually given on the basis of market prices, and the gross product used in weighting in indices of production is usually factor cost.[3] The figures of 'gross domestic expenditure' at constant prices are given in the Blue Book both for market prices and factor cost; the individual industry indices for gross domestic product are on a factor cost basis, but the total is also given on market prices weighting.[4] The 'domestic product' calculation is partly based on work done at the Department

[1] That is, before deducting property income paid abroad and adding property income received from abroad.

[2] The figures for mining and quarrying; manufacturing; building and contracting; and gas, electricity and water, are in fact identical with those given in the index number of production.

[3] That is, net of indirect taxes and subsidies.

[4] The market prices weighting has been dropped in the 1946–1953 Blue Book.

of Applied Economics at Cambridge and much more detailed discussion of the methods used and the significance of the results can be seen in the publications of the staff of the Department who have been responsible for the work.[1]

Consumer expenditure and fixed capital expenditure at unchanged prices are analysed in more detail in the main tables in the Blue Book. Unfortunately there is no similar detailed analysis of public expenditure at unchanged prices, and it is therefore impossible to add to consumers' expenditure at unchanged prices those items of public expenditure which confer benefits on individuals. The table of consumers' expenditure both at current and 1948 prices is given at quarterly intervals in the *Monthly Digest of Statistics*.

THE RELIABILITY OF NATIONAL INCOME STATISTICS

It is not easy to assess the reliability of the figures given in the National Income Blue Book. All the figures are 'processed' statistics, that is, figures which have been amended and adjusted from the original data, both to fit the requirements of particular categories in national income accounting and to cover gaps for which there is little source material. Assessing the reliability of national income statistics is therefore quite different from assessing the reliability of figures on foreign trade in the *Trade and Navigation Accounts* or the figures on production in the Census of Production. For in these the Government departments publish the original data which they collect, merely tabulating, summarizing and arranging them in a convenient form.

Take, for example, the figures of wages in the Blue Book. There are many sources for these: the average earnings inquiries of the Ministry of Labour, the reports of the Censuses of Production and of Distribution, the P.A.Y.E. statistics of the Board of Inland Revenue, and the miscellaneous statistics on earnings in particular industries. The statisticians calculating the national income use all these figures, and others, to estimate the national

[1] See W. B. Reddaway, 'Movements in the Real Product of the United Kingdom 1946–49', *J. R. Statist. Soc.*, series A, vol. CXIII, pt. IV (1950), pp. 435–63; C. F. Carter, 'Index Numbers of the Real Product of the United Kingdom', *J. R. Statist. Soc.*, series A, vol. CXV, pt. I (1952), pp. 82–125, and A. A. Adams, 'The Real Product of the United Kingdom, 1946–52', *London and Cambridge Economic Service Bulletin* in *The Times Review of Industry*, September 1953.

wage-bill, both in total and by industries. To do this the figures from these different sources have to be reconciled, gaps not covered by the basic statistics have to be filled, and the figures have to be adjusted to fit in with the definition of wages which is thought most appropriate for national income calculations. The reliability of the final result thus depends not only on the accuracy of the basic material and how this is used, but also on the methods used to fill the gaps.

To use the National Income Blue Book with confidence one ought, therefore, to know what material is used in compiling each figure or set of figures and how these figures are processed to get the published statistics. The Central Statistical Office has not yet published any detailed explanation of how the estimates are made, and one must therefore proceed mainly on the basis of knowledge of the sources that are available to it and guesses about the methods it is most likely to use to reach the final published estimates. There are many hints, suggestions, and statements in the notes to the Blue Book which are of some help in this procedure, but a full straightforward explanation by the Central Statistical Office would be much more useful.[1] In general, it is probably true to say that year-to-year changes in the various items of national income and expenditure are more reliable than their absolute level.

One way of assessing the accuracy of the estimates is to compare the figures of the totals of national income, expenditure or product arrived at by different methods. As has already been explained,[2] if the appropriate definitions are used, the total of the national income, national expenditure and product should give the same figure. If we estimate each of these separately, using different statistical sources, the difference between the final results would give us some measure, although by no means a conclusive one, of the margin of error in the estimates. The latest Blue Book shows for each year since 1948 the difference between the income and expenditure methods of arriving at the totals of the national income as a 'residual error'. Before 1948 total expenditure was not estimated independently since one item[3] of

---

[1] It was announced in the Blue Book for 1946–1953 that 'a work is now in preparation describing in detail the methods of estimation and the sources from which the estimates are derived'.

[2] See pp. 223 and 226–7.

[3] Stocks.

expenditure could not be calculated accurately, and no figures of 'residual error' appear in the tables for the years before 1948.

It is not easy to discover the exact significance of the 'residual error'. If it measures the margin of error in the estimates of total national income, it would seem to indicate a high degree of accuracy, for the maximum residual error so far has been quite trivial in relation to total national income.[1] But it is doubtful whether it would be correct to interpret the figure of residual error in this way. First, the two estimates—of income and expenditure—do not use completely independent statistical sources. In so far as there is this lack of independence, the results of the two calculations can only be used to check one another within limits. Secondly, it is not easy to discover how far the statistical calculations are done independently. Do one set of people in the Central Statistical Office calculate the expenditure estimates and another the income estimates without communicating with each other during the process? If not, there is bound to be some reconciliation and adjustment of the income and expenditure figures during the actual process of estimation, and the figure of 'residual error' would then merely represent differences which have not been taken into account. The exact significance of the 'residual error' cannot, therefore, be assessed until we know in more detail how the estimates are built up from the original statistics.

The 'residual error' is shown as an item of income and production, so that the total of incomes and production, including the error, add up to the total of expenditure, and they are treated in this way throughout the Blue Book. This means that the total of the national product and national income, before allowing for the residual error, are given as exactly the same figure. But the fact that no difference is shown between these two should not be taken to mean that national product and national income when estimated independently give identical results. It merely reflects the fact that the estimates of gross national product by industry are simply obtained by classifying the various factor incomes by industry of origin.

One advantage of fitting national income estimates into a social accounting system is that figures which cannot be estimated directly can often be obtained as residuals by comparing two sides of an account. Residuals obtained in this way will reflect the error

[1] 0·6 per cent in 1949.

in the figures from which they are derived. It is most important therefore to be able to distinguish residuals from direct estimates in the Blue Book. Unfortunately residuals are not clearly distinguished in the tables themselves, but the notes usually call special attention to residual items.

One of the most important figures arrived at as a residual in this way is the figure of personal saving. The figures of personal incomes and expenditure are set out in an account, both sides of which must by definition add up to the same total. The total of incomes is estimated directly from figures of wages, salaries, professional earnings, the incomes of farmers and other sole traders, rents, dividends and interest paid to persons, and transfer payments to persons. On the payments side only expenditure on consumption and taxation (including insurance contributions) are estimated directly. But since total personal income must equal total personal expenditure, and since by definition what is not spent on consumption or taken in taxation must be 'saved', figures of personal savings can be derived by subtracting the total of consumption and taxation from the total of income. If, as is done in the Blue Book, these figures of 'savings' are then shown on the expenditure side of the account, the total of personal expenditure will necessarily add up to the same figure as the total of income. A residual figure of 'savings'[1] arrived at in this way will necessarily reflect any errors in the estimates of income, consumption and personal taxation; and even a small proportionate error in either of these quite large figures will mean a large error in the residual.[2] It is thus clearly most dangerous to place much reliance on small year-to-year fluctuations in a figure of 'savings' arrived at in this way. Another example of residual figures of this kind is the estimates of stock changes in 1946 and

---

[1] In fact since the total of incomes is estimated before allowing for depreciation and stock appreciation, the residual will include these two items as well as 'net savings'. It is in fact described in the Blue Book as 'Balance: saving and provision for depreciation and stock appreciation'.

[2] For example, in 1952 the 'residual' or 'balance' is the difference between personal income (£12,764 million) and consumption and taxation (£12,058 million), i.e. £706 million. A 1 per cent error in the two figures from which it is derived would give an error of about ±35 per cent in the residual of £706 million. On the other hand such a large error in the figure of personal saving would imply great inaccuracy in the estimates of capital formation.

1947. These are obtained by subtracting the total of consumption, expenditure of public authorities, the foreign balance and fixed capital formation, from the total of incomes.

Another kind of residual estimate is also used in the Blue Book. This can be best explained by giving two examples. Let us take first the figures given for the wage- and salary-bill. The national wage- and salary-bill together can be estimated from the P.A.Y.E. information received by the Board of Inland Revenue. Independent estimates of the wage-bill and salary-bill can then be made for groups of industries from a large range of sources—the Census of Production, accounts of public corporations, Central and Local Government records and so on. There are, however, some trades for which no independent estimates, even on a rough basis, can be made.[1] But a figure of the wage- and salary-bill in these trades as a group can be obtained as a residual, by subtracting the total of wages and salaries in the industries estimated independently from the figure for the national wage- and salary-bill. Apparently the figure of income from employment for 'other services' given in the Blue Book[2] is arrived at in this way. The second example is the estimate of 'additions to tax reserves'.[3] Presumably these figures are obtained as the difference between estimates of provision for taxation,[4] and what is actually paid in taxation as derived from returns of the Exchequer and the tax raising authorities. Any change in these two sets of estimates will be reflected in the residual figures of 'addition to tax reserves', and it is not surprising therefore that there have been very erratic revisions of these figures in successive Blue Books.

The figures for the last year or two in any issue of the Blue Book are bound to be preliminary estimates only and may be substantially revised in later years. Even when there are regular and reasonably accurate sources of information there may be a substantial time-lag before they are ready, and the first estimates for most recent years have to be made on a rough extrapolation.

[1] There is very little information about wages and salaries in most of the service trades (e.g. entertainment, catering, and domestic service).

[2] See Blue Book for 1946–1953 (H.M.S.O., 1954), p. 21.

[3] See p. 220.

[4] These figures are not based on a statistical return received from companies and individuals of what they in fact provide for taxation, but are the Central Statistical Office's estimates of the provision that should be made.

The Board of Inland Revenue figures of assessment of profits for any one year do not appear in their final form until some time after the period to which they relate. Thus when the preliminary national income estimates for 1953 were published early in 1954,[1] the latest income-tax assessment figures were for the financial year March 1952 to April 1953,[2] and these referred in the main to incomes earned in 1951. For 1952 and 1953 rough guesses had to be made which may need substantial revision later. There is some basis for making such estimates in the published accounts of public companies, and apparently a large number of companies now provide up-to-date estimates of their current profits to the Board of Inland Revenue. Both these sources do not provide much information about professional earnings and sole traders and partnerships, and the estimates for these groups for the most recent year or two must be particularly hazardous.

The Census of Production, which is one of the most important sources for estimates of the national product, does not come out until about three years after the year to which it refers. But the authors of the Blue Book no doubt have access to preliminary statements of these and other returns long before they are published.

For some of the estimates there is detailed statistical information for some years only. Thus the Census of Distribution gives detailed information about expenditure for 1950 which is not available for any other year. Similarly the publication of the Census of Population for 1951, even on the one per cent sample basis, makes it possible to check and revise estimates of the occupied and employee population (these are used in calculating incomes) for that year. These two censuses not only help to improve the accuracy of the estimates for the years to which they refer, but they also provide benchmarks against which estimates for other years can be made from other statistical material. Thus the results of the 1950 Census of Distribution can be used not only for the estimates of consumer expenditure in the year 1950, but also to check and improve the way in which such figures as

[1] *Preliminary Estimates of National Income and Expenditure*, 1948 to 1953 (Cmd. 9118, H.M.S.O., 1954).

[2] In fact the *Annual Report* of the Commissioners of Inland Revenue, published in January 1954, gave the assessments for 1951–2, but presumably the Central Statistical Office had by then received preliminary estimates of the assessments for 1952–3.

retail and wholesale trade statistics are used to make estimates for other years.

Assessing the accuracy of estimates of national product and expenditure in real terms, that is, after allowing for price changes, raises many difficult issues. Some of these have already been referred to in discussing index numbers of production and prices in earlier chapters. The special additional difficulty in national product and expenditure calculations is how to allow for changes in prices in that large and miscellaneous group called 'services'. This group covers transport and communications, distribution, insurance, banking and finance, services provided by public authorities, professional services, entertainment, catering, domestic service, and so on, which in total now account for nearly 45 per cent of the national product. The way in which the estimates of changes in the real output of these is made affects substantially the movements in the total, for all these measures of quantities are either difficult to obtain or are of little significance, and allowing for quality presents insurmountable difficulties. The deflation of the figures in current values to figures of output or expenditure at unchanged prices has therefore to be done on a rather arbitrary basis. The services of retail distribution, for example, are measured by the volume of goods distributed, and of medical services by the number of beneficiaries. Value figures for public administration and defence are deflated by an index of costs, which implicitly assumes that there are no changes in efficiency or in the quality of services provided.

This discussion of the reliability of the national income statistics should not be taken as comprehensive. It is merely meant to indicate the sort of considerations to keep in mind in using the figures, and to emphasize the importance of asking the questions: How was the figure arrived at? What basic statistics have been used in its compilation?

EARLIER STATISTICS OF NATIONAL INCOME

Nearly the whole of this chapter has been devoted to the official estimates of the national income, because they are more regular, systematic, accurate and more detailed than anything published before. But the official estimates only go back to 1938, and figures for earlier years are all the work of private research workers making the best of inadequate data. The pioneer workers in this field were A. L. Bowley, Lord Stamp, Sir Alfred Flux and Colin Clark.[1] Bowley's and Stamp's estimates for the period before 1914 extended back to 1860 and were based mainly in the income method. Later estimates for 1924 were made on a similar basis.[2] Flux made the first attempt at estimates of the national product, based on the Censuses of Production for 1907 and 1924.[3] Clark's estimates for the inter-war years from 1924 to 1933 were more detailed and comprehensive than anything done earlier.[4] He attempted not only to estimate the total national income both from the income and expenditure side, but also to analyse the distribution of incomes, the redistributive effects of taxation, the product of industry and capital formation.

It is not easy to piece all these figures together into a continuous series. Fortunately this has been done by A. R. Prest, who has also revised the earlier estimates for 1870–1914.[5] He has also linked these with the later official estimates, so giving a run of annual figures from 1870 to 1946. He also works out figures of income per head, compares the movement of money income and prices, and so derives indexes of changes in total real national income and real national income per head. Prest's tables now provide, without doubt, the most readily accessible and convenient set of national income statistics for the period 1870 to 1946.

[1] For a bibliography of national income publications dealing with estimates before 1938, see A. L. Bowley, *Studies in the National Income, 1924–1938* (Cambridge, 1942), pp. 201–47, and D. Creamer (ed.), *Bibliography on Income and Wealth, 1932-1947*, vol. 1 (International Association for Research in Income and Wealth: Bowes and Bowes, 1942).

[2] A. L. Bowley, *Wages and Income in the United Kingdom since 1860* (Cambridge, 1937); A. L. Bowley, *Studies in the National Income, 1924–1938* (Cambridge, 1942); A. L. Bowley and Sir Josiah Stamp, *Three Studies in National Income* (Series of Reprints of Scarce Works, No. 6, London School of Economics and Political Science, 1938).

[3] Sir Alfred Flux, 'The National Income', *Journal of the Royal Statistical Society*, vol. XCII, pts. I and II (1929), pp. 1–33 and 163–82.

[4] C. Clark, *National Income and Outlay* (Macmillan, 1937), and *Conditions of Economic Progress* (2nd ed. Macmillan, 1951).

[5] A. R. Prest, 'National Income of the United Kingdom, 1870–1946', *Economic Journal*, vol. LVIII (1948), pp. 31–62.

APPENDIX

SINCE the original edition of this book was prepared for publication in 1955 many new statistical reports and articles have been published. Some of these merely give more up-to-date figures on the old basis, but in many cases there have been substantial changes in the methods used in compiling the figures and there are also entirely new sets of statistics not previously available. Fully to take account of all these new and revised statistics would require an entirely new edition of this book. In the meantime a summary is given in this Appendix of the most significant of these, under the chapters and headings used in the main text. This covers the period of up to mid-1958.

CHAPTER I INTRODUCTION

For a general review of important recent developments in economic statistics see Sir Harry Campion, 'Recent Developments in Economic Statistics', *J. R. Statist. Soc.*, Series A, vol. 121, pt. I (1958).

Economic Trends has become an increasingly important publication in recent years. It is now the main source for some special statistics, such as the quarterly estimates of national income and expenditure, and includes articles explaining the basis of important official statistics. See, for example, the articles on 'The Compilation of the United Kingdom Balance of Payments' in the issue for October 1957, and on 'Housing Statistics' in the issue for June 1958.

For a useful general survey of regional statistics see K. S. Lomax, 'Regional Economic Statistics' in *The Sources and Nature of the Statistics of the United Kingdom*, ed. M. G. Kendall (Oliver and Boyd, 1957), vol. 2, pp. 41–58.

CHAPTER II POPULATION

See E. Grebenik, 'Population and Vital Statistics', in *The Sources and Nature of the Statistics of the United Kingdom*, ed. M. G. Kendall (Oliver and Boyd, 1957), vol. 2, pp. 1–11.

CHAPTER III MANPOWER

UNEMPLOYMENT (pp. 67 ff.)

The Ministry of Labour has published for the first time an occupational analysis of unemployment in addition to the usual industrial analysis. See 'Occupational Analysis of Adult Workers wholly Unemployed and of Vacancies Notified to Employment Exchanges and Remaining Unfilled', *Ministry of Labour Gazette*, May 1958, p. 190.

Hours of work, overtime and short time (pp. 77-8)

A new index of weekly hours has been compiled by the Ministry of Labour and is published in the *Ministry of Labour Gazette*. See 'Index of Normal Weekly Hours', *Ministry of Labour Gazette*, September 1957, pp. 330-1.

Since February 1957 figures of short-time working have been published each month instead of quarterly. See *Ministry of Labour Gazette*, February 1957, p. 58.

CHAPTER IV INDUSTRIAL PRODUCTION

THE CENSUS OF PRODUCTION (pp. 80 ff.)

Apart from the publication of the regular reports, there have been the following additional important publications on the Census results.

Census of Production for 1951, Summary Tables Part I and Part II (H.M.S.O., 1956).

'Census of Production shows the Pattern of Change in Industry', *Board of Trade Journal*, 30 July 1955, pp. 262-5.

'Growth of British Industry from 1951 to 1954 Shown by Census of Production', *Board of Trade Journal*, 31 December 1955, pp. 1397-401.

'Census of Production Results for 1956', *Board of Trade Journal*, 20 December 1957, pp. 1273-7.

INDEX NUMBERS OF INDUSTRIAL PRODUCTION (pp. 98 ff.)

The official index of industrial production now includes seasonally adjusted index numbers for 'All Industries' and 'Total Manufacturing Industries'. For the basis used in calculating this adjustment see *Monthly Digest of Statistics*, June 1956, p. ii.

A lot of new work has been done on revising statistics of industrial production for earlier periods. See

B. C. Brown, 'Industrial Production in 1935 and 1948', London and Cambridge Economic Bulletin in *The Times Review of Industry*, December 1954.

T. M. Ridley, 'Industrial Production in the United Kingdom, 1900-1953', *Economica*, Vol. XXII (February 1955), pp. 1-12.

K. S. Lomax, 'New Index Numbers of Industrial Production, 1900–1938', London and Cambridge Economic Bulletin in *The Times Review of Industry*, June 1958.

CHAPTER V AGRICULTURE, DISTRIBUTION AND TRANSPORT

AGRICULTURE (pp. 115 ff.)

For a useful new survey of official statistics on food and agriculture see *Guides to Official Sources No. 4*. Agricultural and Food Statistics (H.M.S.O., 1958).

DISTRIBUTION (pp. 121 ff.)

A Census of Distribution on a sample basis has been taken for 1957. See 'Census of Distribution to be taken for 1957', *Board of Trade Journal*, 17 November 1956, pp. 1201–4.

The basis of the retail trade statistics has been changed and much improved, particularly by extending the sample. See

'Monthly Statistics of Retail Trade to be Improved', *Board of Trade Journal*, 15 January 1955, pp. 81–2.
'Improved Statistics of Sales of Independent Retailers', *Board of Trade Journal*, 1 October 1955, pp. 738–40.
'Improved Monthly Statistics of Retail Sales', *Board of Trade Journal*, 5 May 1956, pp. 561–9.
W. Rudoe, 'Retail Trade Statistics', paper read to the Manchester Statistical Society, 12 January 1955.

CHAPTER VI FOREIGN TRADE

THE VOLUME OR QUANTUM OF MERCHANDISE TRADE, INDEX NUMBERS OF THE AVERAGE VALUE OR PRICE OF IMPORTS AND EXPORTS, *and* THE TERMS OF TRADE (pp. 145 ff.)

The Board of Trade index numbers of volume and price of imports and exports have been revised and are now published with base year 1954 = 100. See

'Volume of Imports and Exports in 3rd Quarter, and Change of Base Year to 1954', *Board of Trade Journal*, 10 December 1955, pp. 1256–8.
'Volume of United Kingdom Imports and Exports in the first Quarter of 1956', *Board of Trade Journal*, 19 May 1956, pp. 678–83.

NON-MERCHANDISE TRADE AND THE BALANCE OF PAYMENTS (pp. 159 ff.). See

'The Compilation of the United Kingdom Balance of Payments', *Economic Trends*, October 1957.
'Overseas Sterling Holdings', *Economic Trends*, May 1958.

Chapter VII Prices

INDEX NUMBERS OF WHOLESALE PRICES (pp. 169 ff.)

The Board of Trade index numbers of wholesale prices have been revised and are now published with the base year 1954 = 100. See

'New Series of Wholesale Price Index Number (1954 = 100) to be introduced next month', *Board of Trade Journal*, 21 February 1958, p. 423.

'Wholesale Price Index Numbers Changed to 1954 = 100', *Board of Trade Journal*, 21 March 1958, pp. 687–93.

For a general analysis of the wholesale price index numbers see H. S. Phillips, 'United Kingdom Indices of Wholesale Prices, 1949–1955', *J. R. Statist. Soc.*, Series A, vol. 119, pt. 3 (1956), pp. 239–83.

INDEX NUMBERS OF RETAIL PRICES (pp. 178 ff.)

An entirely new index number of retail prices, replacing the interim index, has been published by the Ministry of Labour since March 1956. This compares prices each month with 17 January 1956 = 100. The weights used are based on the results of the consumer budget survey for 1953/4. See

Cost of Living Advisory Committee, Report on Proposals for a New Index of Retail Prices (cmd. 9710, H.M.S.O. 1956).

Method of Construction and Calculation of the Index of Retail Prices (H.M.S.O., 1956).

Report of an Enquiry into Household Expenditure in 1953–4 (H.M.S.O., 1957).

R. G. D. Allen, 'On the Decline in the Value of Money', Stamp Memorial Lecture (London, 1957).

R. G. D. Allen, 'Movements in Retail Prices since 1953', *Economica*, vol. XXV (1958), pp. 14–25.

Chapter VIII Incomes

WAGE-RATES (pp. 193 ff.)

A revised index number of wage-rates, with January 1956 = 100, is now published by the Ministry of Labour. See 'New Index Number of Wage Rates', *Ministry of Labour Gazette*, February 1957, pp. 50–1.

For an index of wage-rates by industries since 1948 see Ely Devons and R. C. Ogley, 'An index of wage-rates by industries', *The Manchester School*, vol. XXVI (1958), pp. 77–115.

A useful summary of wage-rate statistics is given in 'Official Indices of Rates of Wages, 1880–1957', *Ministry of Labour Gazette*, April 1958, pp. 132–5.

THE MOVEMENT OF WAGE-RATES AND THE MOVEMENT OF AVERAGE
WAGE EARNINGS (pp. 204–5). See

G. Penrice, 'Earnings and Wage Rates 1948–55', London and
Cambridge Economic Bulletin in *The Times Review of Industry*,
December 1955.

CHAPTER IX NATIONAL INCOME AND EXPENDITURE

A detailed account has now been published of the basis and
methods used in calculating the figures published in the White
Papers and Blue Books on National Income and Expenditure.
See 'National Income Statistics Sources and Methods' (H.M.S.O.,
1956).

Official summary estimates of national income and expenditure
are now published quarterly. See, for example, 'Quarterly estimates of national income and expenditure', *Economic Trends*,
July 1958, pp. vi–xvii.

Gross and net national incomes (pp. 216–7)

Gross and net capital expenditure (pp. 228–30)

In the Blue Book for 1956, estimates were given for the first
time of capital consumption; and national income, product and
expenditure, and fixed capital formation, can now be calculated
on a 'net' as well as a 'gross' basis. See

'National Income and Expenditure 1956' (H.M.S.O., 1956),
pp. 55–9.
Philip Redfern, 'Net Investment in Fixed Assets in the United
Kingdom', *J. R. Statist. Soc.*, Series A, vol. 118, pt. 2 (1955),
pp. 141–92.
T. Barna, 'The Replacement Cost of Fixed Assets in British
Manufacturing Industry in 1955', *J. R. Statist. Soc.*, Series A,
vol. 120, pt. 1 (1957), pp. 1–47.

The Board of Trade now takes a regular enquiry, on a sample
basis, into fixed capital expenditure and stocks. The results are
published in the *Board of Trade Journal*. See

'Changes in Fixed Capital Expenditure 1954–56 shown by new
Board of Trade Enquiry', *Board of Trade Journal*, 4 February
1956, pp. 207–8.
'Stocks and Capital Expenditure of Wholesale Distributive
Trades', *Board of Trade Journal*, 16 February 1957, p. 329.
'New Information on Stocks of Manufacturing Industry',
Board of Trade Journal, 14 January 1956, pp. 47–8.

Savings and investment (pp. 231–2)

The Oxford University Institute of Statistics has undertaken a
series of enquiries, on a sample basis, into personal savings, and the

results have been published in articles in the Bulletin of the Institute from 1954 onwards. See also

D. Cole and J. E. G. Utting, 'Estimating Expenditure, Saving and Income from Household Budgets', *J. R. Statist. Soc.*, Series A, vol. 119, pt. 4 (1956), pp. 371–92.
C. T. Saunders, 'Some Problems in the Estimation of Personal Savings and Investment', paper read to the Manchester Statistical Society, 10 November, 1954.

EARLIER STATISTICS OF NATIONAL INCOME (pp. 244–5)

For a revised set of figures of national income and expenditure at current and unchanged (1912/3) prices see James B. Jeffreys and Dorothy Walters, 'National Income and Expenditure of the United Kingdom, 1870–1952', in *Income and Wealth*, Series V (Bowes and Bowes, 1955), pp. 1–40.

INDEX

253

INDEX

254